The Nordic Wave in Place Branding

The Nordic Wave in Place Branding

Poetics, Practices, Politics

Edited by

Cecilia Cassinger

Lund University, Sweden

Andrea Lucarelli

Stockholm University, Sweden

Szilvia Gyimóthy

Copenhagen Business School, Denmark

Edward **Elgar**
PUBLISHING

Cheltenham, UK • Northampton, MA, USA

Cover image: Kim Simonsen. Courtesy of Adobe Stock/Fotolia

Published by
Edward Elgar Publishing Limited
The Lypiatts
15 Lansdown Road
Cheltenham
Glos GL50 2JA
UK

Edward Elgar Publishing, Inc.
William Pratt House
9 Dewey Court
Northampton
Massachusetts 01060
USA

A catalogue record for this book
is available from the British Library

Library of Congress Control Number: 2019951017

This book is available electronically in the **Elgar**online
Social and Political Science subject collection
DOI 10.4337/9781788974325

ISBN 978 1 78897 431 8 (cased)
ISBN 978 1 78897 432 5 (eBook)

Typeset by Servis Filmsetting Ltd, Stockport, Cheshire
Printed and bound by CPI Group (UK) Ltd, Croydon, CR0 4YY

Contents

List of figures   *viii*
List of tables   *ix*
List of contributors   *x*
Foreword: towards a Nordic manifesto by Britt Kramvig   *xix*
Preface   *xxiii*

1   The Nordic wave in place branding: moving back and forth in
    time and space   1
    Cecilia Cassinger, Andrea Lucarelli and Szilvia Gyimóthy

PART I   POETICS OF NORDICITY

2   Reinvention through Nordicness: values, traditions, and terroir   11
    Lars Pynt Andersen, Frank Lindberg and Jacob Östberg

3   A Nordic perspective on supranational place branding   25
    Jörgen Eksell and Alicia Fjällhed

4   Sparking the Nordic music brand   39
    Jessica Edlom

5   Size matters! Insights from the municipalities of Gothenburg
    and Sorsele   54
    *Sara Brorström, Sarah Degerhammar and
    Kristina Tamm Hallström*

6   Nordic, Scandinavia or Schondia? A commentary on Nordic
    brand constructions   68
    Andrea Lucarelli

PART II   NORDIC PLACE-MAKING PRACTICES

7   Building the slow adventure brand in the northern periphery   76
    *Daniel Laven, Tatiana Chekalina, Matthias Fuchs,
    Lusine Margaryan, Peter Varley and Steve Taylor*

 8 Nordic landscapes in collaborative place-making interventions   91
    Anne Marit Waade, Jens Christian Pasgaard,
    Mathias Meldgaard and Tom Nielsen

 9 Translocal communities and their implications for place
    branding   109
    Rikke Brandt Broegaard, Karin Topsø Larsen and
    Lene Havtorn Larsen

10 THE PRISON: from liability to asset in branding of the
    Danish city Horsens   124
    Ole Have Jørgensen

11 Branding Sámi tourism: practices of indigenous participation
    and place-making   139
    Susanna Heldt Cassel

12 Tactical ruralism: a commentary on Nordic place-making
    practices   153
    Szilvia Gyimóthy

PART III POLITICS OF DISRUPTIVE NORDIC PLACE
          BRANDING

13 Branding on the Nordic margins: Greenland brand
    configurations   160
    Carina Ren, Ulrik Pram Gad and Lill Rastad Bjørst

14 Gastro Scandinavism: the branding of New Nordic Cuisine as
    a discursive space for forging new identities   175
    Kim Simonsen

15 Appropriation of the Nordic brand in the Estonian political
    discourse 1997–2017: consistencies and contestations   191
    Piia Tammpuu, Külliki Seppel and Kadri Simm

16 Phantasmal brand Sweden and make-believe in political speech   207
    Mikael Andéhn

17 Nordic place branding from an indigenous perspective   221
    Anne Heith

18 Market-mediated feminism and the Nordic: a commentary on
    the political dimension of place branding   227
    Cecilia Cassinger

PART IV CONCLUSION

19   The Nordic wave of place branding: a manifesto   236
     Cecilia Cassinger, Andrea Lucarelli and Szilvia Gyimóthy

*Afterword: riding the Nordic wave in place branding – or does the
Nordic exist and will it travel? by Mihalis Kavaratzis*   244

Index   249

Figures

2.1 (a) Restaurant NYT with white tablecloths and comfy chairs, photos of Bodø landscapes on the walls; (b) BRØD with wooden interior, broad benches and homemade tea lights   16

8.1 "Light sabre" design intervention in Hvide Sande, October 2017   91

10.1 The "prison" response in the annual aided TOMA since 2000   126

13.1 Anne Nivíka Grødem featuring a Nordic-style, post-modern re-circulation of an ulu-style knife and traditional Inuit male and female figurines   164

13.2 The roll-ups at the Government of Greenland's official exhibition at Prospectors & Developers Association of Canada (PDAC) convention: "Greenland. Be an explorer. Be a pioneer"   165

14.1 From KOKS, Faroe Islands: sea urchin eggs   176

14.2 From KOKS, Faroe Islands: fermented lamb   178

14.3 From KOKS, Faroe Islands: fermented cod   180

14.4 From the main chef at KOKS, Faroe Islands (1)   183

14.5 From the main chef at KOKS, Faroe Islands (2)   185

Tables

7.1	The relevance of core slow adventure activities for generating annual sales in SMEs	84
10.1	Aided TOMA analysis among people living outside Horsens	127
10.2	Data from "Familiarity Analysis" 2016 and 2018	128
19.1	The Nordic wave in place branding research	238

Contributors

Mikael Andéhn, PhD, Lecturer in the School of Management, Royal Holloway, University of London, UK, is a researcher and educator in the field of business administration, principally marketing. With a focus on the commercial relevance of place, branding, and critical consumption studies. His work has appeared in various journals including: *Tourism Management, International Marketing Review, Marketing Theory, Journal of Marketing Management, Journal of Consumer Behavior, Place Branding and Public Diplomacy*, and *Ephemera*.

Lars Pynt Andersen is Associate Professor of Strategic Communication at Aalborg University, Denmark, Department of Communication and Psychology (Copenhagen Campus). His PhD from Copenhagen Business School was on the rhetorical strategies of television advertising. He has published papers on the uses of irony and personification metaphor in advertising, as well as advertising genre and related effects. Research interests include parental consumption, the 'tween' consumer and vicarious consumption as status negotiation. He is currently researching the (re-) construction of the 'Nordic' and 'Nordic values' in consumer culture and branding strategies.

Lill Rastad Bjørst is Associate Professor at Aalborg University, Denmark, and holds a PhD in Arctic Studies from the Department of Cross-Cultural and Regional Studies at the University of Copenhagen. Recent research has focused on the climate change debate in Greenland and, since 2012, the political debate about Greenland's uranium. She is head of the research center CIRCLA, platform coordinator (AAU Arctic) and academic coordinator for Arctic Studies, a master's programme specialisation at Aalborg University. She has published in leading Arctic journals and since 2016 been the Scientific Editor of Man & Society, a subseries of Monographs on Greenland. Her research interests include Inuit culture and society; climate change and sustainability; mining and industrialisation; and postcolonialism and tourism.

Rikke Brandt Broegaard is a human geographer who has worked with community development, rural areas and inequality all of her professional life. She holds a PhD in international development studies and has worked with access to and control over land and natural resources, and civic rights and gender in rural Latin America, Asia and Africa. Currently, she leads the Danish national team within the research program titled 'Agricultural Investors as Development Actors' (see http://www.diis.dk/AIDA), examining the developmental outcomes of such investments in two African countries. In a Danish context, her research focuses on rural development and peripheralisation processes, including the role of translocal actors for inclusive processes and innovation. She shares her work time between the Institute for Geoscience and Natural Resource Management, Copenhagen University, and the Centre for Regional and Tourism Research, on the Danish Baltic island of Bornholm.

Sara Brorström is Associate Professor of Management and Organisation in the School of Business, Economics and Law at Gothenburg University, Sweden. She has conducted research on public sector organisation, strategy formulation, collaboration and place branding, and communication practices. Her research is published in various journals, such as the *Scandinavian Journal of Management* and *Financial Accountability and Management*.

Cecilia Cassinger received her PhD in Marketing in 2010. She currently works as Senior Lecturer in Strategic Communication at Lund University, Sweden. Her research concerns the consequences and transformative potential of place brand communication in nations, cities and regions, and how it is strategically used to mitigate conflicts among users of these places. She has published articles in academic journals such as *Place Branding and Public Diplomacy*, *Place Management and Development*, *International Journal of Tourism Cities*, and *European Journal of Cultural Studies*.

Tatiana Chekalina is a Post-doctoral Research Fellow in the Department of Economics, Geography, Law and Tourism, Mid Sweden University. Tatiana's research is conducted under the auspices of the university's European Tourism Research Institute (ETOUR), where her research includes destination marketing and branding, customer-based brand equity modelling for tourism destinations, nature-based tourism experience, and the digital tourism experience. Tatiana's current research primarily focuses on dynamic destination brand relationships in the digitalised world. More information about Tatiana's research is available on the web (see https://www.miun.se/Personal/tatianachekalina/).

Sarah Degerhammar is a Researcher at the Royal Institute of Technology, Sweden, and an activist. She has over the past ten years been active in the 'Right to the city-movement' in Sweden and internationally. She is also a founding member of the housing network 'Ort till Ort' and an editor of the magazine *Brand*.

Jessica Edlom is a Brand Strategist with extensive experience of advertising, and has worked with strategic communication for many different public and private organisations. She has an adjunct position at Karlstad University in Sweden and is a licentiate student in Media and Communication. Between 2015 and 2018 she was part of the research team within the European Union (EU)-funded Interreg research project 'Music Innovation Network Inner Scandinavia' (MINS) focusing on the Scandinavian music industry. Since September 2018 she has been part of the research project 'Music Ecosystems Inner Scandinavia' (MECO), which focuses on a music industry in transition and which will continue until 2021. Her research is focused on strategic communication and music artist brand building.

Jörgen Eksell is an Assistant Professor in the Department of Strategic Communication, Lund University, Sweden. He holds a PhD in Service Studies from Lund University. He has experience from multidisciplinary research projects relating to the service sector and public sector. His main research interest is in place branding, value creating processes, hospitality studies, over-tourism, and sustainable tourism.

Alicia Fjällhed is a PhD student in the Department of Strategic Communication, Lund University, Sweden. Her PhD project concerns the assessment and management of misinformation in international public relations. She holds an MA in Public Sector Communication from University of Gothenburg, Sweden, with two theses about the Swedish national brand, and a BSc in Strategic Communication from Lund University, with a thesis about the creation of the Nordic supranational place branding strategy.

Matthias Fuchs is a Professor of Tourism Studies in the Department of Economics, Geography, Law and Tourism at Mid Sweden University. His research is conducted under the auspices of the university's European Tourism Research Institute (ETOUR), where his research includes destination brand equity modelling, economic impact analysis, and electronic-tourism with a focus on big data-based analytics. Matthias is associate editor of the *Journal of Information Technology & Tourism*. He also serves on the editorial-boards of the *Journal of Travel Research*, *Annals of Tourism Research*, *Tourism Analysis* and the *Journal of Hospitality & Tourism Management*. More information about Matthias' research is available on the web (see https://www.miun.se/en/personnel/matthiasfuchs/).

Ulrik Pram Gad is Associate Professor of Arctic Culture and Politics at Aalborg University. He gained his PhD in political science from the University of Copenhagen, Denmark, where he also did postdoctoral work in the Centre for Advanced Security Theory. His Arctic publications include the monograph *National Identity Politics and Postcolonial Sovereignty Games: Greenland, Denmark and the EU* (Museum Tusculanum Publishers, 2016) as well as numerous journal articles and book chapters including, 'In the post-colonial waiting room: How overseas countries and territories play games with the norm of sovereignty', in *Against International Relational Norms: Postcolonial Perspectives* (Routledge, 2017) and 'What kind of nation state will Greenland be? Securitization theory as a strategy for analyzing identity politics' in *Politik* (2017). Before entering academia, he served in multiple roles with the Government of Greenland and with the Danish Ministries of Culture and Foreign Affairs.

Szilvia Gyimóthy is an Associate Professor in the Department of Marketing, Copenhagen Business School, Denmark. Szilvia's primary expertise lies in the intersection of strategic market communications, cultural studies and media geographies. She has carried out both conceptual and empirical research related to transformational placemaking, commodification strategies, and competitive differentiation of regions in the experience economy, highlighting the complex relationships between popular culture, globalisation, tourism and mobility. In the past few years, Szilvia has been working with the cosmopolitanisation of rural place brands, including placemaking practices associated with communitarian walking trails, engineered terroirs and Bollywood imaginaries of the Alps.

Anne Heith is Associate Professor in comparative literature in the Department of Culture and Media Studies, Umeå University, Sweden. She is involved in several projects examining place-making through analysis of constructions of Sápmi and Meänmaa, as well as representsations of migration. In-betweenness, double or multiple identities related to exclusion and belonging in more than one culture, respectively, are central themes in her own reserach.

Susanna Heldt Cassel is a Professor of Human Geography and Director of the Centre for Tourism and Leisure Research at Dalarna University, Sweden. She has published widely in tourism geography and tourism studies. Her research investigates the role of gender, rurality, and heritage issues in tourism, focusing on place-making and the construction of meaning related to places. Branding places and culture through photography and image creation in leisure, tourism, and events are special interests of hers.

Ole Have Jørgensen holds a Master's degree in Ecology from Aarhus University and a Graduate Diploma in Business Organisation from Copenhagen Business School, Denmark. He served as head of administration in Horsens 1989–2007, and earlier worked for the Danish Environmental Protection Agency and different counties and cities. His research interest is Key Performance Indicators and the impact of city branding, urban governance and cooperation with investors and volunteers, and city planning. Earlier papers were on bird migration, chemical residues in birds eggs, water quality and organisation development. He works now as an external senior scientist at the Centre for Research and Development in VIA Business Globalisation, VIA University College, Denmark.

Lene Havtorn Larsen is a Senior Consultant at the Centre for Regional and Tourism Research, Denmark. She holds a BA in Design and a master's in Experience Leadership. Her research field is human resources and voluntary work, connectivity, user-driven innovation and networks as important factors for local and regional development. For several years she has been the project leader of research projects focusing on the value of young out-migrants for the place development of the rural areas they come from in the Nordic Countries. She has recently focused on innovation and marketing of locally produced quality foods, including as tourism and experience products.

Karin Topsø Larsen is a Senior Researcher at the Centre for Regional and Tourism Research, Denmark. She holds a master of arts and a PhD in Geography and Educational Planning. She has been working with local and regional development with a focus on challenged localities and processes of peripheralisation for the past 15 years. Her research centres on young people and their mobilities in relation to the geography of education systems often in rural contexts. In the past five years, she has increasingly come to approach her understanding of challenged localities from a translocal perspective, bringing to light development perspectives in a world of unequal mobility structures and opportunities.

Daniel Laven is an Associate Professor of Human Geography at Mid Sweden University where he also serves as head of the Department of Economics, Geography, Law and Tourism. Daniel's research is conducted under the auspices of the university's European Tourism Research Institute (ETOUR) and explores the intersection between heritage development and sustainable futures. More information about Daniel's research is available on the web (see https://www.miun.se/Personal/daniellaven/).

Frank Lindberg is Professor of Marketing at Nord University Business School, Norway. He gained his PhD in 2001 at Copenhagen Business School, Denmark. Since then he has worked as an associate professor at the University of Nordland and the University of Gothenburg, and Vice-Dean and Dean at Bodø Graduate School of Business, Norway. Lindberg has been Visiting Scholar at Copenhagen Business School, University of California, Berkeley, USA and at the University of Southern Denmark. His research covers areas such as the dynamics of markets and consumption, and focuses on tensions and challenges of consumers and communities during consumption of experiences – especially related to Consumer Culture Theory.

Andrea Lucarelli is Senior Lecturer in Marketing at Lund University and a Research Fellow in the Centre for Sport in Business at Stockholm School of Economics, Stockholm University. His primary research interest is connected to branding applied to the realm of public places (i.e. cities, regions and nations). Andrea's secondary research interest is related to the geographical and historical dimension of consumption, advertising and marketing, the politics of marketing, the role of techno-digital culture in the construction of market phenomena and the commercialisation of sport.

Lusine Margaryan is a Post-doctoral Research Fellow in the Faculty of Environmental Sciences and Natural Resource Management at the Norwegian University of Life Sciences (NMBU). Lusine obtained her PhD from Mid Sweden University. Lusine's research focuses on nature-based tourism, outdoor recreation, and a wide range of topics at the intersection of tourism, nature, sustainability and human experience.

Mathias Meldgaard is an architect and PhD fellow at Aarhus School of Architecture, Denmark, as part of the transdisciplinary research project 'Rethinking Tourism in a Coastal City – Design for new Engagement' (2016–2019, Danish Innovation Fund). He is affiliated to the Research Lab of Territories, Architecture and Transformation, Aarhus School of Architecture. Through the approach of Research by Design, he is interested in architectural ways of mapping and understanding the urban territory as entangled networks of actors and resources.

Tom Nielsen is an architect and Professor of Urban and Landscape Planning at the Aarhus School of Architecture, Denmark, where he has been teaching landscape architecture, urban design and urban planning since 2004. His research focuses on the transformation of the Danish welfare city. This has included research into urban landscapes and public space (i.e. *Formløs*, 2001), suburban transformation, urbanising territories (i.e. *Det urbaniserede territorium*, 2009 and *Den østjyske millionby* (with B.B. Jensen), 2017) and the values and ethics of contemporary models of urban transformation (i.e. *Gode intentioner, uregerlige byer*, 2008).

Jacob Östberg is Professor of Advertising and PR at Stockholm Business School, Stockholm University, Sweden. He gained his PhD in 2003 from Lund University, Sweden. Since then he has taught at the Business Schools at Lund and Stockholm University, and as Visiting Distinguished Professor of Marketing, Aalto University School of Business, Helsinki, Finland, and visiting scholar at Bilkent University, Ankara, Turkey. His research interests revolve around how meaning is created in the intersection of marketing, popular culture, and consumers' lived lives. In particular, Jacob has been interested in questions around gender and masculinity in a Nordic setting, and how the influence of a particular state-sponsored gender ideology has shaped consumer culture.

Jens Christian Pasgaard is an Associate Professor, Cand. arch., PhD at the Aarhus School of Architecture, Denmark. Jens Christian has a special focus on Urban Design, Strategic Planning and the Phenomenon of Tourism. His PhD report on Tourism and Strategic Planning (2012) has been of particular interest for his work on Hvide Sande. He is affiliated to Studio Urban Design, Landscape Architecture (MA Studio) and to Research Laboratory 1 at the Aarhus School of Architecture, focusing on Territories, Architecture and Transformation.

Carina Ren is Associate Professor in the Tourism Research Unit at Aalborg University, Denmark. Carina researches connections between tourism and other fields of the social. Using ethnographic research and focusing on everyday practices, she explores different processes of cultural innovation and value creation, specifically looking at larger events, branding and destination development initiatives. She has published in leading tourism and Arctic journals and is the co-editor of several special issues and books, recently *Co-Creating Tourism Research. Towards collaborative ways of knowing* (2017, Routledge) and *Theories of Practice in Tourism* (2018, Routledge).

Külliki Seppel is an Assistant Lecturer in Media and Social Theories at the Institute of Social Studies, University of Tartu, Estonia. She is a sociologist who has published in the fields of nation building, inter-ethnic relations and democracy, as well as the social aspects of science and technology development.

Kadri Simm is an Associate Professor in Practical Philosophy at the Institute of Philosophy and Semiotics, University of Tartu, Estonia. Having graduated from history, gender studies, and philosophy, her main research interests and publications relate to political philosophy, feminist theory, and bioethics.

Kim Simonsen, PhD and MA University of Bergen, Norway, is a researcher at the University of Amsterdam. He is the leader of the Network on

Romantic Travel Writing to the Far North 1800–1900. He has been the coordinator of the Scandinavian section of the *Encyclopedia of Romantic Nationalism in Europe*. He works with nineteenth-century cultural nationalism, imagology, nationalism, culture in heritage and memory studies, as well the cultural and intellectual history of philology and Scandinavism.

Kristina Tamm Hallström is Associate Professor of Management at the Stockholm School of Economics and Research Fellow at the Stockholm Centre for Organizational Research (SCORE). She has conducted research and published extensively on legitimacy and authority within transnational standards-based governance. Moreover, she is conducting research on the power and consequences of classificatory work used in organising urban planning processes.

Piia Tammpuu is a PhD Candidate and Junior Researcher at the Institute of Social Studies, University of Tartu, Estonia. Having graduated from sociology and nationalism studies, her research interests relate to identity politics, national identity, transnationalism, and transformations of social space.

Steve Taylor is head at the University of the Highlands and Islands' Centre for Recreation and Tourism Research (CRTR), situated in Fort William, Scotland (https://www.whc.uhi.ac.uk/research/current-projects/). His principal roles involve working with international partners on the development and implementation of transnational tourism projects, managing tourism consultancy commissions, and writing articles for an academic audience, on mountain biking development and nature-based tourism in particular. He managed the Slow Adventure in Northern Territories INTERREG project and is the company secretary of the Slow Adventure Co-operative.

Peter Varley is Professor of Consumer Behaviour and Rural Tourism at the Western Norway University of Applied Science. His sociologically informed research centres upon investigations into tourist experiences, contextualised in interaction with places and spaces. These are often explored via studies in gastronomy, travel, adventure tourism, and outdoor leisure. Urban–rural contrasts are used as lenses through which to explore contemporary tensions and dialectics such as slow–fast life, leisure choices, and place-based acts of consumer resistance (see https://www.hvl.no/person/?user=6022837).

Anne Marit Waade is a Professor in Media Studies, Aarhus University, Denmark. Her research includes mediated places, creative industry and promotional culture, landscapes in Nordic Noir, screen tourism travel series and travel journalism. She has published extensively within the field, among others *Locating Nordic Noir* (Palgrave Macmillan, 2017); *Wallanderland* (Aalborg Universitetsforlag, 2013); *'Just follow the trail of blood': Nordic Noir tourism and screened landscapes* (Palgrave Macmillan, 2018). She holds the grant for the large-scale research project 'What Makes Danish TV Drama Travel?' (DFF, 2014–2018), and she is part of 'Rethinking Tourism in a Coastal City' (2016–2019, Danish Innovation Fund), 'Television in Small Nations' (AHRC, 2015–2016) and 'DETECt' (H2020, 2018–2021).

Foreword: towards a Nordic manifesto

Britt Kramvig

Let us start with tasting the metaphor of place branding. Place branding (or the practice of branding places) is a strategic endeavour to make places visible and competitive in the attention economy. Branding creates a visionary platform of becoming; it envisions prosperous viable futures for generations to come. A place can be described as a bounded geographic space, a multiple figure of materialities, politics and investments. A Nordic take on branding augments this view with communitarian perspectives. What we need to relate to is that a place is also *home* for individuals with their hopes, losses, ambitions and everyday lives, and their need to be cared for and recognised as members of a community: a community created by relations and through nodes in a network that we humans cannot do without. A place is always home for humans and other beings, a home where we all instinctively dwell. Previous Nordic studies have taught us that places, even the most remote, expand in time and space. They are not stable, but a vibrant field of diverse actors, governance, materialities, interests, memories and mobilities that inflict place conceptions – that challenge the need to fix a place (Førde, Dale, Kramvig, and Gunnerud Berg 2013). I learned this the hard way, being an anthropological student who settled in a village on the northern Arctic Coast, being possibly the only one not constantly on the move.

Considering these arguments, how are we to think about a place, and how can it be identified as an entity? As researchers, we do create them, even though they exist before we came. This is why place and space is a tricky research object. Space and place is everywhere (or nowhere . . .) following Geertz (1996). So how can we grasp it? A place is always in the making, always in the state of becoming – and we as a research community work to make sense of this. Place branding is a participatory endeavour, as one activity among many in the remaking of a place through multiple narrative, performative and governance techniques. The authors of this book argue that place branding has emerged as an object of study, a specific approach to branding practice and policy, a sensitivity to research and a type of hybrid scholarship that have a specific Nordic flavour. This is an interesting argument.

The study of place-based activity could take inspiration from Ingold (2000), concerned with the relationship between human beings and their environment. He argues against the notion that nature is this empty space constructed by human activity. He criticises the culture vs. nature dichotomy reproduced in the construction paradigm and resists the separation between the built of the human environment and the non-built environment. Instead, he adheres to an indigenous positionality which argues that we are part of nature and we are always in the world. This is a philosophical argument, but it could also be an argument embedded in his ethnographic research in Sápmi. Together with other species, humans instinctively dwell in places. Only through our capability to dwell can we build – because to build is already to dwell, Ingold argues. Just like waves, places are in a constant state of becoming – hence, branding is an act of dwelling; it adds to the becoming of the specificity of places. Waves have no borders or boundaries but they do have undercurrents that pull surfers in specific directions and at moments can pull them down. Writing from coastal Sámi communities, these collective knowledges are part of storytelling events through which the places are remembered and enacted, but also rebranded so to speak, to those that at that moment dwell and at other moments move, in and out of places.

The making of Sápmi as a place for tourism is an interesting case. Organised tourism in Sápmi goes back to 1875 when Thomas Cook & Son started cruises to the North Cape. From there on "Sámi Touristic Camp" became part of what was offered to the travellers at different locations on the coast where siidas dwelled during the summer. The World Exhibition in Paris in 1889 included a group of South Saami from Røros, as did the one held in Chicago in 1893. These exhibitions offered the participants the opportunity to witness the primitive races (Baglo 2001) and brought the curiosity to the fore that later brought new groups of travellers to the North or Ultima Thule. Ultima Thule – the farthest point, and the limit of any journey and people living at the edge of civilisation – was the figure that participated in the European self-image. In addition, these first tourist encounters were organised to reproduce stereotypical images of the Sámi within an ambiguous racial discourse that, as Baglo (2001) argues, supported Social Darwinian ideas. Essentialising ideas about race and culture is very much the foundation of Sámi tourism and the ongoing branding of Sápmi: a settled discourse that indigenous people and companies struggle to resist as well as renegotiate. Often consultants, working through innovation programmes, are not helpful. More than one of the Sámi tourist companies that I work with has been advised to hold on to the problematic clichés of the past, such as the concept of Lappland, because the European travellers know Sápmi as such. Through these reproductions, a culture that is not concerned with authenticity becomes so, within the touristic discourse.

The becoming of a place through branding, and through engaging with the collective acts of remembering or forgetting, contributes to the configuring and forming of places (Ahmed 1999). This is very much so in the Nordic Sámi communities that during the colonial period were forced to collectively give up, or to forget, the Sámi heritage, stories, languages and objects, and accept the branding of the place in line with the authorities. Ahmed (1999: p. 341) argues:

> The lived experience of being-at-home hence involves the enveloping of subjects in a space which is not simply outside them: being-at-home suggests that the subject and space leak into each other, inhabit each other. To some extent we can think of the lived experience of being at home in terms of inhabiting a second skin, a skin which does not simply contain the homely subject, but which allows the subject to be touched and touch the world that is neither simply in the home or away from the home.

The home as skin suggests that the boundary between home and away is permeable and so is the boundary between self and home. In addition, Ahmed argues that movement away is always affective: it affects how "homely" one might feel and fail to feel. The Nordic wave is a figure of thought inspiring many of the writers in this book, undertaking an understanding of the Nordic as a movement whose size and boundaries flow back and forth in time and space. Despite the large number of studies addressing Nordic place brands and branding, little attention has been given to the practices of branding and place branding research within the Nordic welfare states. Place branding is undertaken through strategic political as well as business actors; still, also, the numerous storyings of place that are conducted by less strategic actors should be considered in academic analyses. As Ren, Pram Gad and Rastad Bjørst argue in this volume, place brands are unruly and have multiple sites of enactment. This volume encourages us as researchers concerned with place and place branding to identify and relate to these complexities, as well as always asking the difficult questions about what and whose stories are not told that enact places, homes and brands.

REFERENCES

Ahmed, S. 1999. Home and away: Narratives of migration and estrangement. *International Journal of Cultural Studies*, 2(3), 329–347.
Baglo, C. 2001. From universal homogeneity to essential heterogeneity: On the

visual construction of "the Lappish race". *Acta Borealia*, 18(2), 23–39, DOI: 10.1080/08003830108580524.

Førde, A., Dale, B., Kramvig, B. & Gunnerud Berg, N. 2013. *Å finne sted. Metodologiske perspektiver i stedsanalyser*. Trondheim: Akademika forlag NTNU.

Geertz, C. 1996. Afterword. In S. Feld & K. Basso (Eds.), *Sense of Place* (pp. 259–62) Santa Fe: School of American Research Process.

Ingold, T. 2000. *The perception of the environment: Essays on livelihood, dwelling and skill*. London: Routledge.

Preface

The book is composed of 19 chapters in forms of full text or shorter commentary, and is organized according to three themes: poetics, practices and politics of Nordicity. The introductory chapter apart presenting the structuring logic and framework of the book, it opens with clarification and justification about the academic and popular rationale of the focus of the book, Nordic exceptionalism, from both an ontological and epistemological perspective. The chapters included in the book are grouped based on topicality and their relationship with the different themes, rendering a blending of contrasting or complementary accounts. Each theme ends with a commentary written by one of the editors focusing on some specific issue which has been touched by the preceding chapters, and is of particular Nordic relevance, in speculative manner so to attempt to generate alternative research directions.

The book ends with a conclusion written by the editors in which the peculiarity of Nordic place branding is tackled through a conceptual and contextual meta-analysis of the different contributions included in every chapter. More specifically, the conclusion offers a framework contouring a "Manifesto", which aims to inform researchers, policymakers, and practitioners in their pursuit of more focused, yet critical, place branding research and activities in the Nordic context, but equally extends theorization and contributes to the literature on place branding as traditionally framed by the Anglo-Saxon and European field of research and practice. By theorizing, conceptualizing and analyzing the Nordic, the final chapter offers a discussion on the broader significance and contribution of the book to the international place branding field. The book is bracketed by a "Foreword" by Britt Kramvig and an "Afterword" by Mihalis Kavaratzis, which, from respectively Nordic and non-Nordic scholarship points of view, critically comment on the book and its significance.

1. The Nordic wave in place branding: moving back and forth in time and space

Cecilia Cassinger, Andrea Lucarelli and Szilvia Gyimóthy

This introductory chapter provides a background to the Nordic wave of place branding and its impact on research and practice. The ocean wave is used as a metaphor in the book to emphasize the Nordic as a movement whose boundaries flow back and forth in time and space. The contributors in the book surf the Northern waves in different directions towards increasing the knowledge of the Nordic brand and its implications for place branding. Their contributions emerge from different understandings and ideals of Nordicity, which are used to frame place branding in various ways. The contributions are organized according to three themes – *poetics*, *practices* and *politics* – which are introduced in this chapter.

Nordic place branding is an emerging field of academic research and practice. The evolution, expansion, and geographical spread of place branding in the Nordic region has been studied in several ways and is echoed in recent journal articles and special issues. The strong focus on the Nordic region is evident in the study of Swedish, Norwegian, Finnish, and Danish cases, strategies, and processes, as well as in the researchers' country of origin (see for a review Lucarelli and Berg, 2011; Chan and Marafa, 2013; Lucarelli and Broström, 2013; Andersson, 2014). Similarly, the strong focus on the Nordic as ideological and socio-cultural construct is evident in the analysis of topics and cases that are not only peculiar to the Nordic as a specific academe (e.g. the interest in food), but also more crucially by the recurrence of similar topics and analysis which are translocal (across countries) and international (outside the Nordic).

The Nordic is here understood in broad terms as an idea (Czarniawska-Joerges and Sevón, 2005), an ideological orientation, and myth, as well as a regional space in relation to which theories, concepts, and practices of place branding emerge and develop. The present book is a further step in the evolution, expansion, and geographical spread of place branding in the Nordic region, as well as a timely attempt to consider some of the more nebulous related terms and concept (e.g. Nordic cuisine, gender equality, etc.). It does so by building on and synchronizing the existing body of academic research on the Nordic (e.g. Lucarelli and Hallin 2015; Cassinger and Eksell, 2017; Gyimóthy, 2017), as well as by expanding its empirical outreach to topics, cases and fields of inquiry which have not traditionally been tackled by place branding studies (e.g. brand collaborations, phantasmagoria, feminism, appropriation processes, and ideology).

Despite the large number of studies addressing Nordic place brands and branding, little attention is given to the practices of place branding within the Nordic welfare states. The unusual open access to the field of practice granted to researchers (at least compared to Anglo-Saxon and European standard), and the particular political, institutional, cultural environment of the Nordic has not fully been unpacked. The limited scope of previous studies on place branding paired with a widespread international interest in the "Nordic" as a geographical place, moral orientation, and (normative) discourse calls for more research into the global relevance of Nordic place branding. This triggers a number of questions. How is Nordicity defined in place branding? What characterizes the relationship between the Nordic as an idea, dream and myth and the technocracies of place branding? What are the implications for international place branding studies?

Our main concern in editing this book is to open up space from which the Nordic particularism can be conceptualized, analyzed, criticized, and emulated in an international context. The book is one of the very first attempts to unpack the specificity of "Nordicity" in regards to place branding by collecting, examining, and systematizing diverse instances of the Nordic place branding tradition. It gathers different transdisciplinary accounts written by researchers in different research traditions such as business administration, tourism, geography, communication, sociology, and political science. The contributions demonstrate a certain Nordic place branding scholarship characterized by processes of de-politicization, consensus making, collaboration, and transparency. At the same time, Nordic ideals, policies and values push critical, and, hence far, unexplored issues in place branding, such as feminism, bio-ethics, sustainability, and social justice. It is our contention that these peculiarities may be used for building theories and developing methods, which can be extended to the Anglo-Saxon and European field of place branding research and practice.

PLACE BRANDING PERSPECTIVES

As a form of branding philosophy applied to places, place branding has experienced a rapid growth materializing in different branding strategies, practices and public–private investments. Research on place branding at the same time has created new and interwoven methodologies, and different conceptualizations, in order to shape competitive and winning place branding efforts. Although practices and theories have generally understood "place brands" as a particular phenomenon, one can witness in the international-based research two broadly yet sometime interrelated perspectives. On one hand, one can see studies that conceptualize and analyze place brands as having the same features as corporate and product brands and thus implying place brandings as the practices of strategically creating and enhancing brands. In other words, these studies imply that place brands can be seen as a catalyzer of unifying and coherent communications, strategies and activities structured in different forms such as an umbrella, house of brands, etc. (e.g. Hanna and Rowley, 2011; Iversen and Hem, 2008), embracing the corporate and product branding paradigm (e.g. Ashworth and Kavaratzis, 2009) and emerging as marketing phenomena with some intrinsic characteristics that can be caught and measured (e.g. Insch and Florek, 2008; Zenker, 2011). On the other hand, there are studies where the distinction between place brands and branding is more dynamic and difficult to spot, since brands, rather than being seen as an entity, are instead seen as emerging and becoming process – and therefore branding (or the process of branding) and brands (or the object) does not differ (see e.g. Giovanardi et al., 2013). These studies do not consider pointing out the difference between place brands and branding as a fundamental point of research, and the majority of these studies embrace an interdisciplinary perspective that goes beyond a pure product, service, or corporate branding approach to place branding (Aitken and Campelo, 2011; Kavaratzis, 2012; Pike, 2009; Warnaby and Medway, 2013) which takes into consideration its geopolitical dimension (Eshuis and Klijn, 2012; Lucarelli and Giovanardi, 2016; Ooi, 2004). This offers a grounded spatio-temporal approach which goes beyond the mere application of corporate and product business models to places (Kavaratzis and Kalandides, 2015) where place brands materialize as complex socio-political constructs composed of a multi-contextual understanding both in spatial and temporal dimensions, multi-level interaction among actors and by a legal, political, and aesthetic process.

Despite the fact that the second perspective is more largely endorsed, mainly due to the specific scholarship present in the Nordic research environment, both perspectives are used here as a point of departure in order to spell out the Nordic perspective. In fact, by embracing a cursory view of the literature one can witness that, although a number of studies have addressed Nordic place brands and branding, the peculiarity of brands and branding within the Nordic perspective remains understudied. In this context, on one hand, the present book recognizes that if the unusual open access to the field of practice granted to researchers (at least compared to Anglo-Saxon and European standards), and the particular political, institutional, and cultural environment of the Nordic has not fully been unpacked, on the other hand, the limited scope of previous studies on place branding paired with a widespread international interest in the "Nordic" as a geographical place, moral orientation, and (normative) discourse calls for more research into the global relevance of Nordic place branding.

LOCATING THE NORDIC PLACE BRAND AND NORDIC PLACE BRANDING

Places are imagined and constructed in and through practices for certain purposes and ends. The Nordic region is made up of five countries, Denmark, Finland, Iceland, Norway, and Sweden, and the regions and provinces of the Aaland Islands, Faroe Islands, and Greenland including the Inuit land areas. Sámpi, which belongs to the indigenous Sámi population in the Nordic region, cuts across Finland, Sweden, Norway, and parts of Murmansk in Russia. Sámpi is currently considered as a cultural region without autonomy. The Nordic countries share similarities in terms of language and geographical location, but also in terms of a shared history, culture, values, and ideals. Yet, the Nordic countries differ and have developed unique characters in relation to one another over time (Ehn et al., 1993). In order to examine Nordic place branding, we identify historical and contemporary stereotypes of national and regional differences between the countries. We shed light on the values, ideals, and ideologies that the Nordic countries have used to construct themselves with particular relevance for place branding. Such claimed values include cooperation, consensus, solidarity, democracy, freedom, social cohesion, and gender equality. Equally, the book reflects on the social, cultural, and geopolitical reasons for why these values historically have been emphasized in the region.

We are interested in approaching the construction of the Nordic as an idea, the practices of this construction, and its consequences. This interest is reflected in the three parts that build the book. First, Nordic countries are small and dependent on maintaining good relationships with the surrounding world. Second, the legacy of the Nordic welfare state has recently been called into question. Third, the mythologies and sagas in the regions involve themes of superiority and the obligation to act as a model for other countries to imitate (see Schough, 2008). Scholars have rightly criticized the conception of the Nordic countries as peaceful and benevolent, and challenged the myth of the harmonious Nordic countries by pointing to their violent relationship to former colonies (Adler-Nissen and Gad, 2013), growing problems with right-wing populism (e.g. Pamment, 2016) and involvement in international armed conflicts (Browning, 2007). The Nordic model should thus be understood as an aspirational idea that has more or less impact on Nordic realities.

It follows that the analysis of the relationships between the Nordic and place branding, as it is dealt with in this book, are complex matters. The contributions in the book deal either with the Nordic as a valuable brand which diverse industries (e.g. food, music, tourism) can capitalise on, or the Nordic as a context for place branding practices in which different place branding efforts emerge. Overall, with some exceptions, a practice-based approach to Nordic place branding is adopted with a focus on enactments and processes of becoming, rather than the instruments and effects of branding.

DISCLOSING NEW WAYS OF THINKING AND DOING PLACE BRANDING: POETICS, PRACTICES, AND POLITICS

The contributions in this book exemplify traditions of scholarship that deal with the relation between the Nordic and place branding. Even though each of the chapters provides a unique insight into particular empirical or conceptual aspects of Nordic place branding, they can be clustered along three themes that we refer to as the *poetics*, *practices*, and *politics of place branding* (inspired by Ooi, 2004) The idea is that the Nordic perspective modifies or even challenges place branding's *comme il faut*. Taken together these themes challenge the taken-for-granted concepts and practices within place branding and reveal new ways of thinking and doing research and practice. It should however be noted that the thematization was constructed for the sake of clarity of argumentation and that the themes are interrelated and at times overlapping.

Poetics

The first theme, poetics, deals with ways of constructing and representing Nordicity in place branding practices. But also, given the liaison, in practice, between Nordic as place brand and the branding of Nordic places, the theme deals with the way branding practices are framed in a way that Nordic place branding is considered to be specific, peculiar, and foundational. It follows that the primary focus is given to identifying key narratives, rhetorical strategies, genealogical–historical and emerging storytelling templates in various empirical contexts and on multiple geographic scales. In other words, the contributions included in Part I all at different levels (i.e. not only ontologically and epistemologically but also more crucially empirically) analyze the way Nordic place branding has been in the past and present represented as specific idea, myth and socio-cultural context which is considered to be Nordic. Accordingly, one can see that the different chapters grouped under the present theme all contribute to creating an assembled account. For example, the (pan) Nordic research team composed of Lars Pynt Andersen, Frank Lindberg and Jacob Östberg consider the poetics of enchanting the Nordic *terroir* within the new Nordic cuisine wave. This is followed by Jörgen Eksell and and Alicia Fjällhed who instead take the approach of a diachronic analysis of the Nordic region as a transnational brand based on multilateral agreements across historical and political collaboration. In the next chapter, Jessica Edlom, despite having a similar focus, follows the digital platform Swedish Affair to unveil the how the national brand provides branding synergies for the Swedish creative industries, most notably popular music. Further, the Swedish research team, composed of Sara Brorström, Sarah Degerhammar and Kristina Tamm Hallström, address the specificity of place branding among municipalities in relation to organizational complexity, size, and norms of how to brand in the Nordic context. Finally, Andrea Lucarelli discusses, by manner of a brief historical account of the interlink between Scandinavia and Nordic, how the branding of Nordic reflects difference in both the internal and external pattern of representation of the region.

Practices

The second theme, practices, refers to Nordic ways of doing place branding, and qualifies the characteristics of place branding practices in the Nordic context. Rather than pinning down stereotypical representations and narratives, the chapters in Part II highlight the particularities of branding processes in various empirical and geographical contexts. In addition, it deals with how the Nordic place brand travels, i.e. ways in which the Nordic is appropriated and incorporated into other place branding practices. Accordingly, one can see that the different chapters grouped under the present theme all contribute to creating an assembled account. Part II starts with a large pan-Nordic and non-Nordic research team, composed of Daniel Laven, Tatiana Chekalina, Matthias Fuchs, Lusine Margaryan, Peter Varley and Steve Taylor, examining the processes of building and implementing a label for slow adventure tourism in the Northern territories. Further, in the following chapters the transdisciplinary research team, composed of Anne Marit Waade, Jens Christian Pasgaard, Mathias Meldgaard and Tom Nielsen, present and assess two different modes of collaborative place branding and place intervention approaches in a Nordic rural branding context, while Rikke Brandt Broegaard, Karin Topsø Larsen and Lene Havtorn Larsen investigate the critical role of translocal mobility and relations in branding remote islands. Two further chapters focus on specific issues: Ole Have Jørgensen analyzes the transformation of a Danish city brand, with specific focus on the controversial associations to its former prison and Susanna Heldt Cassel shows how the branding of Sámpi destinations and places can be seen as a complex and contested practice that involves the power to represent and to co-construct the culture and heritage of people and places (not least minority groups and peripheral areas), particularly in a Nordic context. Part II concludes with a commentary by Szilvia Gyimóthy in which she discusses the adoption, interpretation, and rephrasing of values considered to be essentially Nordic.

Politics

The third theme is about the political consequences and implications of Nordic place branding. Previous research predominantly understands the political aspect of place branding as a neoliberal form of governance (e.g. Eshuis and Klijn, 2012; Kaneva, 2011). In Part III, the Nordic is used as an allegory to reveal the politics of place branding in a broader sense, seeking to capture additional configurations of politics (see Lucarelli, 2015). The contributions in Part III consider place branding in relation to Nordic policy-making, ideology, and national identity, and in so doing they make struggles over truth, inclusion, economic interests, and social power visible. Accordingly, one can recognize that the different chapters grouped under the present theme all contribute to creating an assembled account. For example, Carina Ren, Ulrik Pram Gad and Lill Rastad Bjørst, by presenting an analysis of branding approaches in Greenland, present the tensions between Nordicity and postcolonial discourses, highlighting parallel branding processes in four distinct empirical contexts as diplomacy, mining, tourism, and the cultural industries. The following chapter by Kim Simonsen takes a different point of departure in analyzing the politics of Nordic food as a performance and as medialized re-enactment of a nation's inner life, all with the aim of shedding light on food as a reflection and a constant conversation about national identity and identity politics. A similar topic, but related to traditional political discourse, is the topic that the Estonia-based research team, composed of Piia Tammpuu, Külliki Seppel and Kadri Simm, instead highlight in their chapter, which shows how the Nordic brand can be appropriated in a foreign (i.e. Estonian) political discourse. The next conceptual chapter by Mikael Andéhn scrutinizes the use of Sweden as rhetorical placeholder for ideologies in the context of so-called post-truth political discourse. In the chapter by Anne Heith, an indigenous perspective on Nordic Place Branding is offered, in particular by focusing on Sámi and Sámpi and the political uses of immaterial and material resources. Part III concludes with a commentary by Cecilia Cassinger, who reflects on the implications of Nordic feminist politics, in particular Sweden's feminist foreign policy, for mediating the region as a market to invest in and a moral example for others to follow.

REFERENCES

Adler-Nissen, R., & Gad, U. P. (Eds.). (2013). *European integration and postcolonial sovereignty games: The EU overseas countries and territories.* New York: Routledge.

Aitken, R., & Campelo, A. (2011). The four Rs of place branding. *Journal of Marketing Management, 27*(9–10), 913–933.

Andersson, I. (2014). Placing place branding: An analysis of an emerging research field in human geography. *Geografisk Tidsskrift-Danish Journal of Geography, 114*(2), 143–155.

Ashworth, G., & Kavaratzis, M. (2009). Beyond the logo: Brand management for cities. *Journal of Brand Management, 16*(8), 520–531.

Browning, C. S. (2007). Branding Nordicity: Models, identity and the decline of exceptionalism. *Cooperation and Conflict, 42*(1), 27–51.

Cassinger, C., & Eksell, J. (2017). The magic of place branding: Regional brand identity in transition. *Journal of Place Management and Development, 10*(3), 202–212.

Chan, C. S., & Marafa, L. M. (2013). A review of place branding methodologies in the new millennium. *Place Branding and Public Diplomacy, 9*(4), 236–253.

Czarniawska-Joerges, B., & Sevón, G. (Eds.). (2005). *Global ideas: How ideas, objects and practices travel in a global economy* (Vol. 13). Copenhagen: Copenhagen Business School Press.

Ehn, B., Lofgren, O., & Frykman, J. (1993). *Forsvenskningen av Sverige.* Stockholm: Natur & Kultur.

Eshuis, J., & Klijn, E. H. (2012). *Branding in governance and public management.* New York: Routledge.

Giovanardi, M., Lucarelli, A., & Pasquinelli, C. (2013). Towards brand ecology: An analytical semiotic framework for interpreting the emergence of place brands. *Marketing Theory, 13*(3), 365–383.

Gyimóthy, S. (2017). The reinvention of terroir in Danish food place promotion. *European Planning Studies*, *25*(7), 1200–1216.

Hanna, S., & Rowley, J. (2011). Towards a strategic place brand-management model. *Journal of Marketing Management*, *27*(5–6), 458–476.

Insch, A., & Florek, M. (2008). A great place to live, work and play: Conceptualising place satisfaction in the case of a city's residents. *Journal of Place Management and Development*, *1*(2), 138–149.

Iversen, N. M., & Hem, L. E. (2008). Provenance associations as core values of place umbrella brands: A framework of characteristics. *European Journal of Marketing*, *42*(5/6), 603–626.

Kaneva, N. (2011). Nation branding: Toward an agenda for critical research. *International Journal of Communication*, *5*, 117–141.

Kavaratzis, M. (2012). From "necessary evil" to necessity: Stakeholders' involvement in place branding. *Journal of Place Management and Development*, *5*(1), 7–19.

Kavaratzis, M., & Kalandides, A. (2015). Rethinking the place brand: The interactive formation of place brands and the role of participatory place branding. *Environment and Planning A*, *47*(6), 1368–1382.

Lucarelli, A. (2015). *The political dimension of place branding* (Doctoral dissertation). Stockholm Business School, Stockholm University.

Lucarelli, A., & Berg, P. (2011). City branding: A state-of-the-art review of the research domain. *Journal of Place Management and Development*, *4*(1), 9–27.

Lucarelli, A., & Brorström, S. (2013). Problematising place branding research: A meta-theoretical analysis of the literature. *The Marketing Review*, *13*(1), 65–81.

Lucarelli, A., & Giovanardi, M. (2016). The political nature of brand governance: A discourse analysis approach to a regional brand building process. *Journal of Public Affairs*, *16*(1), 16–27.

Lucarelli, A., & Hallin, A. (2015). Brand transformation: A performative approach to brand regeneration. *Journal of Marketing Management*, *31*(1–2), 84–106.

Ooi, C. S. (2004). Poetics and politics of destination branding: Denmark. *Scandinavian Journal of Hospitality and Tourism*, *4*(2), 107–128.

Pamment, J. (2016). Introduction: Why the Nordic region? *Journal of Place Branding and Public Diplomacy*, *12*(2–3), 91–98.

Pike, A. (2009). Brand and branding geographies. *Geography Compass*, *3*(1), 190–213.

Schough, K. (2008). *Hyberboré. Föreställningen om Sveriges plats i världen*. Stockholm: Carlssons.

Warnaby, G., & Medway, D. (2013). What about the "place" in place marketing? *Marketing Theory*, *13*(3), 345–363.

Zenker, S. (2011). How to catch a city? The concept and measurement of place brands. *Journal of Place Management and Development*, *4*(1), 40–52.

PART I

Poetics of Nordicity

2. Reinvention through Nordicness: values, traditions, and terroir

Lars Pynt Andersen, Frank Lindberg and Jacob Östberg

INTRODUCTION

In the aftermath of the New Nordic Cuisine (NNC) manifesto of 2004, the cuisine sector has become interested in invoking Nordicness in many forms related to aesthetics and moralities (Hermansen 2012; Byrkeflot et al. 2013; Leer 2016; Gyimóthy 2017; Neuman 2018). The manifesto-branding strategy used by the consortium behind NNC was inspired by a similar strategy that sparked the New Danish Cinema (the DOGMA manifesto), which also succeeded in creating an 'umbrella' branding effect, or 'wave' for many smaller actors to join (Leer 2016). Both manifesto-invoked 'waves' have been part of an even larger recent interest in the idea of 'the Nordic' in popular culture, but the production of the imagery and mythology of The Nordic Region has been going on for centuries (Harvard and Stadius 2013). It is possible to consider The Nordic Region as an imagined community, but one that also has complex relations to the related imagined communities of Scandinavia, Denmark, Norway, and so on (Anderson 2006 [1986]). Place and destination brands are very complex brand concepts (Ren and Blichfeldt 2011) and consequently we are sceptical of functionalist conceptualizations that call attention to consumer responses, producer contributions or the co-created brand (see Lucarelli and Brorström 2013). Rather, we rely on a post-structural version of the 'appropriation perspective' (Lucarelli and Brorström 2013) in which branding becomes a dynamic and ongoing interpretation of symbolic markers that might 'transgress the traditional boundaries between urban/rural, local/global, traditional/trendy and authentic/invented' (Gyimóthy 2017, p. 1211).

In this chapter we seek to develop the notion of 'the Nordic' as brand further. We propose to see 'the Nordic' as a complex umbrella brand strategy that is based on materializations and performances of Nordicness, even if the different brands under the general umbrella do not explicitly use the term 'Nordic' in the brand name or other central denotations of the product or service. 'Nordicness' can refer to aesthetics, images, myths, social concepts such as 'hygge' or even socioeconomic concepts such as 'Nordic welfare' and the surrounding ideologies and values (Linnet 2011, 2015; Østergaard et al. 2014). In discussing Nordicness it is important not to resort to essentialism by trying to uncover what is authentically Nordic, for example as related to geographical labels or culinary heritage and traditions. Rather, we propose that the 'Nordic' as a brand is a label whose meaning is in constant translation by various institutions such as destination management organizations (DMOs), non-governmental organizations (NGOs) and small and medium-sized enterprises (SMEs), and negotiated through consumption, media, popular culture and politics (Østergaard et al. 2014). On the same note, we suggest that a clear distinction of 'value' or 'tradition' when referring to concepts such as 'Nordic egalitarianism', 'trust' or 'hygge' is difficult or even misleading when trying to define 'Nordicness'. For example 'hygge' is stipulated in the official Danish Canon of Values (Danmarkskanon (https://www.danmarkskanon. dk/ (accessed May 15 2018)), as one out of ten 'Danish values'. But, as pointed out by Linnet (2011): it is the centrality in everyday discourses, the ubiquitousness of 'hygge', that makes up the continuously negotiated, rich meaning for native Nordics. Thus 'hygge' may be discursively constructed as a value, a tradition, a social norm, a context, a performance, a mood, an ambience and a design concept.

As such, there is a pool of Nordicness resources that might be drawn upon to construct and materialize various Nordic brands (Östberg 2011). Some of these resources might be less controversial, such as imagery of Nordic landscapes, whereas others might be highly controversial in certain circles. An example of the latter is the Norse symbols that were appropriated by the Nazis and which are still used by Neo-Nazi groups. This is perhaps an extreme example but the process of creating a Nordic brand can never be entirely apolitical (Escobar 2001) since cultural tension is a precondition for cultural branding (Holt 2004).

Regardless of what particular sets of symbolic resources are drawn upon to connote Nordicness, we can see that this trope has become an important resource of brand meaning for both domestic and non-domestic brand actors, for example in the food and tourism sectors (Hermansen 2012; Gyimóthy 2017; Neuman 2018) and in fashion, furniture and design (Roncha 2008; Östberg 2011). Companies emanating from and/or being based in the Nordic countries can draw upon Nordicness in their brand building endeavours. We propose that 'Nordic branding' as attaching a sense of Nordicness to a market offering is not merely a process of attaching a piece of information that goes into consumer decision-making (Holt

2004; Kornberger 2010). Rather, attaching signifiers of Nordicness might link a market offering to a rich 'product-country imagery' (Askegaard and Ger 1997) that potentially has rich sensory, affective and ritual connotations, that in turn invite consumers to take part in the cultural production of meaning.

The aim of this chapter is to investigate and illustrate how Nordicness is negotiated among firms that are inspired by the New Nordic Cousin. We ask the question: How do firms reinvent the 'Nordic' in their branding, invoking the symbolic resources of Nordicness? We focus on the stories of the human brand actors, primarily the entrepenuers, but we acknowledge the agentic entities such as consumer culture, myths, ideas, brands, traditions, welfare systems and the geographical terroir as the resources for the brand actors to enact. With '(re-)invent' we mean that the brand performances are always constructions that rely on earlier performances and creations of Nordicness. In this sense we lean on Scandinavian institutionalism, and the idea of 'translation' rather than 'diffusion' of the 'Nordic' brand (Czarniawska and Sevón 2005).

THE NORDICNESS OF NEW NORDIC CUISINE

One particularly successful example of *Nordic branding* is the case of NNC, which was initiated by the group behind the restaurant Noma in Copenhagen and the principal actors Claus Meyer and Rene Redzépi (Leer 2016; Thorsøe et al. 2016). The NNC has from the original, programmatic 'manifesto' inception been highly dependent on the notion of terroir for its performance (Hermansen 2012; Byrkeflot et al. 2013; Leer 2016). The NNC manifesto invokes terroir as the main symbolic resource, as NNC aims 'to express the purity, freshness, simplicity and ethics associated with the region [using] produce whose characteristics are particularly excellent in Nordic climates, landscapes and waters' (New Nordic Food 2004, first and third aims). The manifesto's name signifies that something is *new*: NNC was constructed with the aesthetics of simplicity symbolizing the pure and healthy, which, it could be argued, at the time challenged a situation of (global) hybrid culinary tradition (e.g. fast food). The highly aestheticized presentations of the food in cookery books and the media is not without a sensual appeal, but the manifesto underlines that the hedonics of consuming NNC must be balanced with 'modern knowledge on health and well-being' (New Nordic Food 2004, aim 4). Compared to the bright and colourful imagery of Mediterranean food, however, the photos of NNC with, for example, cabbage on wood or stoneware seem somewhat naked and austere, usually dominated by dark green and grey colours (Hermansen 2012). As in the contemporary production values of Nordic Noir crime series, Nordicness is constructed as an aesthetic of 'bleakness' (Waade and Jensen 2016).

Historically, regional branding strategies rely heavily on a rhetoric that cultivates myths, images and ideas of the geographical landscape as terroir (Trubek 2008; Gyimóthy 2017). It is thus important that the symbolic resources of Nordicness are interpreted as standing in a natural relationship to both the geographical location and the market offering at play. If the relationship is interpreted as contrived by relevant audiences, they will not accept the proposition. According to Hermansen (2012), the NNC offers the local urban and modern elites a way of indulging in 'nationalistic' nostalgia otherwise considered contrived or as downright improper ideology (modern elites are supposed to be of a more cosmopolitan mindset). The NNC's Nordicness thus might signify rich symbolic resources for branding and consumption that capacitate construction of regionalism and the accompanied 'terroir fetish' into a modern urban and ethical mode of consumption.

However, the NNC needs to be continuously reinvented if it is to become more than a passing 'fad' (Bech-Larsen et al. 2016; Leer 2016), since the translation of terroir and reliance on novelty wear out or become contrived to the key audiences. The question remains as to how Nordicness influences brand reinvention when cultural symbols, ideologies and values, rather than the geographical typicality, are negotiated.

RESEARCH APPROACH AND CASE DESCRIPTION

We have combined participant observation, photography, online research and observation with semi-structured interviews. The focus during interviews has been on the meaning of Nordicness related to the respective product category and brands. We consider the participants as expert informants who can tell stories and reflect about their professional roles, practices and (branding) strategies in addition to the development of the NNC and related ideas behind the companies. The interviews were all conducted in the professional contexts of the café/restaurant/workshop, the spaces they themselves have at least co-constructed, and therefore likely have imbued with meanings. We consider these ideal settings, as it is easy for informants to be reminded of the constructions and performances, and to point to these or mention them in the interview. The six interviews (manager, head of kitchen, two chefs and two apprentices) at Restaurant NYT (Bodø, Norway) were held in the lounge space or in a dining area of the restaurant (when closed to the public). The two interviews at BRØD

(Odense, Denmark) were held in the café section, but also as part of a visit to the BRØD carpentry workshop (Langeland, Denmark) where the décor is constructed (booths, benches, etc.). During the visits the researchers conducted observations (e.g. dining, café visit) and took photos of exterior and interior areas.

The Norwegian city of Bodø is located north of the Arctic Circle in the region of Nordland. Bodø was founded in 1816 to compete with Bergen in the fishing industry. It has a landscape that perfectly matches the romantic images of Norwegian fjords and mountains, and a long history of nature-based tourism with the emphasis on symbolic elements such as midnight sun, northern lights, mountain hiking and fishing as part of the destination brand (see Visit Bodø n.d.). The shield of the region (like a flag) has the image of a Viking ship. Bodø is a modern city today which is rooted in the history and identity of the landscape that 'gave birth to it', 'nurtured it' and still supports it with the basis for tourism and leisure.

The focus of the study in Bodø is the *Restaurant NYT*, which has been voted the 'best restaurant in Norway' by the patrons and classified as a 'very fine level' of restaurant in the White Guide – The Nordics (White Guide n.d.). Restaurant NYT is managed and owned by two young entrepreneurs who are inspired by the NNC movement. In the decoration of the restaurant, the landscapes of Bodø are ubiquitous: on the walls as large photos. In addition, books and magazines covering varying topics of Nordic Cuisine are found in the lounge areas. Artefacts such as granite rock samples and figurines of birds decorate the space (Figure 2.1(a)). When we were served small portion-sized breads, they were presented on a very large, naturally rounded piece of warm granite rock. The menu is fixed and the customers can choose between four to seven dishes, all based on seasonal ingredients from local resources. The descriptions in the menu are simple explicating only the main content such as 'cod tongue' and 'blue mussels', which is consistent with the restaurant's ideal of creativity and surprise, but also down-to-earth pragmatism. The presentation of each dish details the ingredients with an emphasis on the local origin.

The BRØD chain of bread studios originated in Svendborg (Fyn), and is still at the time of writing opening new branches in Jutland and Fyn. The Odense (Kongensgade) branch was the first full-scale version of the concept. Odense is the third largest city in Denmark, located in the region of Southern Denmark on the island of Fyn. Still, with more of a town-feeling to it, decades of city branding based on the birth place of the writer Hans Christian Andersen has made it a tourist destination. The low housing of the old city centre has many cafés and restaurants that cater for the locals and tourists. Today, there are actually two branches of BRØD in these pedestrian streets.

(a)   (b)

Source: Photos: Lars Pynt Andersen.

*Figure 2.1   (a) Restaurant NYT with white tablecloths and comfy chairs,
              photos of Bodø landscapes on the walls; (b) BRØD with
              wooden interior, broad benches and homemade tea lights*

The BRØD logo has integrated an image of a loaf of bread in the vertical
lines of the 'B' and 'D' ('brød' meaning 'bread'). However, the BRØD
bakery promotes itself as 'a Danish bread studio' on the façade and as an
integral part of the brand name and logo on bags and boxes. The bread
studio is a combined bakery and self-service café with a design that is both
modern and rustic: décor, benches and booths made of 'flamed' pine wood
and little round tables with simple chairs (see Figure 2.1(b)); warm colours
on walls and ceilings and lighted candles on every table (tea lights, as is
customary in Nordic social 'hygge' settings). In many ways, the space and
the organization of self-service counter and seating space resembles the
classic Danish/Nordic version of a Viennese café, which were common
before the sector became dominated by Italian or 'Starbuckified' cafés
(Kjeldgaard and Östberg 2007). The studio has the baker perform his
craft in plain view of the patrons, which differs clearly from the traditional
Danish bakery/Viennese café.

   Everything in the décor is homemade by the people of BRØD, sometimes in collaboration with local artisans, and in their local workshop on
the island of Langeland. From the tea light stands to the leather cushions,
aprons or lamps, everything is locally homemade and has a story.

PRAGMATICALLY (RE)INVENTING TRADITIONS

Paxson (2010) argues that discovering and reinventing traditional production methods are an important strategy of creating terroir. BRØD and
NYT, however, are more pragmatically trying to negotiate the brand as
connected to local traditions. The manager at NYT, Bjørnar, states that
their cuisine is anchored in history and that the Nordic to them means
looking back on Nordland's regional culinary traditions: what did people
do before the fridge and the freezer arrived? To be able to answer this
question they invited the regional media to ask for traditional recipes and
ingredients including the stories behind them. This pragmatic investigation of culinary traditions was an attempt to reinvent not only the purity,
freshness, simplicity and ethics associated with the region (New Nordic
Food 2004), but also the composition of dishes that had been forgotten.
Nordicness, then, implies reconstruction of culinary values, rituals and
traditions, which is closely linked to the North Norwegian cultural identity
(e.g. the 'true north of Norway': harsh living conditions, dramatic nature,
fishing traditions). In this sense, reinventing the Nordic is clearly supported
by a nostalgia of values in traditions, something lost to be recovered.

In BRØD they draw heavily on the central tenets of honest and old-
fashioned bakery. The slightly incongruous mix of Danish and English
in the brand identity is quite indicative of the eclectic 'do-it-yourself' and
'come-as-you-are' approach of BRØD. At the same time they signal local-
ness, no-nonsense, but also presenting culinary ambitions with a globalized
lifestyle concept (bread studio). John (founder/owner) constantly uses the
term 'butter baked' about his idea of honest bread and cakes. Using lots of
butter is also the tenet of the Danish food entertainment show on national
television, and it may be seen as the motto of good, honest (Danish)
cuisine of culinary traditions. John refers to the meaning of the nostalgic
past when telling stories about customers who are reminded about the
'taste of their grandmother's cooking' when eating the butter baked bread.
A central Nordicness element reinventing the Nordic brand involves local
values that 'go more than 100 years back' (John).

The 'honesty' in BRØD goes much further than using real butter: they
use real rum in the cakes, which also means using some level of alcohol.
When asked whether this does not pose some problems, John claims that
they always warn Muslims: 'hey – be aware, we use real rum – but that is
okay, they don't care, believe me!'. The rich food at BRØD is probably not
unhealthy in reasonable levels of consumption, but especially the claim
'butter baked' must be read against the backdrop of lipophobia, the fear
of fat, that has characterized consumers' relationship to food over the
last decades (Askegaard et al. 1999). To explicitly emphasize the butter

component of the baking process is to take a stance saying that culinary values fuelled by nostalgia should trump bodily concerns fueled by vanity. Consequently, BRØD thereby does not align with the tenets of modern healthism of the NNC manifesto but instead cherry-picks notions that align with their nostalgic orientation.

COMMUNAL SPACE: DESIGN FOR 'HYGGE' AND 'KOS'

Both NYT and BRØD have carefully constructed the place to be welcoming, open and inclusive. They have very different ideas of the specific aesthetics that may be appropriate in their context, but the stated intentions and values are very similar. The concepts of 'hygge' (Denmark) or 'kos' (Norway), which is the Norwegian counterpart of the more widespread 'hygge' concept, are probably the most coveted mythologies of Nordicness (e.g. Brits 2017; Wiking 2016). The restaurant NYT re-interprets this myth which is manifest in the organizational culture, décor, ambience and gastronomical design.

As is pointed out by Linnet (2015), while the essence is ever elusive, it is the centrality in Nordic discourses that makes it such a rich symbolic resource as social token and 'standard of social space'. To say about a visit that 'it was hyggeligt' means, simply, we were socializing successfully – 'we had a nice time'. Linnet (2015) writes on the atmospherics of 'hygge':

> In these idealized accounts of feeling at home among other people in public space, it is implied that the ability to relax is served by the informal 'no stiff collar' vibe of the social life unfolding around the subject, which is idealized as removing, from this scene, the status anxiety of urban social consumption.

The construction of communal space is legitimized in different ways by BRØD and NYT as compared to the NNC manifesto because they strive for 'hygge' through negotiating the décor and balancing the comfort of patrons. In contrast, the NNC manifesto draws attention to 'pure' modern design, for example clean natural surfaces, no veneer or Formica, and no superficial elements such as tablecloths. However, the books on 'hygge' often fall into the trap of essentializing the concept to some specific form of décor or recipe, but not so at BRØD and NYT. They do not claim 'hygge', but they have their own versions of the practices related to space and service production that are required.

Baby prams, breastfeeding and crawling toddlers are not always welcome in cafés. The owners of BRØD insist that they want everyone to feel welcome and move tables around to facilitate 'hygge'. They even show flexibility by encouraging the guest to construct a makeshift toddler play corner from what is at hand. When asked about this practice they seem surprised and wonder 'why shouldn't it be like this?'. While BRØD's communal space is inclusive, informal and highly co-constructed by patrons, NYT creates communal 'kos' by emphasizing a friendly fine-dining space. Chefs, as well as assistants, work together in creating the cuisine of NYT, which is inspired by the NNC movement. They reject, however, the 'verfremdungseffekt' that is part of the theatrical element of Noma and other modern forms of haute cuisine (e.g. 'flowerpot with edible dirt'). The goal is rather to meet the patrons with recognizable and 'honest' Nordic food where 'meat tastes like meat', as one chef puts it. Rather than the minimalistic 'New Nordic' staging or the intimidating fine-dining ambience (e.g. 'stiff collar' service, classical music), they would like the ambience of a 'Friday night out with Frank Sinatra and friends'. Reconstructing New Nordic with the right balance of 'fine dining' and 'kos' ambience needs some negotiating. Håkon (main chef/owner) is well aware of the New Nordic Design language, but finds it too austere. He feels the white tablecloths and soft comfortable chairs, mixed with local landscape pictures, feelgood music, fireplace and informal tone, are just some of the things that make patrons relax, 'be themselves' and 'be happy'. This way the space elements usually connoting 'stiff collar' are reconstructed into a *more* informal communality than the simpler and 'naked' wooden table top, and as such reinventing a Nordicness vibe which Norwegians might need for enjoying 'kos' and becoming intimate – in 'public' (Linnet 2015).

THE (UTOPIAN) NORDIC WORKPLACE

NYT are clearly using the symbolic resources of the NNC in the storytelling around the food, and the focus on local produce: they do local foraging as a team in the fjords around Bodø, and they are collaborating personally with local farmers and fishermen. The geographical terroir is clearly an important symbolic resource, but it is contextualized and re-appropriated in a much more pragmatic mode of Nordicness.

The mythology of the egalitarian Nordic workplace (Byrkeflot 2003) is prevalent in the discourses. When the staff at NYT and BRØD feel at home in the space they create and in what they do, it is easier to become more inviting, relaxed and welcoming towards the patrons. They have extremely flexible management, considering the usual hierarchies of traditional businesses like these. When, for example, an assistant or apprentice makes their own culinary creations at NYT they are encouraged to explore and develop it, and they may even personally serve and present what they have made to the patrons. The staff explicitly position NYT as the antithesis of the status hierarchies often experienced in cuisine workplaces. For example, the apprentice and assistants state that there is never any 'yelling', and that their motivation and effectiveness come when they feel respected.

NYT and BRØD both explicitly distance themselves from the profit hungry capitalism and 'mass-marketing machine' in their discourses and practices, even though BRØD clearly states intentions of becoming a widespread chain, perhaps even as a franchise. NYT see themselves as just a group of friends trying to do what they like, no strategy of expanding or competing with Noma or Maaemo (of Oslo) in the Michelin star race. This might also indicate a mode of 'status' denial and perhaps even 'law of Jante': do not get ahead of yourself – *be content.* At the same time, it is important to interpret these statements about not being profit oriented through a lens of authenticity work on part of the respective brands. One of the basic methods employed by brands in order to be interpreted as authentic by consumers is to downplay the profit motive (Beverland 2005). This is not to suggest that the brands are *just* about making a profit, but that the theme of being positioned as 'a group of friends doing what they like' is a business strategy that appears to be successful in this day and age, outside the Nordic setting as well.

CONCLUSION

The question we set out to illuminate in this chapter was how Nordic firms reinvent the Nordic in their branding by invoking various symbolic resources of Nordicness. BRØD and NYT are clearly in the process of reinventing the mythology of NNC, trying to move beyond the dependence on 'new' ways of appropriating the geographical terroir (the purity of the Nordic landscapes, sea, climate) to a notion of Nordicness that is based more on social values and traditions. The traditional construction of terroir was actually never only about the earth, sea or climate in the first place, but just as much a rhetorical genre invoking imagery of people performing 'traditional' modes of production (Paxson 2010, Gyimóthy 2017, Larsen and Osterlund-Potzsch 2015). In these reinventions of Nordicness, the symbolic resources related to the *geographical place* with its tangible, physical focus on product value are pushed even further into the background in favour of *social place* and *cultural values.* Nevertheless, it appears that the seemingly fixed and solid characteristics of a terroir as having a connection to a particular place makes it too valuable as a building block in forging a sense of authenticity to completely abandon (Östberg 2011).

At BRØD and NYT they work very hard to construct an inclusive and egalitarian space for both patrons and employees. The employees are expected to thrive with the openness and transparent services production, as they cannot hide in the back rooms. They are performing the NYT/BRØD brand in all the Nordic, modern egalitarian inclusiveness that resembles the Nordic societal model, which fosters values of 'relatively open markets, strong welfare systems, and a relatively egalitarian stance' (Østergaard et al. 2014, p. 246). This is a mythological resource in itself, also in the form of Nordic exceptionalism (Browning 2007). This reinvented Nordicness is a resource for the cultural production of *The Social Utopia*, no less. Claus Meyer, of Noma and NNC fame, has already conquered New York with Danish Hot Dogs, which are not as 'made in Denmark' but made with 'Nordic welfare values' in the workplace.

The ambition to be inclusive can also be detected in the respective brands' orchestration of their customer experience. By rejecting some of the conventions of haute cuisine, such as the theatrical elements of food presentation at, for example, Noma, they aim to construct an experience where everyone should feel included. In essence, the aim is that patrons should not feel that they need a certain amount of cultural capital to be able to understand and enjoy what is being offered. Instead, everyone should be able to enjoy themselves regardless of their cultural background, aiming for an atmosphere of 'hygge' where people can 'be themselves' and 'be happy'. To understand these tendencies of rejecting the bourgeoisie's 'cultured' taste expressions in which substance is replaced by surface décor, we can draw a parallel with another manifesto published almost three quarters of a century prior to the NNC manifesto. In the aftermath of the 'Stockholm Exhibition' in 1930 where Swedish functionalism was introduced to the world, a number of influential architects and other key players authored the *acceptera* manifesto of design and architecture (Asplund et al. 1931). Largely, the manifesto was a rejection of bourgeoisie values including the tendency of the lower classes to mimic aesthetic expressions of the upper classes in order to gain status. Both BRØD and NYT refuse to be held hostage by conventional haute cuisine or bakery cultures. Instead, they try to reinvent their brands as a kind of dialectic of opposition between the superfluous ornamentation of bourgeoisie aesthetics at one end of the spectrum and the supposed low quality of mass production on the other (Husz 2012).

Our findings show that reinvented Nordicness is less about posing as a counterculture to globalized and industrialized food culture (Kjeldgaard and Östberg 2007), or even as a form of counterrevolution to the NNC manifesto (a symbolic resource that is interpreted). The branding actors reported on in this study insist on the viability and intrinsic value and meaningfulness of 'Nordicness' for them as 'Nordics'. Nordicness is not just 'another lifestyle trend to exploit'; they insist on a much larger perspective on Nordic values: on egalitarianism, gender, parenting, restoring Nordic food quality and traditions. As in the original manifesto (New Nordic Food 2004), they believe in their reinvention as a moral imperative, although stated in a much less revolutionary rhetoric, which may indeed be the ideal symbolic marker of 'true Nordicness': no-nonsense 'humbleness', or – as the 'Law of Jante' goes – 'do not think you are something special' (while, paradoxically, still marketing this as 'special').

In this brief chapter, we have probed the reconstruction of Nordicness in brand actors in just two contexts. In future investigation of the Nordic branding it may be pertinent to analyse the challenges of reinventing Nordic dialects and study other sectors such as design, fashion and culture, delving more deeply into the 'terroir of values' invoked to construct Nordicness beyond cuisine and tourism. Also, we have tried to show how place branding can thrive by tapping into a very diverse 'pool of symbolic resources', thus allowing more complexity than prevalent notions of 'One Clear Brand Identity' allow (Ren and Blichfeldt 2011).

REFERENCES

Anderson, B. (2006 [1986]), *Imagined Communities: Reflections on the Origin and Spread of Nationalism*. London: Verso.

Askegaard, S., and Ger, G. (1997), 'Product-country images as stereotypes: A comparative study of Danish food products in Germany and Turkey'. Working Paper, Aarhus School of Business, MAPP Centre.

Askegaard, S., Jensen, A. F., and Holt, D. B. (1999), 'Lipophobia: A Transatlantic Concept?', in L. M. Scott and E. J. Arnould (Eds.), *Advances in Consumer Research*, vol. XXVI. Provo, UT: Association for Consumer Research, pp. 361–365.

Asplund, G., Gahn, W., Markelius, S., Paulsson, G., Sundahl, E., and Åhrén, U. (1931), *Acceptera*, Stockholm: Tiden.

Bech-Larsen, T., Mørk, T., and Kolle, S. (2016), 'New Nordic Cuisine: Is there another back to the future? – An informed viewpoint on NCC value drivers and market scenarios'. *Trends in Food Science & Technology* **50**, 249–253.

Beverland, M. B. (2005), 'Crafting brand authenticity: The case of luxury wines'. *Journal of Management Studies*, **42** (5), 1003–1029.

Brits, L. T. (2017), *The Book of Hygge: The Danish Art of Contentment, Comfort, and Connection*. New York: Penguin.

Browning, C. S. (2007), 'Branding Nordicity: Models, identity and the decline of exceptionalism'. *Cooperation and Conflict*, **42** (1), 27–51.

Byrkeflot, H. (2003), 'Nordic management: From functional socialism to shareholder value', in B. Czarniawska and G. Sevón (Eds.), *The Northern Lights—Organization theory in Scandinavia*. Copenhagen: Copenhagen Business School Press, pp. 17–39.

Byrkeflot, H., Pedersen, J. S., and Svejenova, S. (2013), 'From label to practice: The process of creating new Nordic cuisine'. *Journal of Culinary Science & Technology*, **11** (1), 36–55.

Czarniawska, B., and Sevón, G. (Eds.) (2005), *Global Ideas: How Ideas, Objects and Practices Travel in a Global Economy*, vol. 13. Copenhagen: Copenhagen Business School Press.

Escobar, A. (2001), 'Culture sits in places: Reflections on globalism and subaltern strategies of localization'. *Political Geography*, **20** (2), 139–174.

Gyimóthy, S. (2017), 'The reinvention of terroir in Danish food place promotion', *European Planning Studies*, **25** (7), 1200–1216.

Harvard, J., and Stadius, P. (2013), eds. *Communicating the North: Media Structures and Images in the Making of the Nordic Region*. London: Routledge.

Hermansen, M. E. T. (2012), 'Creating terroir: An anthropological perspective on new Nordic cuisine as an expression of Nordic identity'. *Anthropology of Food* (S7), accessed 20 November 2018 at http://aof.revues.org/7249.

Holt, D. B. (2004), *How Brands become Icons: The Principles of Cultural Branding*. Cambridge, MA: Harvard Business Press.

Husz, O. (2012), 'The morality of quality: Assimilating material mass culture in twentieth-century Sweden'. *Journal of Modern European History*, **10** (2), 152–181.

Kjeldgaard, D., and Östberg, J. (2007), 'Coffee grounds and the global cup: Glocal consumer culture in Scandinavia'. *Consumption Markets & Culture*, **10** (2), 175–187.

Kornberger, M. (2010), *Brand Society: How Brands Transform Management and Lifestyle*. Cambridge: Cambridge University Press.

Larsen, H. P., and Osterlund-Potzsch S. (2015), 'Islands in the sun: Storytelling, place & terroir in food production on Nordic islands'. *Ethnologia Scandinavica*, **45**, 29–52.

Leer, J. (2016), 'The rise and fall of the New Nordic Cuisine'. *Journal of Aesthetics & Culture*, **8** (1), 33494, DOI: 10.3402/jac.v8.33494.

Linnet, J. T. (2011), 'Money can't buy me hygge: Danish middle-class consumption, egalitarianism, and the sanctity of inner space', *Social Analysis*, **55** (2), 21–44.

Linnet, J. T. (2015), 'Cozy interiority – the interplay of materiality and sociality in the constitution of cozy 3rd place atmosphere', *Ambiances, Perception – In situ – Ecologie sociale*, (June), accessed 20 November 2018 at http://ambiances.revues.org/543.

Lucarelli, A., and Brorström, S. (2013), 'Problematising place branding research: A meta-theoretical analysis of the literature', *The Marketing Review*, **13** (1), 65–81.

Neuman, N. (2018), 'An imagined culinary community: Stories of morality and masculinity in "Sweden–the new culinary nation"'. *Scandinavian Journal of Hospitality and Tourism*, **18** (2), 149–162.

New Nordic Food. (2004), 'The New Nordic Kitchen Manifesto', accessed 9 November 2018 at http://newnordicfood.org. [Direct link to archived version of original manifesto: http://en.arkiv.nynordiskmad.org/about-nnf-ii/new-nordic-kitchen-manifesto/].

Östberg, J. (2011), 'The mythological aspects of country-of-origin: The case of the Sweedishness of Swedish fashion'. *Journal of Global Fashion Marketing*, **2** (4), 223–234.

Østergaard, P., Linnet, J. T., Andersen, L. P., Kjeldgaard, D., Bjerregaard, S., Weijo, H., Martin, D., Schouten, J., and Östberg, J. (2014), 'Nordic consumer culture: Context and concept', in M. Schouten and R. Belk (Eds.), *Consumer Culture Theory*. Bingley: Emerald Group Publishing, pp. 245–257.

Paxson, H. (2010), 'Locating value in Artisan cheese: Reverse engineering terroir for new-world landscapes'. *American Anthropologist*, **112** (3), 444–457. DOI: 10.1111/j.1548-1433.2010.01251.x.

Ren, C., and Blichfeldt, B. S. (2011), 'One clear image? Challenging simplicity in place branding'. *Scandinavian Journal of Hospitality and Tourism*, **11** (4), 416–434. DOI: 10.1080/15022250.2011.598753

Roncha, A. (2008), 'Nordic brands towards a design-oriented concept'. *Journal of Brand Management*, **16** (1–2), 21–29.

Thorsøe, M. H., Kjeldsen, C., and Noe, E. (2016), 'It's never too late to join the revolution! – Enabling new modes of production in the contemporary Danish food system'. *European Planning Studies*, **25** (7), 1166–1183.

Trubek, A. B. (2008), *The Taste of Place: A Cultural Journey into Terroir*. Berkeley, CA: University of California.

Visit Bodø (n.d.), Website, accessed 20 November 2018 at https://visitbodo.com/home.

Waade, A. M., and Jensen, P. M. (2016), 'Nordic noir production values: The Killing and The Bridge'. *Academic Quarter*, **7**, 189–201.

White Guide (n.d.), White Guide – The Nordics, accessed 20 November 2018 at http://www.whiteguide-nordic.com/.

Wiking, M. (2016), *The Little Book of Hygge: The Danish Way to Live Well*. London: Penguin.

3. A Nordic perspective on supranational place branding

Jörgen Eksell and Alicia Fjällhed

It's all part of Nordic Cool 2013, a month-long festival beginning Tuesday and featuring 750 artists who will sing, dance, act, cook and exhibit their way to illuminating the cultures of Norway, Sweden, Finland, Iceland and Denmark, as well as Greenland, the Åland Islands and the Faroe Islands. [. . .] Beyond flora and fauna, the festival includes a Lego exhibit, music from the next-big-thing launching pad Iceland Airwaves festival, a cinematic Norwegian thriller, a panel on the region's ever-popular crime novels and a taste of New Nordic cuisine. "Nordic Cool will be a way of showing that the Nordic countries are more than Ikea and 'The Scream,' which perhaps are two things that many people would associate with us," says Hadia Tajik, Norway's minister of culture. "It's hard to put words on what is specifically Nordic." (Merry, 2013)

This chapter concerns the supranational place branding work initiated by the Nordic countries after the Nordic Cool festival in Washington, DC. The festival was arranged by the John F. Kennedy Center for the Performing Arts, in close collaboration with the Nordic countries and the official Nordic co-operation that through a multi-layered presentation of the Nordic region sought answers to the question: What is Nordic? Events, seminars, meetings, conferences and debates were arranged around political issues of Nordic interest such as equality, education, research, values, economy and the Nordic model. With over 200 000 visitors and an extensive media coverage, the Nordic Cool festival was considered a success. But the internal evaluation revealed the need for a common strategic platform amongst the Nordic members to enable future similar collaborations and make them both more time and cost efficient. The Nordic countries have a long history of political collaboration, but the management of "the Nordics" as an asset for place branding had hitherto been unexplored as a joint strategic asset. Thus, the festival resulted in an invigoration of the brand work of the Nordic region and the Nordic prime ministers gave the green light to the creation of a common strategy for international profiling in 2014/2015. The process initiated a negotiation of themes amongst the Nordic members that would comprise a common supranational place branding strategy.

The brand strategy of the Nordic countries, *The Nordic Perspective,* represents a unique example of a group of nations that have agreed on a supranational place branding strategy. It is a rare collaboration that allows us to identify critical aspects in the supranational place branding work. Hence, the purpose of this chapter is to develop knowledge on place branding by exploring significant antecedents and factors of the creation of the Nordic supranational place branding strategy. The study is based on an analysis of policy documents such as a pilot study (Nordic Council of Ministers, 2014) and the strategy *The Nordic Perspective* (Nordic Council of Ministers, 2015), six interviews with national representatives from the Nordic countries (henceforth referred to as "representatives") engaged in both the reference group to the supranational place brand and engaged in the nation branding initiatives for the respective countries, and two interviews with the communicators and project leaders at the Nordic Council.

The chapter is structured in the following way. First, the concept of supranational place branding is introduced; second, the antecedents and decisive factors of the initiation of the Nordic supranational place brand are presented; third, the process of negotiating a strategy and agreeing on the themes in the strategy is discussed; and, last, the consequences of *The Nordic Perspective* are presented.

SUPRANATIONAL PLACE BRANDING

During the twenty-first century, place branding initiatives have become ubiquitous as countries, regions and cities of the world compete to attract tourists, investors, media attention, residents and a qualified workforce. Still, the development of supranational place brands – that is, regional place brands that stretch over several entire nations – have only recently become of interest to researchers in spite of repeated calls for more research and papers by influential academics. In 2000, O'Shaughnessy and O'Shaughnessy argued "that regions are as important in branding nation state", where for example "the idea of Latin America may be more important than any of its regional components" (p. 58). Two years later, Anholt made a call for more papers about "supra-national branding; the effects of branding countries in groups" (2002, p. 231). Nevertheless, studies on supranational place branding remain scarce.[1] Supranational

---

[1]   A number of related concepts have been used to describe the branding of different countries together. For example, concepts such as *regional branding* (Andersson 2007), *supra-national branding* (Anholt 2002; Therkelsen and Gram, 2010; Andersson and Paajanen, 2012) and *inter-regional place branding* or *transnational place branding* (e.g. Zenker and Jacobsen,

regions that have received some attention from academics include Europe (i.e. van Ham, 2005; Anholt, 2007; Pieterse and Kuschel, 2007), the Baltic Sea Region (i.e. Andersson, 2007; Andersson and Paajanen, 2012) and Africa (i.e. Wanjiru, 2005; Osei and Gbadamosi, 2011).[2] However, these studies foremost highlight the difficulties initially described by Anholt in 2005, as a place branding strategy requires (1) a clear mutual understanding of what the brand is, (2) what it wants to become, (3) a strategy on how to get there, and (4) the leadership necessary to carry it out. On a similar note, Therkelsen and Gram (2010) argue that stakeholders' ability to agree on these matters is an important challenge in any place branding initiative where "reaching agreement clearly becomes all the more difficult as the geographical size and complexity increases" (Therkelsen and Gram, 2010, p. 115). It has even been stated that "in regions composed of several sovereign states, imposing a brand strategy is politically impossible" (Anholt, 2005, p. 225). At the same time, researchers (e.g. Therkelsen and Gram, 2010) propose a number of possible advantages for the nations engaged in a supranational place branding initiative, such as a shared and coherent profile and economics of scale. The idea of supranational branding is thus considered a potentially prosperous place branding activity, which highlights the importance of understanding the factors that enable such an initiative. The process of creating a supranational brand strategy has likewise been poorly studied. A few prevalent studies of cities and regions point to the fact that place branding cannot be separated from its political governance context (e.g. Lucarelli and Giovanardi, 2016; Cassinger and Eksell, 2017; Zenker and Braun, 2017) and any branding initiative of regions needs to take these characteristics into account. In alignment with this argument, Braun (2012) claims that place branding is the subject of political decision-making and deals with regional or municipal organization(s) and policy-making procedures. In regional and supranational place branding initiatives these aspects are clearly even more decisive to the brand strategy process.

2015) have been used by researchers in recent years. In this chapter, the term *supranational branding* is used to put specific emphasis on the regional collaboration of several independent countries.

  [2] In addition, the promotion of supranational regions from a tourism perspective has been investigated through supranational *destination* branding in relation to Europe (i.e. Therkelsen and Grams, 2010), Scandinavia (i.e. Flagestad and Hope, 2001) and the Baltic Sea Region (i.e. Paajanen, 2014).

ANTECEDENTS OF THE NORDIC PERSPECTIVE

The following section sheds light on the factors that enabled the creation of a Nordic supranational place brand strategy. The section explores both antecedents of the relationship between the Nordic countries as well as decisive factors explaining the commencement of the initiative.

From Conflict to Collaboration

The relationships between the Nordic countries have not always been close or friendly. For hundreds of years, the countries were engaged in recurring bloody conflicts when striving for power and dominance within the region. Nonetheless, as a result of the 200 years of inter-regional peace, the region is presently characterized by both political and commercial cross-national collaborations, and multiple common denominators such as a cultural, societal and linguistic affinity. The cross-national collaboration between the Nordic countries is "one of the oldest and most extensive types of regional cooperation in the world" (Magnus, 2016, p. 195) with a common body for inter-governmental co-operation (the Nordic Council of Ministers) founded in 1952 closely followed by the official body for formal inter-parliamentary co-operation (the Nordic Council) in 1971. The Nordic countries thereby represent a supranational collaboration with more than 50 years of experience in common cross-national product development, perceived as a matter of course within the region as northerners consider other Nordic nations as the natural basis for political, economic and cultural international co-operation (Petersson, 2005). Historically, the political Nordic co-operations have focused on internal development and inter-regional harmonization. For example, a common passport union and labour market was founded in the 1950s and later on the creation and export of the idea of a "Nordic Model" as it emerged during the Cold War. One could argue that this was in fact the first example of Nordic supranational branding. However, it was created with the purpose of keeping the region out of conflict by branding the Nordic as a model region, presenting it as a region characterized by peace and prosperity. The core lay in the thought of "exceptionalism" in relation to the Nordic foreign policy and the international moral and social justice that created a "Nordic model" fit for export (Browning, 2007). Admittedly, the history of the Nordic collaboration has formed a basis for the creation of the supranational place brand of today.

In spite of the established collaboration and contemporary unity amongst the Nordic countries, the Nordic Council of Minsters wanted to evaluate whether a joint Nordic place brand was worth investing in, and ordered a pilot study from a brand agency to answer the question of whether an external and internal idea of something distinctly Nordic existed. The pilot study concluded that "through its inheritance [the Nordic countries] share a lot of common ground and in large parts common identity among the citizens" (Nordic Council of Ministers 2014, p. 31). Whilst the Nordic nations have strong national identities, common Nordic characteristics are also described in the pilot study to have influenced the national identities of the respective countries. Furthermore, the pilot study highlights that, "from those with an outside perspective, the Nordic countries constitute a 'homogenous masse' – not only geographically but also culturally, historically, politically and economically" (Nordic Council of Ministers 2014, p. 13). Furthermore, the Nordic brand is considered positive and coherent and "[m]ost of the participants paint the picture of the Nordic as a region with a well-managed government, being open and transparent, and a society with sound welfare, high level of equality and extensive environmental awareness" (Nordic Council of Ministers 2014, p. 17). Undoubtedly, there are examples of negative associations highlighted in the pilot study. However, they are few and non-conclusive, for example:

> High tax-levels and neutrality in conflicts are not perceived as necessarily a good thing, and the integration of immigrants is not working optimally in the Nordic countries which have been noted in foreign media. (Nordic Council of Ministers 2014, p. 18)

The appreciation about something distinctly Nordic within and outside the region is also reflected in the interviews with the representatives from the Nordic countries engaged in the branding initiative and the communicators and project leaders at the Nordic Council. And so, the prevalent image of the Nordic countries is one of the enabling factors for the creation of the supranational place brand strategy.

Nordic Attraction and Global Competition

A common Nordic history and a beneficial collaboration between its nations have resulted in prosperous conditions for formulating a supranational place brand strategy, but these conditions have existed for decades. So one might ask: Why was the initiative to create a joint place brand strategy taken in 2013?

One of the factors that explains why the process of creating a supranational place branding strategy was initiated at this particular time is the booming interest in all things Nordic during the twenty-first century.

Everything from *Nordic noir*, which includes novels, films and TV series such as *The Millennium Trilogy, Bron* and *The Killing*, or *Nordic cuisine* with restaurants like *Noma* and the new food-philosophy *New Nordic Food*, and *Nordic lifestyle* concepts such as as *hygge* and *lagom*, are described as key driving forces in bringing the world's attention. Parallel to this development, the Nordic Model (presented in the previous section) was reborn in the aftermath of the global financial crisis of 2007–2008, and announced as "The next super model" by *The Economist* in 2013 based on the clusters of Nordic nations in top league tables in regard to everything from income to education, press freedom and equality (Allern, Blanch-Ørsten, Kantola and Pollack, 2012), global competitiveness (World Economic Forum, 2014) and quality of life (*The Economist*, 2013). In light of this external interest, the Nordic co-operation recognized the need to take charge of their brand presentation abroad. The spark that is described, by the pilot study as well as several interviewees, to have lit the flame was the above-mentioned festival Nordic Cool in Washington, DC. This new type of place branding potential was at the time also recognized by external actors such as András Simonyi, Johns Hopkins University, and Erik Brattberg, Visiting Fellow at Johns Hopkins University. In an article published in *Huffington Post* under the headline "Nordic Cool Power in Washington: What the Nordics Teach About Nation Branding" the authors concluded:

> Clearly, what is unique about the Nordics is not just their cultural appeal, but also their successful "nation branding" efforts underpinned by strong attention to both soft and hard power. [. . .] The fact that they hold hands is a victory of reason. None of them alone can wield as much power and influence as in unit. [. . .] Their strength lies in turning their diversity into a joint message. (Simonyi and Brattberg, 2013)

Another factor that explains why the process of creating a supranational place branding strategy was initiated at this time is the internal evaluation of the festival. The evaluation pointed to a need for a common strategy and strategic platform that made future collaborations more time and cost efficient. Clearly, the festival and its evaluation were decisive factors of the commencement of the supranational place branding initiative. Another factor was international development, with increased competition between places on a global arena. As the pilot study later concluded: "Competition for a place on the international arena is tough, and small countries like ours can work together to generate greater visibility and influence" (Nordic Council of Ministers, 2015, p. 9). A supranational place branding strategy is described by interviewees as the possibility to present the Nordics as a region with 25 million inhabitants that constitutes the twelfth largest economy in the world. It is emphasized by several representatives in interviews that such a strategy is useful in reaching distant markets. The latter opportunity is also highlighted in the strategy and described as particularly relevant "in markets where awareness of the region is greater than awareness of the individual country" (Nordic Council of Ministers, 2015, p. 9). From this point of view, one could find individual incentives relating to Therkelsen and Gram's (2010) suggestion that a supranational place branding initiative could hold image-transfer possibilities between nations. Similarly, the Nordic representatives describe the possibility of not only being affiliated with the overall Nordic brand, but also with other Nordic entities. One representative explains that the larger Nordic countries might be famous locally (for example in Europe) and thus appreciate being presented as Nordic in the foremost remote markets, whilst smaller areas are more famous in remote markets and might benefit from being connected to the Nordic brand in a more local setting.

> It is not always the country with the greatest power that makes it famous or not. It might as well be Greenland's polar bears or areas with amazing nature. And Iceland has the volcanos that people remember. If you show pictures of Denmark, it could very well be any other city in Europe.

Another representative paints a similar picture, pointing to the fact that Iceland is the only country in the Nordic region with its own sign in the Chinese language. At the same time, the representative questions whether the pressing issue always is related to whether the country or territory is famous or not, and argues that it is also a question of what it is famous for. In the case of people's recognition of Iceland in distant markets, the person asks, "Is it only because they know about the geysers or the waterfalls? Or do they know that there are people living in the country?" In sum, the representatives value a supranational belongingness for different reasons. At the time of the decision to initiate the supranational place brand, benefits for countries of different sizes and needs were presented.

THE NORDIC PERSPECTIVE

The following section focuses on the construction of the strategy *The Nordic Perspective*. Given the difficulties other supranational place branding initiatives have encountered it is reasonable to ask: How were the Nordic countries and autonomous territories able to accomplish the negotiation and agree on the themes of the strategy?

An Established Nordic Policy Process

A pre-existing supranational identity and/or common experiences of cross-national product initiatives, such as political collaborations, are presented in previous studies as possible solutions to overcome the obstacle of agreeing on a supranational place branding strategy (cf. Andersson, 2007; Therkelsen and Gram, 2010; Andersson and Paajanen, 2012). In the case of the Nordic region, there is a common Nordic history and the region is characterized by cultural, societal and linguistic affinity across the national borders. In consequence, the shared affinity has created a foundation for political collaborations which has been decisive in the building of the internal and external sense of Nordicness historically as well as today. The Nordic countries also have similar preferences concerning policy-making, and the countries are often characterized as a group with common interests and policies that could be labelled as Nordic (e.g. Laatikainen, 2003). The Nordic common ground and aligned national interest seem to have led the way for a smooth negotiation process amongst the representatives in the reference group for the supranational brand strategy. As stated previously in this chapter, the Nordic nations have a previously established collaboration on political issues from culture and education to healthcare. Thus, even before the decision of the prime ministers of the Nordic countries in 2013, there was a supranational political programme in place that had been negotiated through the Nordic Council which served as a departure point for the supranational place branding reference group. In contrast to the way previous studies portray the negotiation process amongst stakeholders involved in a supranational place branding initiative, interviews with the stakeholders involved in the Nordic supranational branding work rather paint the opposite picture. As one interviewee describes the negotiation:

> Nordic co-operation is very consensus based. So that one chooses not to co-operate in areas where one or more countries do not want to co-operate. So all decisions are made with the consensus principle and the strategy is based very much on the official Nordic co-operation in areas where we already have a co-operation. But I think, if the strategy had been more specific or concrete, it would probably have been more problematic.

The interviewees highlight that the Nordic political co-operation is based on a consensus-driven approach, and the branding initiative focused on areas which all representatives agreed upon as an important part of the brand. As the interviews suggest, there will also be areas of differences within the supranational region which included stakeholders do not wish to include in the common presentation of the supranational entity – in which case the Nordic strategy for negotiation has been that they would not include issues or characteristically traits which the representatives could not agree upon. This approach would, of course, also have contributed to the productive conversation, as it cleared out topics that might otherwise have led to unproductive disagreements. On this note, one might conclude that in order for the supranational place branding strategy to become a reality, the region would have to disagree on very few issues in order to have enough mutual denominators to build their common presentation.

National Differences as Productive Capital

In spite of the apparent similarities between the Nordic countries and autonomous territories that were decisive to the process of completing the Nordic supranational brand initiative, the aim of the strategy is not to present the nations as identical. This represents an interesting challenge in the presentation of the Nordic supranational place brand, as the region is characterized by both similarities and differences amongst the Nordic entities, and the place branding strategy has to walk a fine but important line between conveying the picture of a united region and not overlooking the distinctive features of each country. On that note, the balance between supranational similarities and national differences is described in the strategy as follows:

> The objective is not to convey a homogenous picture of the countries in the Nordic region, nor to give an impression that all Nordic citizens, organizations and governments think and behave in the same way. Instead of emphasizing the distinctive features of each country, our aim is to promote what we have in common – our Nordic perspective, our values, and a culture that has grown out of a common history. (Nordic Council of Ministers, 2015, p. 5)

As previously stated, national differences are described by the interviewees as an important incentive for engaging in this supranational place branding initiative for both common Nordic and individual national reasons. In sum, national differences contributed with a collective productive supranational capital. In this respect, one representative describes the process of creating a supranational brand as simpler than the nation branding initiative in her country:

> I believe, when you arrive at a national level, it is [more difficult]. Then special interests get more power. The Nordic is on an all-inclusive, perhaps abstract level. That may be the explanation, I am not saying that it is the whole explanation, but I think that is one explanation.

Apparently, there were no obstacles to include differences as far as they were agreed by the representatives to provide productive capital to the common supranational brand. For example, several interviewees point to the variations in nature and rural and urban landscape as a supranational strength in creating incentives for tourism, and the strategy describes how the diversity within the region offers branding possibilities for the included nations being a part of "a large and diverse range of industries and culture, not to mention a varied and fascinating natural environment" (Nordic Council of Ministers, 2015, p. 10).

Furthermore, it is clear in the interviews with the representatives in the reference group that both similarities and differences amongst the Nordic members contribute to the distinct character of the region. In consequence the countries' similarities and differences are considered to all contribute to the Nordic supranational place brand. From this perspective, one interviewee highlights the relationship between the branding of the supranational region and the branding of the individual countries within the region, and that "In the branding of the country you will brand the region, and in the branding of the region the countries will be characterized by different strengths. [. . .] all countries have different strengths and together they could create the common impression of the Nordic as positive in many different areas." The supranational place branding strategy's ability to take the national place branding strategies into account thus constitutes another important reason behind the success of the strategy, as it allows the representatives to see the symbiotic relationship in engaging in place branding on a supranational level as it is in line with the national ones.

CONSEQUENCES OF THE NORDIC PERSPECTIVE

The following section discusses the conclusions and knowledge contribution of the study and the implications of the antecedents and factors affecting the initiation, negotiation and completion of the supranational brand strategy of the Nordic countries.

A number of antecedents of the relationship between the Nordic countries and decisive factors explaining the decision of the Nordic Council of Ministers to create a supranational brand strategy for the Nordic countries are discussed in this chapter. The 200 years of inter-regional peace and an established long-term political collaboration in official organs of political decision-making between the countries is an important antecedent of the decision. Furthermore, the initiative originated also from a heightened international interest and hype in

'Nordic' culture, lifestyle, cuisine and economic model, as the execution and evaluation of the Nordic Cool festival in Washington, DC in 2013 created an understanding of the benefits of an increased co-operation and lit a spark for the creation of the supranational place brand strategy *The Nordic Perspective.*

The long-term and continuous co-operation paved the way for a productive consensus-driven policy process that formed the supranational place brand strategy. The strategy conveys a picture of a united supranational region and at the same time allows the distinctive features of each country to present itself as productive capital in both the strategy and the nation branding of the respective countries. In consequence, both the negotiation process and the strategy can be characterized as productive, inclusive and pragmatic in a Nordic sense.

The Nordic Perspective provides a unique case of supranational place branding, as it not only points to the challenges associated with constructing a strategy, but also shows that it is possible to complete such an initiative. Previous studies on supranational branding depict the construction and negotiation amongst the nations as a difficult, if not impossible, endeavour. The process is challenging in any place branding initiative, still "reaching agreement clearly becomes all the more difficult as the geographical size and complexity increases" (Therkelsen and Gram, 2010, p. 115) and this has occasionally been described as impossible on a supranational level (Anholt, 2005). The core of the challenge relies on the country's ability (or disability) to agree on a set of common values or a core idea of the brand (Andersson, 2007).

Previous studies on the strategy work of cities and regions emphasize that place branding cannot be separated from its political governance context (e.g. Lucarelli and Giovanardi 2016; Cassinger and Eksell 2017; Zenker and Braun 2017). The conclusions presented in this study indicate that context must be understood in its broadest sense in order to understand its significance for the strategy work. The immediate governance context at the Nordic Council and the policy process of negotiations established by the continuous political collaboration by the countries and autonomous territories does not explain the strategy work executed. Moreover, the study highlights the significance of historical, cultural and societal antecedents that in this case formed a foundation for both internal and external understanding of the countries as a region with adequate similarities to be able to form a joint place brand. Even highly contemporary contextual factors represented by the need for improved future collaboration at the evaluation of the Nordic Cool festival and the experienced hype regarding Nordic culture, literature, food and economic model were instrumental in the decision to commence the strategy work.

Hence, the study indicates that different types of antecedents and factors were in interplay and were vital to the initiation, negotiation and completion of the strategy.

As a result, the Nordic supranational branding strategy confirms the recommendations presented by previous place branding studies related to different spatial levels. A place brand cannot be an artificial desk product, but has to be anchored in the perception of the region as a region by its stakeholders. As Andéhn and Zenker (2015) point out, "A place is a brand often long before it is formally branded" (p. 25). Latin America, Europe and Africa are a few examples where geographical proximity, similarities in culture and societal structures, linguistic affinities and/or other mutual denominators have led the world to view nations as part of a common supranational entity – a supranational brand. From this standpoint, the Nordic supranational place brand is not a novel creation or even re-invention, but rather a continuation and enhancement of a co-operation, ideas and values already established in the Nordics.

Lastly, we want to repeat Anholt's call from 2002 for more research on supranational place branding. There is still a need for studies on the branding practices of independent countries that choose to brand themselves together and the effects of these endeavours, as well as more studies on the antecedents and factors that enable strategy work of place brands in regions of the world, and other academic exploration of the Nordic supranational place branding initiative.

REFERENCES

Allern, S., Blanch-Ørsten, M., Kantola, A. and Pollack, E. (2012), 'Increased scandalization', in S. Allern and E. Pollack (eds), *Scandalous! The mediated construction of political scandals in four Nordic countries*, Göteborg: Nordicom, pp. 29–50.

Andéhn, M. and Zenker, S. (2015), 'Place branding in systems of places: On the interrelation of nations and supranational places', in S. Zenker and B. P. Jacobsen (eds), *Inter-regional place branding: Best practices, challenges and solutions*, Cham: Springer, pp. 25–38.

Andersson, M. (2007), 'Region branding: The case of the Baltic Sea Region', *Place Branding and Public Diplomacy*, **3** (2), 120–130.

Andersson, M. and Paajanen, M. (2012), 'Common or competing products? Towards supra-national branding in BaltMet Promo', *Journal of Place Management and Development*, **5** (1), 56–69.

Anholt, S. (2002), 'Foreword', *Brand Management*, **9** (4–5), 229–239.

Anholt, S. (2005), 'Nation brand as context and reputation', *Place Branding*, **1** (3), 224–228.

Anholt, S. (2007), '"Brand Europe": Where next?', *Place Branding and Public Diplomacy*, **3** (2), 224–228.

Braun, E. (2012), 'Putting city branding into practice', *Journal of Brand Management*, **19** (4), 257–267.

Browning, C. S. (2007), 'Branding Nordicity: Models, identity and the decline of exceptionalism', *Cooperation and Conflict: Journal of the Nordic International Studies Association*, **42** (1), 27–51.

Cassinger, C. and Eksell, J. (2017), 'The magic of place branding: Regional brand identity in transition', *Journal of Place Management and Development*, **10** (3), 202–212.

Flagestad, A. and Hope, C. A. (2001), '"Scandinavian Winter": Antecedents, concepts and empirical observations underlying a destination umbrella branding model', *Tourism Review*, **56** (1), 5–12.

Laatikainen, K. V. (2003), 'Norden's Eclipse: The impact of the European Union's Common Foreign and Security Policy on the Nordic Group in the United Nations', *Cooperation and Conflict*, **38**, 409–441.

Lucarelli, A. and Giovanardi, M. (2016), 'The political nature of brand governance: A discourse analysis approach to a regional brand building process', *Journal of Public Affairs*, **16** (1), 16–27.

Magnus, J. (2016), 'International branding of the Nordic region', *Place Branding and Public Diplomacy*, **12** (2–3), 195–200.

Merry, S. (2013), Nordic Cool 2013 takes over the Kennedy Center, *Washington Post*.

Nordic Council of Ministers. (2014), *Team up to do something big: En förstudie kring behovet av en gemensam nordisk varumärkesstrategi*, Oslo: The Communication Department of the Nordic Council and Happy Forsman & Bodenfors.

Nordic Council of Ministers. (2015), *Strategi för internationell profilering och positionering av Norden: 2015–2018*, Oslo: The Communication Department of the Nordic Council and Happy Forsman & Bodenfors.

Osei, C. and Gbadamosi, A. (2011), 'Re-branding Africa', *Marketing Intelligence and Planning*, **29** (3), 284–304.

O'Shaughnessy, J. and O'Shaughnessy, N. J. (2000), 'Treating the nation as a brand: Some neglected issues', *Journal of Macromarketing*, **20** (1), 56–64.

Paajanen, M. (2014), 'Accessibility of cities and regions in supranational branding: The case of the Rail Baltic', in M. M. Mariani, R. Baggio, D. Buhalis and S. Longhi (eds), *Tourism management, marketing, and development: Volume I. The importance of networks and ICTs*, New York: Palgrave Macmillan US, pp. 197–220.

Petersson, O. (2005), *Nordisk politik* (6th edition), Stockholm: Norstedts juridik.

Pieterse, V. and Kuschel, A. (2007), 'Supra-national origin marketing schemes', *Place Branding and Public Diplomacy*, **3** (3), 222–233.

Simonyi, A. and Brattberg, E. (2013), 'Nordic cool power in Washington: What the Nordics teach about nation branding', *Huffington Post*, 23 February.

The Economist (2013), 'The Nordic countries – The next super model', 24 February.

Therkelsen, A. and Gram, M. (2010), 'Branding Europe: Between nations, regions and continents', *Scandinavian Journal of Hospitality and Tourism*, **10** (2), 107–128.

van Ham, P. (2005), 'Branding European power', *Place Branding*, **1** (2), 122–126.

Wanjiru, E. (2005), 'Branding African countries: A prospect for the future', *Place Branding*, **1** (22), 84–95.

World Economic Forum (2014), 'The global competitiveness report 2014–2015'. World Economic Forum, Geneva.

Zenker, S. and Braun, E. (2017), 'Questioning a "one size fits all" city brand: Developing a branded house strategy for place brand management', *Journal of Place Management and Development*, **10** (3), 270–287.

Zenker, S. and Jacobsen, B. (eds) (2015), *Inter-regional place branding: Best practice, challenges and solutions*, Cham: Springer International Publishing.

4. Sparking the Nordic music brand

Jessica Edlom

INTRODUCTION

The Nordic countries are successful exporters of popular music and seen as influential on the global music scene. The music industry is multifaceted and complex, strongly affected by digitalisation in the last decades, but nevertheless it keeps growing steadily each year (Musiksverige, 2017). This development is explained by a flourishing concert market and successful music artists, songwriters and producers. There are a lot of outstanding Nordic examples, for example Kygo, Tove Lo, Aviccii and Max Martin, who has been No. 1 in the Billboard list 21 times, only beaten by the Beatles. In the streaming era, music usage is being spread over multiple services, which increases the impact. In January 2016, for example, Nordic music generated 1.4 billion streams on Spotify – 60 percent of it being streamed outside the region (Music:)ally, 2016 on By:Larm in Oslo). When music creates substantial and tangible value for the nation states, what role does popular music play and how can it be used strategically in building the Nordic nation brands?

The aim of this chapter is to examine the use of popular music and the music industry in building the brands of the Nordic countries. It will particularly focus on the organisational aspect of the strategic brand building; how joint efforts and collaborations between music actors and organisations (both private, industry organisations and governmental organisations) are created and steered in order to brand the Nordic region as an important music region; a creative hub and music innovator.

Globalisation, marketisation, digitalisation and a transition to the experience economy have changed the conditions of nation branding (Aronczyk, 2008; Bolin and Ståhlberg, 2015; Campelo, 2017). "Soft" factors, such as culture, leisure, and attitudes like innovation and creativity, are getting more important in differentiating a nation (Morgan, Pritchard and Pride, 2002). There is a growing strategic significance of cultural export and popular culture as brand value – cultural products appeal to people's shared habits and tastes according to Morley and Robin (1995)

and therefore help build the image of a nation and strengthen its economic competitiveness in the global market (Huang, 2011). Digitalisation
has made it more important to clarify national identity in a coordinated,
strategic and audience-centred way (Melissen, 2005; Bengtsson, 2011;
Balakrishnan, 2009). The modern digital consumer is generally connected
and hyper-informed, which creates new challenges regarding the management of nation branding. But it also creates possibilities. Popular music
is a digital and global commodity that is central in consumers' lives and
on digital platforms where they interact on a daily basis. Music could
therefore be seen as a suitable and even important commodity, adding to
the brand values of the Nordic countries.

This chapter is divided into four sections, which together analyse the circulation of nation brand values such as music through media technologies
and audiences, and with a specific focus on collective and participatory
aspects. First, there is a short introduction to the conditions and context of
the Nordic music industry of today and why this is interesting for branding a nation. Then follows a section that covers recent theoretical debates
on the strategy and management of nation branding. Following that, the
common nation branding effort of the Nordic countries, with a focus on
music, is introduced and two cases where this is done are presented and
analysed. Finally, the concluding section discusses the empirical findings
in relation to strategic and contemporary nation branding theories.

A METHODOLOGICAL APPROACH TO UNPACKING A NORDIC BRANDING EVENT

The empirical context of the study is the joint Nordic effort of branding
the Scandinavian music scene at the 2016 and 2018 South by South West
(SXSW) in Austin, Texas, USA – one of the most influential festivals and
conferences on innovation and culture of today. These cases are studied
regarding both the role of music in nation branding and the branding
process. The purpose is not primarily to evaluate the results of the projects
(even though the results will be discussed), but the focus is on the strategy,
planning, management and execution of the projects.

To be able to understand different aspects of the complex branding
process, the study has a qualitative approach in analysing strategy, activity
and content in the branding event. Semi-structured interviews were done
with key informants from Nordic nation branding actors: government
officials, representatives from tourist and export organisations, music
companies, music artists/groups and communication/marketing/branding
consultants. In addition to the interviews, formal reports dealing with gov-

ernmental strategies, websites of different organisations and companies, as well as social platforms on the internet were analysed. There was also an ethnographic part of the project: visiting the event and taking part in the activation of the brand on site.

THEORISING COLLABORATIVE NATION BRANDING IN THE DIGITAL ERA

Contemporary nation branding is a complex process. It is important to have a coherent approach to the branding process to make it work (Hanna and Rowley, 2015; Kavaratzis, Giovanardi and Lichrou, 2018). A well-functioning nation branding should be well executed, have a mix of marketing elements and channels, present appealing content, and stimulate creative and innovative "on-brand" ideas to be able to attract target groups, stir co-creation, and inspire lifestyle choices among brand publics (Arvidsson, 2006; Jenkins, 2006; Dinnie, Melewar, Seidenfuss and Musa, 2010). Here popular music is a good example of an "on-brand" idea that meets people on an everyday level (Anholt, 2003).

As nation brands have become an essential part of the strategic assets of a state, they need to be treated strategically (Dinnie et al. 2010; Szondi, 2008; Kotler and Gertner, 2002). The nation strategy is normally created by national, regional or local governments in partnership with the private sector (Govers and Go, 2009). The nations being branded today require new and dedicated structures to coordinate, develop, maintain and promote the brand. The traditional apparatus of trade or government is no longer fit for such a purpose, according to Anholt (2013). Many parties can be involved in this: promotion boards, destination marketing organisations, export, trade and investment agencies, ministries of foreign affairs, chambers of commerce, financial institutions, corporations, and marketing or communication experts. They have to cooperate extensively with each other, as well as with other public and private actors, to make it work, according to Govers and Go (2009). There can be a tension between cultural identity, governmental goals and commercial interest. But Pamment and Cassinger (2018) argue that the nation brand in itself allows actors with different and even conflicting agendas to work together. Complex networks of actors are often developed over a long period of time, aligned to safeguard and develop the image of nation.

Nation branding should be collective – there are many stakeholders that need to come together to plan and manage their investments. In such a dynamic process, management and leadership is central. The nation brand leadership is taken by, or given to, key stakeholders (which can be governmental organisations, industry organisations and commercial actors), often in partnership with each other (Govers and Go, 2009). This often shared leadership emerges from trustful relationships between key partners, from what they create jointly. But leaderships, partnerships and collaboration can also be challenging – it is necessary to be able to negotiate successfully and agree on a shared purpose and common goals. Hanna and Rowley (2015) propose a Strategic Place Brand Management model, where the importance of brand leaders understanding the complex relationships between the parts of the process, is underlined. Brand leaders should work with and engage the stakeholders on all levels to discuss the brand identity and its values, to have a shared view on the values built into it. The objective is to align and coordinate the strategy and the communication. In the digital age of today, when communication and branding is often two-way and co-creational, brand leadership should also manage the opportunity that the digital arena creates to collaborate and co-brand. The complexity of a nation branding process calls for a collaborative effort, which brings together the wishes of all stakeholders involved in the process (Hanna and Rowley, 2015; Kavaratzis et al., 2018). The key to make it work is more integration and an inclusive approach. The nation branding process should be dynamic, collective and participatory: the multiple stakeholders on different levels – connected to different interests – represent an eco-system in which multiple resource-integrating service-exchange activities are being undertaken by multiple actors and actor-to-actor networks, from different perspectives (Kavaratzis, 2012; Kavaratzis et al., 2018; Morgan et al., 2002). A brand value that is being co-created in open eco-systems provides flexibility and inclusiveness, and allows several interwoven processes to take place at the same time, which is much needed in the digital arenas of today where brands are seen as dynamic and social processes.

CO-BRANDING THE NORDIC COUNTRIES VIA MUSIC

During the early twenty-first century, the Nordic countries (Sweden, Denmark, Finland, Norway and Iceland) have been at the forefront of nation branding practices. No other region in the world has embraced nation branding like the Nordic region, according to Pamment (2016). All Nordic countries work intensively with their respective nation brands. They have created institutions for managing consensus over national image promotion across the public and private sectors and are ranking high in the Anholt-GfK Nation Brand Index (Pamment, 2016). There are also efforts in branding the Nordic area as a whole. Nordic countries have a long tradition of collective export promotion. The place branding tradition of these countries has been characterised by cooperation rather than competition. For many years, they have carried out joint marketing efforts, for instance in the United States, via the Scandinavian Tourist Board (Lucarelli and Hallin, 2015).

Central here is the fact that the Nordic region is rather culturally homogenous, with high standards in terms of income, social welfare, level of education, freedom of press and equality. Characteristics such as progressive and innovative, as well as appearance, lifestyle, culture and politics are also common to the region. As nation brand core values, these are seen as attractive to the rest of the world and it is seen as important to create an image around these values (Pamment, 2016; Koponen, 2016).

The Nordic nations are rather small and dependent on export. During the 1980s, for example, the Nordic country-of-origin brands tended to be manufactured foods and goods like Volvo, IKEA and Lego. There is today considerable growth in many sectors, but particularly in the culture and creative sector. During the 2000s there was an increasing emphasis on the cultural and creative industry and export. The music export sector in all the Nordic countries is increasing steadily each year. Swedish music export, for example, reached 2 billion Swedish crowns in 2016, which was the highest ever. Music export also creates many indirect economic effects that are hard to measure. The value of creative export can be measured, but not the value of intangible assets and rights, or cultural value (Tillväxtverket, 2017).

All Nordic countries have an organisation that supports and promotes their music export: Export Music Sweden, Music Norway, Iceland Music Export, Music Export Denmark and Music Finland (Nordic Council of Ministers, 2015). The size of the organisations, the way of organising and the funding varies between the countries. The organisations' efforts in promoting the respective nations via music is also coordinated with the effort of branding the countries as a whole, although different approaches are being used. Nordic countries all have created institutions for managing consensus over national image promotion across government and the private sector, such as the Norwegian Public Diplomacy Forum, the Council for Promotion of Sweden Abroad, the Fund for the Promotion for Denmark, the Finland Promotion Board and Promote Iceland. But further efforts have been made in order to coordinate all the different stakeholders and the core values.

In Sweden, *Team Sweden* was launched in 2015 – a collaborative platform and network of 19 authorities, governmental organisations (for example Business Sweden, Visit Sweden and the Swedish Institute) and companies, all of which work to promote Sweden under a common brand platform and strategy – called Brand Sweden. In branding Sweden there are many different stakeholders, with strong common values: openness, progressivity, innovation and creativity. There is a clear focus on creative industries. According to the Swedish export strategy from 2015, from the Government Offices of Sweden, the cultural and creative industries have a particularly important role to play in presenting a positive image of Sweden and the wish is to build on the successful music export and the reputation of a music force (Swedish Institute, 2008, 2015).

In Norway, many publicly supported stakeholders promote Norway and Norwegian companies abroad, for example Innovation Norway, Norwegian Arts Abroad, Norwegian Energy Partners, Visit Norway and also the City of Oslo. There are cooperation efforts, for example *Merkevaren Norge* (Brand Norway) by Innovation Norway (Innovasjon Norge, 2018), which brings together governmental and commercial organisations in order to promote export and investments. In a recent report, though, The Industrial Policy Council for cultural and creative industries in Norway highlights the importance of taking the creative industries more into account in the ongoing work on Brand Norway, as the creative industries have high-profile potential (Norwegian Ministry of Culture, 2017). This resonates with the increasing focus on Norwegian music as important on the export market (Johansen and Storaas, 2016).

In Finland a new operating model around the nation brand was created in 2012, the Team Finland network, with tasks to help organisations to go global, providing services and networks and with the aim of bringing together centres for Economic Development, Transport and the Environment, Business Finland, Finnvera and Ministry for Foreign Affairs (Finland Promotion Board, 2017). The current Country Branding Strategy is created by the Finland Promotion Board and the promotion is centred around the website 'This is Finland'. Art and culture have a central part on the official Finland website, signalling its importance to the Finnish Nation Brand (Ministry for Foreign Affairs of Finland, 2018).

The Danish government's nation branding initiative Action Plan for the Global Marketing of Denmark, launched in 2007, brings together the Ministry of Economic and Business Affairs, Ministry of Foreign Affairs, Ministry of Education and Ministry of Culture. The various initiatives in the Action Plan are carried out in comprehensive dialogue with a wide range of both public and private actors with different focuses, for example Visit Denmark promoting Denmark, focusing on tourism, but also with a clear focus on working with the creative industry (Merkelsen and Kjaergaard Rasmussen, 2015; Visit Denmark, 2018).

Iceland, the fastest growing nation brand according to Brand Finance (2017), is promoted by Promote Island – a public–private initiative carried out in partnership with, for example, Visit Iceland and Iceland's Creative Centers, to promote Iceland as a country of origin for creative industries and to support promotion of the Icelandic cultural scene – highlighted as dynamic and original (Island, 2018).

Efforts in branding the Nordic countries are also made on a Nordic level, following the traditions of Nordic cooperation. In 2008 the five Nordic music export offices decided to create a common platform for sharing information and best practices, building on prior more informal dialogue and collaboration. The platform came to be a place for developing pan-Nordic strategies and analysing changes and challenges in the music sector, in order to complement and strengthen each other. The Nordic Music Export Programme (NOMEX) began its formal operation in February 2012 with a programme called Strength in Unity (2011–2015), which was funded by the Nordic Council of Ministers, in order to create a more unified voice for Nordic music. NOMEX initiated a range of projects, such as Ja Ja Ja Music (Nordic club nights in London and Berlin) and the Nordic Playlist (presenting tailor-made playlists on Spotify), creating publicity via viral content and connecting with artists, media and music industry professionals. There have also been so-called trade missions – getting the Nordic music industry to meet representatives from other countries. In a study by Arto Koponen (2016), the actors point out the well-functioning collaboration, knowledge sharing on the platform and an openness and willingness to share working methods as important. Business practices, frameworks and working methods are shared in order to develop music export collaboration on a Nordic scale. This makes artists and culture export actors want to work more towards a Nordic brand rather than a national brand, according to Koponen (2016). These projects have helped the Nordic countries to compete globally through a stronger marketing profile, shared risk and shared investment in spreading Nordic music abroad (Williams, 2010). NOMEX today continues to be a pan-Nordic platform administrated through Music Finland, but owned by all the music export offices in the Nordic countries. The organisation keeps conducting cooperation projects and studies about music export on the Nordic level. It also continuously collaborates in branding Nordic music via Nordic club nights, playlists and export activities.

NORDIC EVENTS ON SOUTH BY SOUTHWEST

This chapter is focused on the Nordic countries getting together to promote and co-brand the region at the annual festival and conference South by South West (SXSW), in Austin, Texas, USA. SXSW brings together the areas of interactive media, web, gaming, innovation, film and music and is considered one of the most important and interesting meeting points on digital culture, creativity and innovation today. It is a melting pot of creativity and innovation. The conference and festival more or less takes over Austin for ten days in March every year, with more than 2000 music acts performing, several hundreds of sessions, lectures and workshops and hundreds of films being screened. The number of attendants is around 100 000 from around the world according to SXSW – professionals from many different sectors, not only the creative industry, but all kinds of industries and trade interested in innovation and the digital.

The Nordic countries have been present at SXSW in different ways in different years: sometimes just visiting as a country and/or company delegations, sometimes participating to promote the country, region or company. In 2016 a Nordic joint venture at SXSW took place at the pop-up venue "The Nordic Lighthouse", a place for meetings, showcases, jam sessions, exhibitions and installations, workshops, talks, conversations and networking for the Nordic creative industry. It was funded by both governmental and private actors in Sweden, Denmark and Finland, and the Nordic Innovation House in Palo Alto. The different Nordic countries taking part in the programme acted both together and separately at the site. Team Sweden, for example, launched the concept The Swedish Affair and the digital platform Showcase Sweden, a digital collection of creative works and companies from Sweden, showing Swedish music, games, clothes, films, advertising or TV drama. The expectations of the Swedish participants being interviewed in this study were several: to be noticed and build the brand of Sweden as a country, to make people go there, to connect to creative business from other countries, to discover Nordic music (or listen to it more), and for music artists attending to be signed and booked. One aspect here is the impact of personal connections and experiences: "The live music touches you in another way than you talk about it or listen to it on Spotify", as a participating representative from a Nordic export organisation puts it. The other Nordic countries made similar efforts during the festival. Finland, for example, invited 30 Finnish companies to showcase their innovations at the SXSW Interactive EXPO, Team Finland and Oslo Lounge (Norway) showed their respective countries' start-up, music and film industries. Denmark chose not to be part of SXSW in 2016. The following year some Nordic countries were present at SXSW, but not in a joint or powerful effort.

In 2018, though, the Nordic countries decided to make a more unified presence at SXSW. The background to this was a common group trip to Austin in 2017 with Nordic companies, organised by the City of Oslo. The city then (in September 2017) invited large companies and organisations that usually take part in SXSW to a meeting with the purpose of creating further cooperation in order to build the Nordic brand. The number of participants grew like a snowball – first, companies that were already partners and cooperating and then one led to another. Both governmental organisations and regional and local organisations from the Nordic countries, as well as different companies that fit the common Nordic or Scandinavian brand, and of course music creators and companies, joined the collaborative effort. The work was done by governmental organisations such as Visit Denmark, Innovation Norway, the music export organisations and some of Scandinavia's leading brands – such as Scandinavian Airlines (SAS), Carlsberg, Osos, Arcus, Himkok, The North Alliance (NoA), Doberman, Dansk Markedsføring, and Swims. An important driving force in this became SAS, who took the lead and issued invitations to strategy and planning meetings, came to hold the project leading role, created and hosted a common site in Austin and also held meetings after the event to evaluate it. The common site, a café near the conference transformed into a "House of Scandinavia", was their idea and initiative, but this grew bigger and bigger. As one participant puts it: "It was a dream idea, and I don't think they understood in the beginning the impact it would have and the amount of interest it would attract from organisations and companies." SAS had noticed an increasing interest from all Scandinavian countries to participate in the festival and conference and organised four direct flights from Stockholm to Austin to make it easier to get to the SXSW. Their incentive was to use the platform for building their brand. According to Fredrik Henriksson at SAS: "Many of our customers are innovative, creative and very keen on digitization, which is completely in line with what we are doing at SAS" (SAS Group. 2018). These brand values aligned with the nation brand values and strategies, according to participants.

House of Scandinavia was supposed to be a spot for networking and daily happenings, presentations, curated entertainment and showcases with leading Scandinavian artists and entrepreneurs – "all in the spirit of Scandinavia". A great many different types of content and projects took part in the House of Scandinavia, hosted by various organisations and companies. There were, for example, Nordic start-up presentations and meet-ups for creatives. There were Scandinavian breakfasts every day, dinners hosted by the world famous Michelin-starred restaurant Noma, and parties with royals attending (HRH Crown Prince Haakon of Norway). Above all, there was a big focus on music. Different Nordic music organisations created matchmaking sessions with music industry professionals, song listening parties (presenting song-making collaborations created during a song writing camp) as well as showcases with a wide range of Nordic artists, presented by Music Norway, Music Finland and Live at Heart, a music festival from the Swedish town Örebro.

All the things happening at the site made it possible to produce content: to film, record and photograph the different parts of the event, to create content with the focus on promoting both the event and the brands at the same time. As part of the marketing strategy for the Nordic participation at SXSW, Sony Sweden, for example, collaborated with SAS in presenting a live show and the world premiere of a new single by Swedish artist Kim Cesarion and his band in the air, on the direct flight SK 6953 between Stockholm and Austin. The event started at the Arlanda airport, with red carpets for the travellers and cheering pilots. In the air the show was filmed, and the film, edited during the flight, was released on social media directly after. The film of the unique music event went viral (the film has reached over 30 000 views after a few weeks) and became an important part of the campaign. Activities in social media, connected to the Nordic event at SXSW 2018, were taking place in the open Facebook group of House of Scandinavia (managed by SAS), as well as on all the different partners' pages. There were no Instagram or Twitter accounts for the House of Scandinavia, but organisations, companies, creators and private persons could and did create and share content from the different parts of the busy schedule of the House of Scandinavia. By "hashtagging" intensively (for example #houseofscandinavia, #swedenlive, #superfinland, #nordicmade) the posts built on the digital social presence of the Nordic countries at SXSW.

DISCUSSION AND CONCLUSION

This chapter has focused on the role that music and the music industry play in branding the Nordic countries and, more specifically, the strategic and managerial side of branding the Nordic region as a music region. The aim was to provide insight into the complex, organisational process of branding that needs a clear strategy and collaborative approach, even over national borders. The main focus in this study has been to understand the relationship between actors in this specific branding partnership. The setting of Nordic countries collaborating before, during and after a large event, with a clear focus on creativity and music in particular, created a common ground where collaboration seemed to function rather well. This study shows that collaboration not only between countries but also between governmental organisations and corporations is important, even a success factor. Previous work with, for example, cooperation on the music scene and in different projects and organisations, at a Nordic level, has been important for making the Nordic branding initiatives successful. NOMEX, seems to have been important as a "hotbed" for collaborations like on SXSW, by creating platforms and common strategies for music export and branding.

There are some differences in the investments of the SXSW events in 2016–2018. In 2016 the overall impact of the Nordic countries was considered fairly good – not excellent, according to participants. There are several explanations given to this: the low participation of organisations and the level of cooperation between those who participated. The planning of the events could be better, the communication and content could be more exciting to "stir" the right target groups, according to participants. The content was also centred to a great extent on individual countries, not building the Nordic region/Scandinavia, according to one interviewee in this study. Other critiques put forward by participants in the 2016 event was that SXSW is too big to make an impact, and that these kinds of events steered by governmental organisations tend to create low interest, both from visitors and from the different actors involved in the project. Participants also blamed low governmental knowledge about music. "The music export strategy is not always rooted in reality, as it should be", as one music company representative puts it. If the music export is highlighted in the strategies, there is a need for more funding and more involvement of the industry in the nation branding process.

In 2018 a more collaborative and co-creational way of working became a success factor. The common branding agenda of the House of Scandinavia in 2018 was central to the outcome and this spilled over into the digital arenas in an integrated way. A holistic and integrated approach to nation branding is needed, but also exciting and engaging content is crucial (both on the physical and digital sites). Both in 2016 and 2018 the Nordic marketing projects had this objective. The later version seems to have managed it better. "We really managed to create a feeling of FOMO (fear of missing out)", as a strategist put it, "We created something outside the ordinary. And that is needed today."

The mere commercial side of these Nordic nation branding initiatives should not be overlooked. At the 2018 SXSW, SAS is seen as a unifying force and a mediator in the campaign. Its brand values are close to those of the Nordic countries in a way that maybe no other companies' values could be. No other actor could play that part, according to one interviewee in the study. The driving force in this project has been common, shared interests and target groups, as well as the interests of each participant organisation, driven by business goals. There are a great many trying to connect to the same people, that have more or less the same target groups and benefit from communicating together and having joint forces and funds. Joint communication efforts are becoming more and more common, and this is is one important aspect of the well-functioning cooperation in these cases, according to this study. The event at SXSW in 2018 seems to have been this dynamic, collective, and participatory event that Kavaratzis et al. (2018) say is key to successful nation branding. The companies and organisations taking part in branding the Nordic countries see it as a creative partnership with common interests that should be continued. As one participating strategist puts it: "That it turned out to be this successful [. . .] given relatively limited resources in time and money, is great! If this is done next year, which I hope, and with the experience gathered, it will get even better and have even higher impact."

In a fast and digital market, there is also a need to be agile. A market and communication plan for today needs to be constantly changing. This creates a need for cooperating with other actors that are agile as well. This could be one explanation as to why the SXSW participation in 2018 worked out well. Also the fact that a resourceful actor took the lead, and managed to bring in different (and maybe the right?) partners, was clearly very significant. But is it problematic that a company takes the lead in a joint nation branding event? One participating company turns the question around: Could this have been done successfully by a governmental organisation? Large commercial organisations seem to be agile enough, and have the expertise in reaching target groups and interacting with them. They also have the resources and the driving force to come ashore with a complex branding process like this. The key seems to be shared interests in creating business value and building brand, not only on a nation branding level, but on a company level. The fact that both governments and commercial organisations participate brings credibility, stability and nation strategy as well as marketing and communication know-how. The question then is who is building and steering the strategy of the Nordic music scene onwards? NOMEX continues to function as a platform, but is in practice only one of several leaders in the branding process. When having nation brand strategies for the Nordic countries in place that align with each other, practice in collaborating on a Nordic level seems to keep building on common know-how and shared values in the co-branding, as well as a wish to keep working together.

REFERENCES

Anholt, S. (2003). *Brand new justice: The upside of global branding.* Oxford, UK: Butterworth-Heinemann.

Anholt, S. (2013). Beyond the nation brand: The role of image and identity in international relations. *Exchange: The Journal of Public Diplomacy,* 2(1), 1–7.

Aronczyk, M. (2008). Living the brand: Nationality, globality, and the identity strategies of nation branding consultants. *International Journal of Communication,* 2, 41–65.

Arvidsson, A. (2006). *Brand, meaning and value in media culture.* Padstow, UK: Routledge.

Balakrishnan, S. (2009). Strategic branding of destinations: A framework. *European Journal of Marketing,* 43(5/6), 611–629.

Bengtsson, S. (2011). Virtual nation branding: The Swedish embassy in Second Life. *The Journal of Virutal Worlds Research,* 4(1), 1–26.

Bolin, G. & Ståhlberg, P. (2015). Mediating the nation-state: Agency and the media in nation-branding campaigns. *International Journal of Communication,* 9, 3065–3083.

Brand Finance (2017). Nation brands. Retrieved 1 December 2018 from http://brandfinance.com/images/upload/bf_nation_brands_2017.pdf.

Campelo, A. (Ed.) (2017). *Handbook on place branding and marketing.* Cheltenham, UK and Northampton, MA, USA: Edward Elgar Publishing.

Dinnie, K., Melewar, T. C., Seidenfuss, K., & Musa, G. (2010). Nation branding and integrated marketing communications: An ASEAN perspective. *International Marketing Review,* 27(4), 388–403.

Finland Promotion Board (2017). *Finland's country branding strategy.* Retrieved 1 December 2018 from https://toolbox.finland.fi/wp-content/uploads/sites/.

Govers, R. & Go, F. (2009). *Place branding: Glocal, virtual and physical identities, constructed, imagined and experienced.* Basingstoke, UK: Palgrave Macmillian.

Hanna, S. A. & Rowley, J. (2015). Rethinking strategic place branding in the digital age. In M. Kavaratzis, G. Warnaby & G. J. Ashworth (Eds.), *Rethinking place branding: Comprehensive brand development for cities and regions* (pp. 85–100). Cham, Switzerland: Springer International Publishing, AG.

Huang, S. (2011). Nation-branding and transnational consumption: Japan-mania and the Korean wave in Taiwan. *Media, Culture & Society,* 33(1), 3–18.

Innovasjon Norge (2018). *Merkevaren Norge.* Retrieved 1 December 2018 from https://www.innovasjonnorge.no/no/merkevarennorge/.

Island (2018). Press. Retrieved 1 December 2018 from https://www.iceland.is/press.

Jenkins, H. (2006). *Fans, bloggers, and gamers: Exploring participatory culture.* New York: New York University Press.

Johansen, C. K., & Storaas, V. (2016). *Vekst 2020 – et fremtidsbilde at norske musikkselskaper.* Oslo, Norway: Music Norway.

Kavaratzis, M. (2012). From "necessary evil" to necessity: Stakeholders' involvement in place branding. *Journal of Place Management and Development,* 5(1), 7–19.

Kavaratzis, M., Giovanardi, M., & Lichrou, M. (2018). *Inclusive place branding: Critical perspectives on theory and practice.* New York: Routledge.

Koponen, A. (2016). *Benchmarking Nordic music export operations* (bachelor's thesis assigned by Music Finland). Jyväskylä, Finland: JAMK University for Applied Sciences.

Kotler, P. & Gertner, D. (2002). Country as brand, product, and beyond: A place marketing and brand management perspective. *The Journal of Brand Management*, 9(4), 249–261.

Lucarelli, A. & Hallin, A. (2015). Brand transformation: A performative approach to brand regeneration. *Journal of Marketing Management*, 31(1), 84–106.

Melissen, J. (2005). Public diplomacy: In tandem with branding. In *Government Communication: The Dutch* Experience. Government Information Service, Ministry of General Affairs. The Hague, Netherlands: Opmeer Printing.

Merkelsen, H. & Kjaergaard Rasmussen, R. (2015). The construction of Brand Denmark: A case study of the reversed causality in nation brand valuation. *Valuation Studies*, 3(2), 181–198.

Ministry for Foreign Affairs of Finland (2018). This is Finland. Retrieved 1 December 2018 from https://finland.fi.

Morgan, N., Pritchard, A., & Pride, R. (Eds.) (2002). *Destination brands: Managing place reputation*. Oxford, UK: Elsevier Science.

Morley, D. & Robin, K. (1995). *Spaces of identity: Global media, electronic landscapes and cultural boundaries*. London, UK: Routledge.

Music:)ally (2016). Spotify hails Nordic exports: 1.4bn streams in January alone. Retrieved 9 July 2019 from https://musically.com/2016/03/04/spotify-hails-nordic-exports-1-4bn-streams-in-january-alone/.

Musiksverige (2017). Musikbranschen i siffror. Statistik för 2016. Retrieved 1 December 2018 from https://statistik2016.musiksverige.org.

Nordic Council of Ministers (2015). *NOMEX – Nordic Music Export Programme. Final report*. Retrieved 1 December 2018 from http://www.nomex.com.

Norwegian Ministry of Culture (2017). The Industrial Policy Council for Cultural and Creative Industries in Norway. Retrieved 1 December 2018 from https://www.regjeringen.no/contentassets/8aeb67b6217d41b29b18b5584a87f61c/recommendations_industrial_policy_council_.pdf.

Pamment, J. (2016). Introduction: Why the Nordic region? *Place Branding and Public Diplomacy*, 12(2–3), 91–98.

Pamment, J. & Cassinger, C. (2018). Nation branding and the social imaginary of participation: An exploratory study of the Swedish Number Campaign. *European Journal of Cultural Studies*, 21(5), 561–574.

SAS Group (2018). SAS offers direct flights to the South by Southwest (SXSW) tech and music festival. Retrieved 1 December 2018 from https://www.sasgroup.net/en/sas-offers-direct-flights-to-the-south-by-southwest-sxsw-tech-and-music-festival/.

Swedish Government (2016). The Swedish Affair på SXSW. Retrieved 1 December 2018 from https://www.regeringen.se/artiklar/2016/03/the-swedish-affair-pa-sxsw/.

Swedish Institute (2008). *Brand Sweden. The Road to an Updated Image of Sweden Abroad*. Stockholm: Swedish Institute.

Szondi, G. (2008). *Public diplomacy and nation branding: Conceptual similarities and differences*. The Hague, Netherlands: Netherlands Institute of International Relations "Clingendael".

Tillväxtverket (2017). *Kreametern. En guide till svensk statistik för kulturella och kreativa näringar*. Stockholm, Sweden: Tillväxtverket.

Visit Denmark (2018). Global marketing of Denmark. Retrieved 1 December 2018 from https://www.visitdenmark.dk/da/danmark/global-marketing-denmark.

Williams, M. (2010). NOMEX Strength in Unity, A Music Ally report. Retrieved 22 September 2018 from http://nordicmusicexport.com/wp-content/uploads/2014/04/NOMEXstrategyandconstituion.pdf.

5. Size matters! Insights from the municipalities of Gothenburg and Sorsele

Sara Brorström, Sarah Degerhammar and Kristina Tamm Hallström

INTRODUCTION

> Does size matter for how branding activities are carried out and what consequences they have? And are there some specific challenges in the Nordic context when it comes to branding places of different sizes?

These are the questions we aim to answer in this chapter by studying two Swedish municipalities of different sizes and their efforts at branding towards, first and foremost, their inhabitants, but also indirectly towards an external audience. The basis of this interest is an understanding that Nordic place branding differs from place branding in other contexts and is thus especially salient to draw insights from (Lucarelli and Hallin, 2015; Cassinger and Eksell, 2017), and that the matter of size is rarely discussed. In general, it is claimed that the specifics of local governments in the Nordic countries are heavy service responsibilities, broad autonomy, collective decision making (Haveri, 2015) and collaboration within the local governments as well as with other local governments (Brorström and Parment, 2017). Moreover, Haveri (2015: 138) mentions the "strong tradition of consensus-seeking between different interests and avoidance of open conflict" as something that is characteristic for the Nordic countries. On top of this, there is often a belief that population growth is desirable, and pro-growth strategies have been adopted, in terms of steering documents such as vision statements, in many local governments in the west (Loftman and Nevin, 1996; Brorström, 2010). In this chapter we aim to contribute to an increased understanding of how the Nordic institutionalised values and practices are expressed and reflected in branding and communication activities for small and large municipalities.

We illustrate this by analysing two Swedish municipalities of very different characteristics and size, both representing the Nordic ideals and both part of the larger Nordic region. The city of Gothenburg, located on the west coast, is the second-largest municipality in Sweden with around 570,000 inhabitants and a steady growth. Sorsele, in the far north, is with its 2,500 residents one of the smallest and continuously decreasing municipalities population-wise, but one of the largest in land area. We see these two municipalities as together illustrating the use of branding in a Nordic context. The chapter is structured as follows: first, we introduce the framework used, then we provide a description of the two municipalities, how branding is organised and how the practices of branding affected them, and finally we discuss in what way branding activities depend on the size of the two municipalities.

FRAMEWORK – NORDIC PLACE BRANDING FOR MUNICIPALITIES OF DIFFERENT SIZES

Municipal organisations today face pressure from different stakeholders, such as inhabitants, companies and authorities, to expand their services and to become more attractive. The resulting changes are often seen as aligned with New Public Management (NPM) ideas (Hood, 1991; Lapsley, 2008), and the rise of the "brand society" (Kornberger, 2010; Lucarelli, 2018). However, the likelihood of successfully increasing the attractiveness of a place depends on the characteristics – social, economic and environmental – of the area in question (Brorström and Parment, 2016). Logan and Molotch (1987) described cities as "growth machines", where growth in population has been considered a purely positive thing and is therefore often also claimed to be a reason for investments in branding activities in the Nordic countries (Brorström and Parment, 2016). However, most cities and local governments cannot affect the pace of their growth (Leo and Anderson, 2006; Syssner, 2015). Hence, while large accumulations of people may lead to an increase in societal problems and an increased need for investments, growth is still considered a key to an attractive future (Lombardi et al., 2011). Furthermore, branding activities are thus becoming increasingly common in municipalities, irrespective of size (Syssner, 2015; Brorström and Parment, 2016). One issue, however, is that there is no conceptual agreement on how place brand identity is built and communicated (Ruzzier and de Chernatony, 2013). A key characteristic of developing an identity for a place is that a place brand needs to accommodate the diverse interests of multiple stakeholders (Cassinger and Eksell, 2017) and that this process differs significantly between a small rural municipality and a larger city.

Kavaratzis and Hatch (2013: 74) argue that the place branding literature has a static view of identity, that it is something that can be "tapped, defined, and manipulated" and that branding then becomes the attempt to communicate the place identity. Our approach aims to add nuance by considering identity as the outcome of a process of decision making, where it is possible to break down a place's identity into elements which are manageable and can be communicated. We also agree with Giovanardi (2015), who argues that place branding should be seen as a multiscalar phenomenon and can emerge from actions on different scales. Moreover, according to our framework, some values and aspects are destroyed or hidden along the path of shaping or articulating the identity. Bertilsson and Rennstam (2018) call this the "destructive side of branding", which implies that branding not only builds but can also destroy values. Echeverri and Skålén (2011) illustrate how values are both co-created and co-destroyed among several actors. Their study is not in the place branding context, but co-destruction is still useful as a concept to understand how the management of values can lead to either the creation or destruction of values among involved actors and thus lead to tensions between values. Value creation is about creating a narrative, a story, about the place, at the same time as different development projects are running. This can be summed up in what Therkelsen et al. (2010) call the "city of words" versus the "city of stones", a metaphor useful in the two municipalities that are presented here, since both municipalities were working on plans to be implemented in the future.

BRANDING GOTHENBURG AND SORSELE

In this chapter, we use qualitative data collected from the city of Gothenburg and from the municipality of Sorsele. In Gothenburg 20 interviews were carried out with civil servants at the communication unit that is organised as part of the city management office and with civil servants responsible for large city development projects. In addition, steering group meetings of the River City (Älvstaden) project were observed, as branding efforts were part of their agenda for discussion. In Sorsele, 11 interviews were conducted with civil servants in leading positions in the municipality, including the head of communication and one communication officer temporarily employed in 2016–2018 for the project and tasked with developing a comprehensive plan for the municipality. In addition, observations of meetings between the municipality and inhabitants about the development plan for the municipality were carried out. As noted, Swedish municipalities have a large degree of autonomy towards the state and are responsible for a large share of public services such as social services, education and infrastructure (Bergström et al., 2008; Haveri, 2015). Swedish municipalities are also free to brand and communicate in a way they find appropriate. Nevertheless, both municipalities have recently invested in different means of communicating their brands and we can see similarities, but also differences, that we argue it is important to highlight. Lucarelli (2012) illustrates five different city branding elements: events and activities; history and heritage; graphics and symbols; processes and institutions; and artefacts and spatial planning. In Gothenburg and Sorsele we have studied first and foremost events and activities, mainly in relation to spatial planning.

Gothenburg – Two Planning Visions and a Railway Tunnel

The current communication and branding of Gothenburg started, according to the interviewees, with a need for something that could "hold the city together". This was after the city council, in 2012, had adopted two visions: the River City Vision and Vision 2021. The River City vision reads: "River City Gothenburg – Open for the World" and is accompanied by three strategies: Connect the City, Reinforce the Regional Core and Meet the Water. This vision had been developed in a collaborative mode across traditional city boundaries: within the city, with external stakeholders and with citizens. There were several aims behind this initiative; one was to start collaborating more within the city, and another was to create an image of Gothenburg that portrayed the city as forward looking, innovative and sustainable. The Gothenburg 2021 vision started as a means to decide on how to celebrate the city's four-hundredth anniversary in 2021. Vision 2021 had been developed with a focus on citizens' dialogue and resulted in many ideas for how to celebrate the actual year and what to do in the meantime. With these two visions, a need to create a more holistic way of communicating and branding the city emerged and a decision was made by the city council to organise branding and communication efforts holistically from the city management office. A communication director was appointed and a communication unit created. One of the interviewees from this new organisational unit commented that there was a great responsibility to make sure "the traffic office doesn't say one thing and then the park and landscape administration says something else, about the same place".

Another articulated motive behind the reinforced communication and branding in Gothenburg related to the plans for the West Link (*Västlänken*), a railway tunnel that would run below the city centre in the future.[1] Criticisms of this project had been raised by inhabitants

---

[1] The construction of the West Link railway tunnel started in spring 2018 and will be concluded by 2026.

and others, one argument being that the city had not been transparent about the development plans. Interviewed civil servants, however, argued that the inhabitants who later became critical had shown little interest during the actual planning. The long planning process was thus to blame. However, the interviewed civil servants also argued that they needed to become better at communicating what the city was planning and, perhaps even more important, at communicating *why* they were planning it.

Sorsele – One Vision, Core Values and Crucial Developments

In Sorsele, there were several expressions of the intensified branding and communication efforts: the internal work of drafting a municipal vision; the process of creating core values for the municipality which would serve as a frame in the communication processes; the establishment of the new position of a communication officer; the development of a branding strategy; and a work process with the purpose of developing a comprehensive plan for the whole municipality. Behind these initiatives was a perceived need to change the negative trend of the past decades, with a significant decrease in the number of inhabitants and services closing down. One civil servant commented that there was both a need to formalise the development work that had been initiated in recent years and a need to make Sorsele visible on both the "national and global map". Another civil servant stressed that spreading the existing image of Sorsele as a sparsely populated municipality is not very beneficial from a branding perspective. Moreover, as in Gothenburg, the interviewees in Sorsele expressed the view that it was time to make decision-making processes in the municipality more transparent, and to develop the work of communicating with relevant stakeholders, such as inhabitants and the business community, which consists of a large number of entrepreneurs. The winter car testing industry is a leading business here and the general opinion is that there are benefits for the municipality when automotive companies establish testing sites for ice driving. However, while this business generates work within the municipality during the winter season, it also means that parts of the frozen lakes are fenced off and closed for other activities, such as ice fishing. Another growing seasonal industry in Sorsele is the summer fly fishing tourism, which also means that certain stretches of the rivers are regulated and restricted exclusively to this type of fishing, banning traditional fishing for food. The fishing industry, along with other outdoor activities, is crucial for the image of the place according to the interviewees, but does not lead to many jobs for the inhabitants. This suggests a tension between the image of the place and the industries that are important for creating work. Industries are important, as they may contribute to the growth and development of the municipality, yet the presence of these industries has led to discussions among inhabitants about who the municipality and its surrounding countryside is for – people attracted for shorter visits, or those already living there on a permanent basis?

Despite this type of tension between different values, several interviewees express a need to brand the municipality and improve communication in order to attract new residents. In both Gothenburg and Sorsele, the interviewees do not make any distinction between branding, communication and information. It is all part of the overall work of creating an image of what the municipalities are. In Gothenburg, interviewees talk about how the brand of the city is "built up" by communication. And the best result is if there is an understanding of why the city invests in a certain development and how it is connected to other changes in the city.

THE NORDIC SPECIFICS AND THE TWO MUNICIPALITIES

In the Nordic context there is generally assumed to be a closeness between a municipality and the inhabitants – they are to be involved and listened to, as a part of a democratic process (Haveri, 2015). However, what this means in practice differs between Gothenburg and Sorsele. In Gothenburg, people identify themselves more with the city district they live in than with the city as a whole. Moreover, the size of the city makes target groups abstract. It is thus not possible to address all citizens at the same time. One of those interviewed explained:

> It is about creating a specific niche when we do things. Maybe like . . . now we do this towards that target group. We cannot be too general, then no one cares. That is a challenge.

The city can thus "hide" behind the abstraction of citizens, with general categories of target groups. According to the city's communication plan of 2016, there are external target groups, such as citizens, visitors, businesses and the surrounding areas, as well as internal target groups such as elected politicians, managers and employees of the city organisation. These target groups are uncontested, everyone is involved but no one is designated.

In Sorsele, a trial and error mode was used to divide stakeholders into target groups. In 2016, for example, the municipality organised an open meeting with inhabitants in the main village, but no one turned up. However, three meetings held in the three smaller villages were more successful. Moreover, the municipality tried to reach and attract inhabitants through dialogues around certain themes, some of which were connected to protected "national interests",[2] while others were connected to local business activities. Moreover, separate meetings were organised for the municipality's Sami population, with a specific focus on the reindeer industry. Although this format was described as worth developing, it also caused problems. Some debates became infected and difficult to resolve, for example around practical issues such as fishing, as touched upon earlier. Some stakeholders used sustainability arguments to push for the introduction of fly fishing where the caught fish is thrown back into the water, while others made references to traditions of keeping the rivers open for conventional fishing, where the fish is taken home. Other forum debates, such as the one about protected mountains, were harder to define or summarise in a simple way and were perceived as too abstract, which in turn led to few people attending the meetings. Yet other groups perceived that they were not listened to, even though the municipality tried to create space for interaction. One example regards the timing of the dialogue meetings with the Sami population working within the reindeer industry. As these meetings were organised in the winter when the entire reindeer business is moved to the coast 350 kilometres away from Sorsele, nobody representing this group showed up. In a planning process, one interviewee explained, there are deadlines for comments, which apparently clashed with the reindeer herding schedules. In other words, the bureaucratic model of the municipality did not match the business run by the Sami population.

The small size of Sorsele, with its decreasing population and limited resources, makes the municipality sensitive when different values are in conflict and tensions arise. The issue of land use is a unique subject matter for a small rural community like Sorsele. Another example from Sorsele which demonstrates the tension caused by different values occurred in 2010 and concerned the establishment of a wind farm consisting of close to 100 wind turbines, in addition to the 100 or so already in place. Several aspects around these developments were criticised – among them the fact that part of the property used for the first wind farm was owned by the leader of the city council who earns money from the rental income; the noise of the turbines, which is disturbing for the people living in a nearby village; and the fact that the wind farms do not generate any new jobs for locals – together creating trust problems. To address these problems, efforts were undertaken to improve both transparency and communication.

---

[2] National interests are regulated by the state as such with reference to extraordinary values linked to culture or the natural environment.

Branding Visions and Other Steering Documents

In Gothenburg, even though much is being planned, most of this will take place in the future and the challenge is thus to make people buy into the future image of the city. Interviewees explained that, from a communication perspective, it is crucial to consider the time aspect and, more precisely, to make the inhabitants see *why* the city is investing in different developments now, when it will be a long time before they see the result. In other words, the city actors are creating the 'city of words' and later they will have to align it with the 'city of stones' (Therkelsen et al., 2010). The issue of the railway tunnel, the West Link, was frequently brought up, which was partly held to be a way to respond to critical voices coming from inhabitants in Gothenburg who were against this development and who, according to several of those interviewed, took up too much time in the debate. Professionals working at the branding and communication unit described how they ended up in the middle. One of them expressed it as follows:

> There are also people that are positive towards the West Link [. . .] but they are not as loud and then we are in the middle and have to communicate facts.

The interviewees described how this debate entailed that, whatever "fact" they wanted to communicate in various fora, it always ended up being about the West Link. One of the civil servants present at an exhibition at the central station, presenting the future city, says that when asked about what people want to know:

> Most people want to talk about the West Link, but they do not ask things: they already know all there is to know, they just want to confirm that [the West Link] is not a good project.

Even so, the fact that the city of Gothenburg is growing makes it possible for the future to contain all kinds of developments, since, according to the interviewees, investments will be needed as people continue to move to the city. The growth ambition, expressed in visions and strategies, also informed the communication plan and information policy, documents that were meant to coordinate branding of the city to provide a holistic and unified image. This development of steering documents can furthermore be seen as a means to increase collaboration within the city organisation as well as to develop information sharing across boundaries. The possibility of using the future as an argument for investments is not unique to the Nordic countries, but the consequences of an expressed need for increased collaboration do indicate a striving for the Nordic ideal (Haveri, 2015).

In Sorsele, facing de-growth, it has been more difficult to plan for the future in an abstract manner, since attracting new inhabitants and businesses is a crucial issue. The interviewees talked about the general problem of making the municipality attractive for people to live in, and the urgency linked to this, since it would affect decisions about whether to maintain public services at a basic level or close them down completely in certain parts of the municipality. In contrast to Gothenburg, it seemed crucial to be very specific about the attractions of the municipality of Sorsele and the motives for staying or moving there. One civil servant working with communication in Sorsele is, however, hopeful:

> The natural environment here is amazing. There is all kinds of accommodation, for example, both close to nature and in villages. So, if you're an outdoor person, for example, it's a great place to live. There is work. Yes, there are good communications, like the motorway that runs close to the airport. There is actually no reason why the number of inhabitants should drop in Sorsele.

At some of the citizen consultation meetings held by the municipality, it became clear that many people in Sorsele thought that it was necessary to invest differently – taking into account a more unique quality of the site – in order to create value and attract citizens from other parts of Sweden. One inhabitant commented that the municipality should be more selective in its branding tactics and less keen to please national ideals, and instead identify the unique aspects of Sorsele. There is a feeling among some of the residents that the municipality does not support them and their initiatives and that the municipality should decide what kind of place they want to be and not just follow in the footsteps of Stockholm. Despite the fact that many of the residents see the advantages of living in a small municipality, politicians, civil servants and employees in the municipality insist on, and work first and foremost, with the growth agenda, in almost all of their sectors. However, the fact that the municipality's population is decreasing creates a "sense of urgency" – a feeling that action is necessary and that the inhabitants need to accept initiatives that may help the municipality to grow. In that sense, when comparing Gothenburg and Sorsele, both growth and de-growth could be said to support branding activities, and the actual effort lies in creating a narrative that illustrates this. In Sorsele, where the future is not as positive as in Gothenburg growth-wise, a paradox occurs: the municipality brands what it thinks are the best things to attract people, the natural environment and the fishing, but this does not necessarily correspond with what the people living there actually experience as good, namely industries creating jobs. There is a possibility that while the municipality is trying to become more attractive through various communication efforts, the result might be the opposite.

In other words, by creating one value, another is destroyed (Bertilsson and Rennstam, 2018).

CONCLUDING DISCUSSION – THE BIGGER AIM OF PLACE BRANDING: SIZE MATTERS

To conclude, while more efforts are being put into branding and communication in general in the municipalities studied, they are intended to resolve different issues. What these issues are, we argue, depends on the size of the municipality and the direction of growth. If we start with the similarities, in both municipalities discussions about a lack of transparency and distrust on the part of citizens reinforced the perceived need for branding and communication. Moreover, in both municipalities this reinforcement of communication and branding started with the development of formal documents such as a vision and a comprehensive plan. These documents clarified that there was a need for communication if these were to be realised in the future. They also justified reinforced branding efforts, since they were described as creating external images of the municipalities. This conclusion confirms the argument put forward by Kavaratzis and Hatch (2013): revisiting and redefining a place vision provides stimulus for the construction of place brands. This development also took organisational form. In Gothenburg, the adoption of two new visions led to the development of a communication unit at the city management office and an investment in communication across the city organisation. The aim was to make sure the whole city "talked with one voice". This echoes what Hatch and Schultz (2008) have highlighted: the importance of the internal brand aligning with the corporate. In Sorsele, the establishment of a communication unit was justified in a similar way; however, given the small size of the municipality, there was less focus on communication efforts and organisational solutions across departments. Yet in both municipalities, the branding and communication during the process of formulating and spreading the new documents became closely connected to the idea of collaboration and an ambition to reach consensus between different organisational units (Brorström and Parment, 2017). In Sorsele, there was a perceived need to become more transparent and more coherent, and to improve the way the municipality talks to the inhabitants as a result of the development of a municipal vision and the work with the comprehensive plan. In other words, the documents produced implied a need for communication, as a means to make the people buy into the municipality's investments and plans for the future, or accept the constructed "city of words" (Therkelsen et al., 2010).

However, as we stated at the beginning of the section, communication and branding were means to resolving different issues. In Gothenburg, there was a concern about the internal coordination, and the idea of collaboration took precedence, whereas the issue prioritised in Sorsele concerned the decrease in population, which affected the provision of public services, which in turn opened up for debates regarding the contents and message of the communication work surrounding the development of the comprehensive plan. One conclusion that can be drawn from this is that with size comes a complexity of organisation, and with increased organisational complexity we see that the message of branding efforts becomes more fluid and vague – something that it should be possible to communicate and see accepted by a plenitude of target groups. Thus, the internal organisational work, rather than the actual content and its consequences, becomes the focus of attention in a city the size of Gothenburg, but not in Sorsele. Yet in Gothenburg, we see that the argument that the city is growing is used in favour of large investments, such as the West Link. This implies that it is possible to argue in favour of investments and municipal developments with both a growing and a decreasing population. Place branding can thus be seen as the frame within which these different developments can be met. At the same time, with these choices come consequences; some aspects and groups are not highlighted. As Bertilsson and Rennstam (2018) argue, brands are understood as distillates of larger wholes, expected to mark quality rather than making people delve into the substantial aspects of a product. Brands are furthermore supposed to simplify rather than encourage an investigation of alternatives. What can be concluded from both Gothenburg and Sorsele is that this distillation and simplification in practice creates tensions and conflicts between different values. Creating the "city of words" that was not always regarded by the inhabitants as being in line with the "city of stones" (Therkelsen et al., 2010) led to tensions being created. One important conclusion is thus that, by inviting people to co-create, there is inevitably also a risk that values are co-destroyed (Echeverri and Skålén, 2011). What is regarded as a "fact" at the communication office in Gothenburg might be seen by others as debatable. Moreover, the very creation of "facts" might be a tool for making different tensions visible. This was evident in both Gothenburg and Sorsele, where it could be argued that the small size of Sorsele made these tensions more visible than in the larger city of Gothenburg. In Gothenburg, the size made it possible to be abstract, whereas in Sorsele the tensions of value became almost personal. Even so, the communication in Sorsele, aimed at creating a solid story about the place, dimmed the history of the place and of other depopulated places – the real politics behind why this was happening in the first place, as well as how this issue could be resolved for the people living there.

In both municipalities, the idea of creating a "consensus" and an understanding among citizens about why a development is favoured was strong, something that also puts pressure on internal collaboration. The strong focus on both consensus and collaboration could therefore be one explanation as to why some issues are not discussed as much as others. It becomes more important to agree than to address the many different issues at hand. However, it seemed difficult in both municipalities to make the inhabitants "forget" issues, in other words to actually destroy values (Bertilsson and Rennstam, 2018), as was also described above. The discussions on the West Link in Gothenburg or the wind farm in Sorsele that came up no matter the targeted discussion are examples of this and illustrate that communication and branding is a co-creational process (Echeverri and Skålén, 2011). This also confirms Giovanardi's (2015) claim that place branding takes place at different scales.

However, in theory the idea of collaboration/consensus did not seem to go together with the idea of politics, in the sense that they do not include a debate and a "clash of ideas" (Vanolo, 2014). Instead there was a striving to create a unified value that as many people as possible could agree on, resulting in abstract and neutral communication. In that sense, the two Nordic ideals – collaboration and democratic values – seem to be paradoxical, since place branding, although described as democratic, was also a way of depoliticising the development of a place and the image of the municipality; communication was described as something neutral and the communicators described their work in terms of communicating "facts". In other words: place branding in our cases paradoxically became a means to spread political decision making by depoliticising the developments at hand.

To sum up, the Nordic ideals are present in both our case municipalities, although the effects depend on the size and the direction of growth. The future might be more abstract in Gothenburg, but in Sorsele it has more to do with tangible problems; yet the developments in both municipalities appear to support different developments and investments. This chapter contributes to the place branding literature by illustrating how the hegemonic Nordic ideals are affecting branding activities in municipalities of different sizes, and what consequences will follow. We have illustrated that local governments by adopting to the Nordic ideals communicate and brand the municipalities in various ways. Yet at the same time the development at hand is depoliticised through being articulated as fact and as neutral. However, the place branding process is always co-creational, implying contesting, co-creation and co-destruction of values.

REFERENCES

Bergström, T., H. Magnusson and U. Ramberg (2008), 'Through a glass darkly: Leadership complexity in Swedish Local Government'. *Local Government Studies*, 34(2): 203–220.

Bertilsson, J. and J. Rennstam (2018), 'The destructive side of branding: A heuristic model for analysing the value of branding practice'. *Organization*, 25(2) 260–281.

Brorström, S. (2010), *Kommunala satsningar av betydelse – en fråga om identitet, förnuft och tillfälligheter.* Gothenburg: Akademisk avhandling, Förvaltningshögskolan vid Göteborgs Universitet.

Brorström, S. and A. Parment. (2016), 'Various-sized municipalities dealing with growth issues: Different issues but the same solutions?' *Scandinavian Journal of Public Administration*, 20(4): 73–89.

Brorström, S. and A. Parment. (2017), *Attraktiva platser bortom urbanisering och tillväxt. En studie av hållbar utveckling.* Lund: Studentlitteratur.

Cassinger, C., and J. Eksell, (2017), 'The magic of place branding: Regional brand identity in transition', *Journal of Place Management and Development*, 10(3): 202–212.

Echeverri, P. and P. Skålén, (2011), 'Co-creation and co-destruction: A practice-theory based study of interactive value formation', *Marketing Theory*, 11(3): 351–373.

Giovanardi, M. (2015), 'A multi-scalar approach to place branding: The 150th anniversary of Italian Unification in Turin', *European Planning Studies*, 23(3): 597–615.

Hatch, M. J., and M. Schultz (2008), *Taking Brand Initiative: How Companies Can Align Strategy, Culture, and Identity Through Corporate Branding.* San Francisco, CA: Jossey-Bass.

Haveri, A. (2015), 'Nordic local government: A success story, but will it last?', *International Journal of Public Sector Management*, 28(2): 136–149.

Hood, C. (1991), 'A public management for all seasons?' *Public Administration*, 69(1): 3–19.

Kavaratzis, M. and M. J. Hatch, (2013), 'The dynamics of place brands: An identity-based approach to place branding theory', *Marketing Theory*, 13(1): 69–86.

Kornberger, M. (2010), *Brand Society: How Brands Transform Management and Lifestyle.* Cambridge: Cambridge University Press.

Lapsley, I. (2008), 'The NPM agenda: Back to the future', *Financial Accountability & Management*, 24(1): 77–96.

Leo, C. and K. Anderson (2006), 'Being realistic about urban growth', *Journal of Urban Affairs*, 28(2): 169–189.

Loftman, P. and B. Nevin (1996), 'Going for growth: Prestige projects in three British cities', *Urban Studies*, 33(6): 991–1019.

Logan, J. R. and H. L. Molotch (1987), *Urban Fortunes: The Political Economy of Place.* Berkeley, CA: University of California Press.

Lombardi, D. R., L. Porter, A. Barber and C. Rogers (2011), 'Conceptualising sustainability in UK urban regeneration: A discursive formation', *Urban Studies*, 48(2): 273–296.

Lucarelli, A. (2012), 'Unraveling the complexity of "city brand equity": A three-dimensional framework', *Journal of Place Management and Development*, 5(3): 231–252.

Lucarelli, A. (2018), 'Co-branding public place brands: Towards an alternative approach to place branding', *Place Branding and Public Diplomacy*, 14(4): 260–271.

Lucarelli, A. and A. Hallin (2015), 'Brand transformation: A performative approach to brand regeneration', *Journal of Marketing Management*, 31(1–2): 84–106.

Ruzzier, M. and L. de Chernatony (2013), 'Developing and applying a place brand identity model: The case of Slovenia', *Journal of Business Research*, 66(1): 45–52.

Syssner, J. (2015), 'Planning for shrinkage: Policy implications of demographic decline', *Journal of Depopulation and Rural Development Studies*, 20(1): 7–31.

Therkelsen, A., H. Halkier and O. B. Jensen (2010), 'Branding Aalborg: Building community or selling place?' In G. Ashworth and M. Kavaratzis (eds), *Towards Effective Place Brand Management* (pp. 136–155). Cheltenham, UK and Northampton, MA, USA: Edward Elgar Publishing.

Vanolo, A. (2014), 'Smartmentality: The smart city as disciplinary strategy' *Urban Studies*, 51(5): 883–898.

6.   Nordic, Scandinavia or Schondia? A commentary on Nordic brand constructions

Andrea Lucarelli

The relationship and duality between Scandinavia and Nordic is the main focus of the present commentary. More specifically, in the present commentary the modified representation of "Scandinavia" as a concept, idea or, as in the present book, brand, is juxtaposed to the other brand, of the Nordic, as is predominately used in this book. As can be seen in many contributions in the book, at different levels of analysis many of the chapters in Part I deal with the two in a direct or indirect manner, in a way that "Scandinavia" and "Nordic" cross-cut the main geographical, cultural, linguistic, culinary, popular, political and social aspects of the specific, imaginary or real brand, which might refer to Scandinavia and/or Nordic.

While there is no space here to do justice to any specific details on the narrative or mythological construction of these two, by merely referring to the arguments presented in the different chapters included in the first part of this book, one can recognize how the two are used for analytical, conceptual and empirical reasons interchangeably in many different contexts, by researchers and informants, in public debates and in popular culture, both locally and internationally. For example, why does music in the USA capitalize on Scandinavia as a brand (Edlom), whereas Northern culinary experiences and their brand construction are referred to as Nordic (Andersen, Lindberg and Östberg)? Or, why is Nordic mainly used in foreign politics and soft diplomacy, not Scandinavian (Eksell and Fjällhed)? How and where are the different branding projects built according to the typical Nordic consensus model and analysed following Scandinavian Institutionalism (Brorström, Degerhammar and Tall Hallström)? And again, broadening the view to other chapters and contributions inside as well as outside this book, how can Scandinavia and the Nordic region equally be associated to food (Simonsen) and even design, while Scandinavia might be more specific to fashion (e.g. Melchior, 2011)? And, equally, the way the European Union (EU) region building process affects geographical regions and their inhabitants could be Nordic (Heldt Cassel and Ren, Gad and Björst) but also Scandinavia(n) (e.g. Löfgren, 2008)?

To start with I want to stress that, despite the multiple explanations one can argue that there are, at least at a popularized level, there are two common types of argumentation. The first is related to fashion and time, which is also possibly in line with the argument of the present book. Nordic is the "new one": it is the brand that is increasingly used in any field, from food to travel, from politics to the creative industries. Thus, Nordic is in vogue, a rising brand, it is used both "because of" and "due to" its wide usage, hence it is constructed in different fields. Scandinavia(n), on the contrary, is the "older one": it is still employed because of its links to a specific industry or timeframe and its main narrative works for specific fields like, for example, in the popularization of design and furniture as exemplified by IKEA and Scandinavian Airlines in the 1960s–1970s, or specific generational music like that produced in the 1970s by ABBA. The second common argument presents the Nordic, or Nordicity, as an internal brand whereas Scandinavia, or Scandinavian, is an external brand. In branding terms this argument could be translated as a process that sees Nordic as "brand identity" for the area, as analysed in this book, for example, in many chapters, and Scandinavian as "brand image". Or even, taking a brand organizational point of view, Nordic refers to internal branding practices that can be used by different regional stakeholders (i.e. inhabitants, politicians, organizations) to build a sense of common belongingness, while Scandinavia refers to external branding practices to be used for communication purposes internationally with different stakeholders such as tourists, foreign investors and diplomats.

Although both these arguments have their points of strength and their flows, my task here is not to assess their validity, but rather, by using the case of Stockholm, to unpack the conjunctures and disjunctures between Scandinavia and Nordic. The case of Stockholm is useful here, especially in branding terms. Following the launch of the new brand "Stockholm, the Capital of Scandinavia" (SCA), in 2005 and in a similar way to many corporations, the City of Stockholm Communication Office published a brand manual to be used by any paying stakeholder (i.e. the 51 municipality members belonging to Stockholm Business Alliance (SBA)) for future internal and external marketing communications. Internally, the slogan, the logos and the different design and layout elements included in the brand manual should in fact be used by the municipalities and their subsidiary organizations, such as municipal water and waste companies, in their daily communication practices when, for example, designing websites, drafting documents and creating communication outlines relating to their daily activities. Externally, the slogan, the logos and the different design elements should rather be used by any municipalities and their subsidiary organizations, such as tourism bureaus and convention centres, in their international promotional materials, in pamphlets and marketing campaigns aimed at attracting tourists and business investment. In addition to these dimensions, the external international dimension was stressed by the Communication Director of SBA at that time, Monica Ewert, as reported in the manual, which highlights her point of view: "Stockholm the Capital of Scandinavia is not merely a slogan, it is a message . . . a message that is conveyed through the brand"; the adoption by any stakeholder should reinforce the main message, namely: "Our message is simple: Stockholm is the Capital of Scandinavia" (see Stockholm Business Region, 2005, p. 5).

And yet, as also pointed out by several researchers (see Metzger, 2013), the internal, local and intra-regional dimensions are visible, by not only taking the manual into consideration but also other policy and official documents. In fact, embracing a cursory semiotic analysis of the SCA brand, one quickly realizes that the use of capital letters when referring to the three "legs" (i.e. Central Capital, Business Capital and Cultural Capital) does not just contain aesthetic and stylistic motives, but may also contain and point to other underlying motives. The use of the word "Capital" in the slogan and throughout the brand manual could be understood as a way to prepare the ground for the creation of a brand narrative (see Koller, 2008) not only targeting those stakeholders interested in using the brand, but also as an attempt to build an iconic political brand (see Holt, 2002). In fact, by looking at how through the use of text and pictures in the brand manual and in other virtual and printed material the issue of "Centrality" and "Capital" are juxtaposed it is clear how, on the one hand, Stockholm, as city, is presented depicting an area which cuts across the administrative–political borders of the Stockholm Municipality and current Stockholm and, as the Capital of Scandinavia, as a larger area located around Lake Mälaren (see Lucarelli and Hallin, 2015). On the other hand, it demonstrates that presenting Stockholm as the Capital of Scandinavia is a representation in itself – of a modified and renewed version of the idea of Scandinavia.

PAN-SCANDINAVISM AND CAPITAL OF SCANDINAVIA

What can the case of Stockholm help us to grasp in terms of the intersection between Nordic and Scandinavia? The following section is aimed at contextualizing the multiple intersections between them in a way that historically points at their convergence and disjuncture. If we look back to when I glimpsed at the internal and external dimensions of "Stockholm, the Capital of Scandinavia" and the presentation of a newer definition of Scandinavia, a historical conjuncture and disjuncture can be observed. In fact, apart from the marketing fad that covers the idea of the new definition of Scandinavia, which might be based on, among other things, the reference to its presence in international tourist guides such as the *Lonely Planet*, as pointed out by Simonsen in the present book, there is an interesting additional point to be stressed about Scandinavia. "Scandinavia" in relation to Sweden, Norway and Denmark not only has a contemporary appeal and usage, but may also be anchored historically in sixteenth-, seventeenth- and eighteenth-century Pan-Scandinavism, with its political, cultural and linguistic long-tails on the contemporary construction of Nordic and its usage in fields such as films, novels, and also social affairs and politics. This ironically, I should say, is in a way that the "ancient" Pan-Scandinavism not only has much richer and more widely used resources for the contemporary construction of the Nordic compared to Scandinavia, but also vice versa, as in the case of Norse mythology and the Viking era, which is instead used more directly with regard to Scandinavian tourism – at least if we look at the chapters in the present book. This interlinkage of present and past images, narratives and resources, which not only enable a retro-brand to be built (see Brown et al., 2003), but also allow "Scandinavia" and "Nordic" to be reproduced in a different context, time and space so that they are dialogically, yet dualistically, historically juxtaposed, allows us to see, via the Stockholm case, an interesting example of a possible "proto-brand". A proto-brand is thus not only a brand that employs history as resources but is actually "frozen" into its continuous spatial-temporal re-construction in a way that is both old and new, ancient and young, solid and malleable, fixed and fixing as well flexible and modulating.

But how can this be observed in the Stockholm case? First, let's consider the pairing of Stockholm with "Capital" and "Scandinavia". In this coupling we can find at least two different discourses: one about a historical movement (i.e. Pan-Scandinavism) claiming Scandinavian commonality and exceptionalism, which could take the form, as Andéhn suggests, of banal nationalism, and the other about Stockholm as the geographical, cultural and economic political "Centre" of the entire Scandinavia, represented as geo-politically equivalent to the Nordic Countries (Andéhn et al., 2014). By both being present in the contemporary branding efforts of Stockholm as "the Capital of Scandinavia", these two discourses can be seen as the representation of an action of unleashing, and at the same time concentrating, the historical and contemporary, as well as local and international, political, cultural and social tensions. This is because these discourses and images are relational not only in their essential features and attached meanings but also, crucially, in the meanings carried by other images and discourses that precede or surround them (Rose, 2014). In other words, the historical conceptualization and way to represent Scandinavia, as well as its link to Nordic, is at the same time linked with the contemporary manner in which Scandinavia is presented by popular culture and by commercial market(ing); but also, and this is another interesting observation, it is linked by the irony of the usage of a sports metaphor – which is, per se, an interesting choice given the usual emphasis on Nordic-based collaboration/support, as in the case of football fan-ships, and at the same time conflict/incongruence, as in the case of winter sports claims of worldwide excellence – all this resorting to one of many discourses included into the construction of Nordic as brand.

These two discourses cross-cut the presentation, in the brand manual, of Stockholm as political "Centre" performatively, in a sense that the production of the "new" spatiotemporal conceptualization of Scandinavia has to do with peculiar inherent political, spatial, as well as socio-cultural environments (see Lucarelli and Hallin, 2015). Beyond the "cocky tagline", as suggested by the consultant helping to create the SCA brand, Julian Stubbs, the notion of "Capital", paired with attempts to present something that geographically does not in reality exist (i.e. a Capital of Scandinavia), creates the context in which the SCA performs a re-definition of the terri-toriality and the historical belonging of Stockholm, now as "the Capital of Scandinavia", in the shape of an alliance of 51 municipalities (SBA), which is in dissonance with both the original territorial definition, as framed by Stockholm–Mälarregion on one side, and with the national and adminis-trative definition of Stockholm as municipality or as county, as defined by the Swedish State, on the other. "Stockholm, the Capital of Scandinavia", in its function and symbol as brand, by attracting municipalities up to 250 km from Stockholm to be members of the alliance, has overcome such physical and ideological borders, indeed creating a totally "new space", not only geographical but also ethereal. Here, again, such performative action thus can not only be seen as a transformation of a regional vision into a brand, but also as a power–political laden trajectory (e.g. Massey, 1992) of a brand that, for what it stands for and how it is able to mobilize and create communities of followers, can be seen not only as icon (see Holt, 2002), but also as "thing per se" (e.g. Lash and Lury, 2007) emerg-ing as different and divergent compared to both historical and popular conceptualizations of Stockholm, Scandinavia and Nordic.

This brings us to the second observation of the historical conjuncture and disjuncture. This refers to the historical background in which the

SCA emerged as the new brand for the Greater Stockholm. In fact, with its newest brand, Stockholm Municipality planned a shift from leveraging natural, historical and technological assets, as in previous branding efforts, towards more geo-political, international popular cultural-based assets, thus highlighting the local area around which Stockholm is located (Ågren, 2013). Although this is important to stress for the contemporary debate which emerged around the brand (see Gromark, 2017), what is more important here is to point out that what characterized the new assets, or brand elements (Lucarelli, 2012), in both contemporary and historical terms, is the selective portrait of Stockholm city around its main brand elements. In fact, not much changes if the discourse on Stockholm is that of places of sexual liberty, frivolity and joviality, as in the 1960s, or of progressive social and urban engineering, as in the 1970s, because much of the branding and marketing of the city refers to these elements. What is important is the discontinuity of different themes in the continuity of selective commercialization of Stockholm across history. This suggests that the brand construction of Scandinavia, or Nordic, is dialogical and always in-play.

This loop out does not stop here but goes back in time and space. In fact, across the years, different slogans, marketing campaigns and brands have appeared and disappeared in Stockholm. During those years different organizations and collaborative networks with different aims and functions have appeared in Stockholm's political, touristic and business life. Different authorities and different discourses and images emerged and intertwined. Different temporal periods reflect different orientations, from the managerial city to the entrepreneurial city; different marketing and branding campaigns reflect different paths and logics, with different impacts both locally and internationally. In this context, then, how could one interpret the Scandinavia–Nordic duality in the light of the capital of the Scandinavia brand? In line with the view of a proto-brand, as noted earlier, we might engage in a dialogical de-re-con-transformation of these brands by, as in the Stockholm example, maybe resorting to Stockholm's (possibly) oldest and historical brand, "Venice of the North", which emerged as a popular reinterpretation popularized by Erik Dahlberg's work Suecia Antiqua in the 1920s, and which, in turn, referred to the very first representation of Stockholm that emerged in 1523 for the German theologian Jakob Ziegler's treatise "Schondia". The proper idea that Stockholm can be the "Nordens Venedig" or "Venice of the North" has not left the popular common debate, as can be seen in the petition presented in 2012 by a local politician to represent Stockholm as "Nordens Venedig", but for our argument it might better to try to tread the path of Ziegler's book, especially in its description of the entire Nordic territories as "Schondia". Whether this is an ancient "neutral" way to conceptualize and denote the Nordic region or rather another way to brand it has yet to be further discussed. What is, however, important is that, by treading the path of "Schondia", we might be able to both demystify the contemporary brand myth and contextualize its mythological trajectory.

REFERENCES

Ågren, K. (2013). *Att sälja en stad: Stockholms besöksnäring 1936–2011*. Stockholm: Stockholmia förlag.

Andéhn, M., Kazeminia, A., Lucarelli, A., & Sevin, E. (2014). User-generated place brand equity on Twitter: The dynamics of brand associations in social media. *Place Branding and Public Diplomacy*, *10*(2), 132–144.

Brown, S., Kozinets, R. V., & Sherry Jr, J. F. (2003). Teaching old brands new tricks: Retro branding and the revival of brand meaning. *Journal of Marketing*, *67*(3), 19–33.

Gromark, J. (2017). Stockholm: The narcissistic capital of Sweden. In M. Kavaratzis, M. Giovanardi, & Maria Lichrou (Eds.), *Inclusive Place Branding* (pp. 148–162). Abingdon: Routledge.

Holt, D. B. (2002). Why do brands cause trouble? A dialectical theory of consumer culture and branding. *Journal of Consumer Research*, *29*(1), 70–90.

Koller, V. (2008). "The world in one city": Semiotic and cognitive aspects of city branding. *Journal of Language and Politics*, *7*(3), 431–450.

Lash, S., & Lury, C. (2007). Global culture industry: The mediation of things. *Historian*, *403*, 15.

Löfgren, O. (2008). Regionauts: The transformation of cross-border regions in Scandinavia. *European Urban and Regional Studies*, *15*(3), 195–209.

Lucarelli, A. (2012). Unraveling the complexity of "city brand equity": A three-dimensional framework. *Journal of Place Management and Development*, *5*(3), 231–252.

Lucarelli, A., & Hallin, A. (2015). Brand transformation: A performative approach to brand regeneration. *Journal of Marketing Management*, *31*(1–2), 84–106.

Massey, D. (1992). Politics and space/time. *New Left Review*, *1*(196), 65–84.

Melchior, M. R. (2011). From design nations to fashion nations? Unpacking contemporary Scandinavian fashion dreams. *Fashion Theory*, *15*(2), 177–200.

Metzger, J. (2013). Raising the regional Leviathan: A relational–materialist conceptualization of regions-in-becoming as publics-in-stabilization. *International Journal of Urban and Regional Research*, *37*(4), 1368–1395.

Rose, G. (2014). On the relation between "visual research methods" and contemporary visual culture. *The Sociological Review*, *62*(1), 24–46.

Stockholm Business Region. (2005). *The Stockholm brand book*. Stockholm: Stockholm Municipality.

PART II

Nordic place-making practices

7. Building the slow adventure brand in the northern periphery

**Daniel Laven, Tatiana Chekalina,
Matthias Fuchs, Lusine Margaryan,
Peter Varley and Steve Taylor**

INTRODUCTION

The use of tourism as a sustainable regional development strategy, particularly for rural and/or peripheral areas, has been a focus of academic debates and policy discourse for nearly 30 years (e.g., Briedenhann & Wickens, 2004; Hall & Boyd, 2005; Lane, 1994; Müller & Jansson, 2006). At the same time, scholars have noted that rural and peripheral areas face specific challenges in tourism brand development, which are important to overcome because rural regions are often dependent on joint branding in order to develop effective place brands (Cai, 2002; Vuorinen & Vos, 2013). In addition, Europe has seen a rise in interregional cross-border place branding, incentivized by the European Union (EU) cohesion policy and its specialized funds (Braun, 2015; Witte & Braun, 2015). In this context, Nordic peripheries emerge as an interesting example, characterized by both typical challenges (e.g., outmigration, aging population, deindustrialization) and unique opportunities (e.g., high aesthetic, environmental, cultural value, comparatively high quality of life). Nordic peripheries, therefore, comprise 'the other' facet of the Nordic place brand, not being part of the 'slick' image of the hypermodern, progressive and dynamic urban Nordic spaces. All of the aforementioned makes Nordic peripheries particularly attractive for tourism, which is increasing in popularity in terms of tourist arrivals and media coverage as well as academic research (Brouder, 2013; Berglund, 2017; Hall & Boyd, 2005; Hall et al., 2009; Lee et al., 2017).

This chapter explores branding in the context of Nordic and northern peripheries through a case study of Slow Adventure in Northern Territories (SAINT).[1] SAINT was a cross-border project funded by the EU Northern

---

[1] http://saintproject.eu/ [Accessed 15 May 2018].

Periphery and Arctic Cooperation Program (NPA),[2] aimed at the geographical area sometimes called the Nordic and Celtic northern Europe (Danson & de Souza, 2012). The main goal of the SAINT project was to help local tourism small and medium-sized enterprises (SMEs) overcome the challenges of peripherality in their branding and marketing efforts, and advance the development of an interregional cross-border place brand. Project participants were from four Nordic countries (Iceland, Norway, Sweden and Finland) and three non-Nordic countries (Scotland, Northern Ireland and Ireland), all areas with, according to the NPA, typical features associated with northern peripheries. SAINT draws directly from Varley and Semple's (2015) concept of *Nordic slow adventure*, in turn rooted in the Nordic philosophy of outdoor recreation and the international slow movements.

Our chapter aligns with the second theme of this book, i.e. place-making *practices* of place branding. We unpack the course of developing and testing a slow adventure brand in the geographical context of the Nordic and northern periphery of Europe as an emergent and unfinished process. The chapter specifically focuses on the appropriation of the Nordic outdoor recreation tradition, while merging it with the ethics of the slow movements, which are further applied to the cross-border region of the northern periphery of Europe. This chapter starts with a theoretical discussion where we provide the background to the outdoor recreation tradition in the Nordic countries, the special place of the northern peripheries in the tourist imagery of the Nordics, and the process of negotiating various concepts while creating the slow adventure brand. We proceed with a brief overview of the SAINT project results, followed by a discussion and conclusion which positions the slow adventure and the interregional place branding initiatives in a broader picture of regional, international and global trends.

OUTDOOR RECREATION IN THE NORDIC COUNTRIES

Outdoor recreation in the Nordic countries is more than just a leisure pastime. Known in Sweden and Norway as *friluftsliv*, literally translated as 'life in the open air', outdoor recreation is a tradition, a belief system and a way of life. The term is believed to have been coined by the great Henrik Ibsen, himself a passionate wanderer, who captured the spirit of the age in his epic poem 'On the Heights' in 1859 (Leirhaug, 2009). Nordic

---

[2] http://www.interreg-npa.eu [Accessed 15 May 2018].

outdoor recreation has been referred to as 'a philosophical lifestyle based on experiences of the freedom in nature and the spiritual connectedness with the landscape. The reward of this connectedness with the landscape is this strong sensation of a new level of consciousness and a spiritual wholeness' (Gelter, 2000, p. 78). The emphasis on outdoor recreation in the Nordic countries has conventionally been based on fairly simple and straightforward outdoor activities as practiced by the general population in a non-competitive context. These include activities such as walking, hiking, swimming, skiing, camping, mushroom- and berry-picking (Aasetre & Gundersen, 2012; Sandell & Sörlin, 2000).

Since the nineteenth century, nature has been a key component in the construction and mobilization of national identities in the Nordic countries. Outdoor recreation has shown the capacity to bridge different social classes and distant communities through circulation of publications, stories, photos, paintings and other media, resulting in what Sandell and Sörlin (2000) called 'discovery of recreation landscape'. In addition, several contextual elements contributed to the popularization of outdoor recreation in the Nordic countries. First, there is the Right of Public Access (or 'freedom to roam'), which offers all citizens nearly unlimited access to nature for recreation purposes. Second, Nordic societies underwent urbanization relatively recently compared to the rest of Europe. The skills of living off the land (e.g., hunting, fishing, bush craft), and links to the countryside have stayed strong among the general population (Hörnsten, 2000). Finally, the Nordic countries are sparsely populated, which leaves vast uninhabited areas, particularly in the peripheries. These and other factors have ensured a specific place for outdoor recreation in the Nordic cultures.

Outdoor recreation, like any other social phenomenon, has undergone substantial transformations during the last century. Departing from the traditional modes of engaging with nature, the current trends include increasing commercialization, diversification, sportification, motorization, and a growing emphasis on adventure, performance and equipment (e.g., Elmahdy et al., 2017; Fredman et al., 2014; Varley & Semple, 2015). Furthermore, changes in demographics and lifestyle along with economic and technological developments have resulted in a growing preference for short and high-quality forms of recreation that rely on infrastructure, comfort and accessibility (Fredman et al., 2012; Wall-Reinius & Bäck, 2011). In conclusion, a review of the outdoor recreation trends indicates that the interest in outdoor recreation in the Nordic countries remains high while the modes of engagement with nature have exploded in diversity, among which the factors of speed and adventure are important. SAINT aims to tap into this opportunity while offering an alternative *slow* adventure, capitalizing on the Nordic recreation traditions.

OUTDOOR RECREATION IN THE NORTHERN PERIPHERIES AS A NORDIC TOURIST BRAND

The north and northern peripheries have been historically exoticized and romanticized as places of untouched, awe-inspiring wilderness, magic and mystery that invite exploration, discovery and adventure (Gunnarsdóttir, 2011; Margaryan & Zherdev, 2011; Ísleifsson, 2011). These are also the landscapes that offer opportunities to face sublime nature's forces, test one's limits, and celebrate endurance, perseverance and achievement, all of which are rooted in the glory of Arctic explorations of the nineteenth century. Romantic ideals were especially important in establishing northern peripheries as spaces where one can experience freedom and authenticity, and discover what is pure, true and real as opposed to the supposedly decadent and corrupt centers of civilization in the urban south. For instance, Ísleifsson (2011) has identified the following stereotypes associated with the north, persistent in the twenty-first century: utopian, creative, authentic, progressive, wealthy but also unemotional, and even immoral. Danson and de Souza (2012, p. 98) state:

> North as far away (this also comes with some meanings of remoteness, cold climate and, possibly, sparsely populated which are all 'taken-for-granted'; or even more drastically: 'a vast emptiness'). The characteristics of remoteness and emptiness also appear in the most common definitions of the concept of periphery itself.

Perpetuation of this and a similar repertoire of contradictory stereotypical representations and performances in relation to north and northern peripheries has been conceptualized as *borealism*, an analogy of Said's (1979) famous *orientalism* (Schram, 2011). Consequently, these themes are omnipresent in the tourism marketing media, which is known for its propensity to reproduce stereotypical narratives (Alessio & Jóhannsdóttir, 2011; Gunnarsdóttir, 2011; Rakić & Chambers, 2011; Pritchard & Morgan, 2000).

Idealized northern nature has been one of the most dominating themes when it comes to tourism in the northern peripheries. The north of the Scandinavian Peninsula is frequently described as 'Europe's last wilderness' and 'Europe's Alaska' (Sylvén, 2015); tourists are invited to experience 'the magic of Lapland',[3] 'the dream of winter wonderland' in Finland,[4] or 'troll

---

[3] http://supemenlatu.fi [Accessed 15 May 2018].
[4] http://visitfinland.com [Accessed 15 May 2018].

hunting' in Iceland.[5] An analysis of marketing media in Iceland demonstrated that the majority of promotional images represents nature without any visible human impact (Hermans, 2016; Margaryan & Zherdev, 2011). As a recent marketing stunt, Sweden's tourism board has listed the entire country as a 'place to stay' on the Airbnb accommodation-sharing platform, capitalizing on the Right of Public Access. By doing so, the national tourism board states that tourists are welcome to enjoy Sweden's vast nature as an ideal and limitless 'relaxation area', where cliffs are terraces, lakes are infinity pools and rivers are bathrooms (Visit Sweden, 2017). Overall, the social construction of peripheral nature as hedonic places of tourist enjoyment and relaxation, known in the tourism literature as 'pleasure peripheries' (Turner & Ash, 1975), has been well-documented and is still very much present in the tourism media (Brown & Hall, 2000; Hall & Boyd, 2005; Müller & Jansson, 2006).

MERGING NORDIC AND NORTHERN IN THE 'SLOW ADVENTURE' BRAND

In the discussion on place branding, particular attention needs to be paid to the spatial aspect of this process (Boisen et al., 2011). The importance of geographical perspectives in marketing and place branding have been extensively pointed out (e.g., Ermann & Hermanik, 2017; Giovanardi & Lucarelli, 2018). Moreover, branding has been recognized as 'a profoundly geographical type of commodification process' (Ermann & Hermanik, 2017, p. 12), which tightly braids products, places and nations. In the case of the slow adventure brand and its application in the SAINT project, we see the following examples of geographic negotiations. First, the slow adventure brand is semantically embedded in two major areas – the Nordic friluftsliv tradition, and the more recent slow movement. The Nordic friluftsliv is bound to a specific place (i.e., the Nordic region). Varley and Semple (2015, p. 74) explicitly point out that slow adventure is 'a concept particularly suited to the wide, wild expanses of many parts of the world, and specifically to the outdoor living and journeying experience potential in Nordic countries'. They further emphasize (p. 87):

> [S]low adventure fits well with the people, landscapes, cultures and skills of the Nordic countries, and emerges as an opportunity to facilitate high value, unique and memorable experiences. It may also be a concept that makes Nordic tourism distinctive and highly valued for those on the outside – a

---

[5]   http://guidetoiceland.is [Accessed 15 May 2018].

sustainable, eco-sensible tourism rich in the skills and cultures of the region and its peoples.

The slow movement ideologies, on the other hand, have spread beyond its geographic roots. Originating in Italy in the 1980s, the Slow Food movement was a reaction to the expansion of global fast food chains. This philosophy can now be found in a multitude of production and consumption processes in more than 150 countries including tourism, agriculture, architecture, fashion, learning and creating, as well as simply being (see, e.g., Clancy, 2018; Dickinson & Lumsdon, 2010; Fullagar et al., 2012; Honore, 2004). The spatial extension of this thinking is exemplified by the Slow Cities network (known as Cittàslow, also of Italian origin), which strives to revitalize and protect traditional urban life and public spaces. As of 2017, the Cittàslow network consists of 238 cities in 30 countries (Clancy, 2018). Overall, slow movements symbolize resistance to the ever-accelerating hypermodern society that propagates a cult of speed in every aspect of human life. Similarly, Varley and Semple (2015) define slow adventure through four key components: *time, nature, passage* and *comfort*. Attention to nature's rhythms, bodily experiences of nature's elements, and mental and physical immersion into a journey through historical, cultural and natural landscapes are all parts of a tourist adventure when done slowly. In other words, taking time to create insightful, deeply meaningful and transformative experiences in the outdoors, rooted in the local ethics, culture and history is at the heart of slow adventure.

The SAINT project considers the concepts of slowness and peripherality as complementary. Peripheries, or, very loosely, the outermost boundaries of an area, are by definition the spaces of resistance to the fast-paced hypermodern, hypermobile and hyper-globalized 'core'. Peripheries of the European North are places of vast, relatively unmodified natural areas of high ecological and aesthetic value, of rich cultural heritage, especially when it comes to the traditional knowledge of nature use and interpretation. Along with the presence of the typical disadvantages of the peripheries, the countries of the European North, and especially the Nordics, are known for their high levels of social welfare and equality (e.g., high levels of gross domestic product (GDP) per capita (World Bank, 2018) in combination with low Gini coefficients (OECD, 2018) and high levels of sustainability (SDG, 2017)). This indicates that the peripheries in question are comparatively well supplied in terms of the access to modern infrastructure, technology penetration, facilities and general attributes associated with a high quality of life, setting these societies apart from their peripheral counterparts in other parts of the world. As stated by Danson and de Souza (2012, p. 102), '[h]owever measured, whether in terms of income or

GDP per head, happiness, quality of life, rates of innovation, political and social freedom and stability, low levels of inequality, or gender balance, the Nordic countries individually and collectively rank at or near the top of any global ranking'. Even though Ireland and the UK perform less well, following an Anglo-Saxon development model, and are not part of the Nordic 'Ark of Prosperity', they are part of the NPA region due to other aforementioned similarities (Danson & de Souza, 2012). Based on this, the NPA even aspires to turn the northern peripheral area into a '1st class region to live, study, work, visit and invest' (NPA, 2016, n.p.). The NPA, in other words, aims to create a transnational region and a place brand, delineating and promoting an image of one dynamic region with certain common properties.

In general, the rise of transnational regions and the development of interregional brands is primarily a European phenomenon, which has specific political goals within the cohesion policy of the EU, namely to 'promote a harmonious economic, social and territorial development of the Union as a whole' (NPA, 2016, n.p.). The typical form of transnational regional cooperation in the EU aims at reducing administrative, cultural-linguistic or infrastructural barriers separating the governments, businesses and residents of border regions, for which specially allocated funding is available (e.g., INTERREG initiative (Braun, 2015; Witte & Braun, 2015)). Slow adventure deals with two interregional brands, Nordic and Northern European peripheral, which, despite significant overlaps, represent different historical and cultural trajectories as well as political goals (for an in-depth discussion on interregional place brands see Zenker & Jacobsen, 2015).

The SAINT project, with its slow adventure brand, works with an amalgamation of all three brand levels discussed by Ermann and Hermanik (2017), namely product (activities related to the ethics of slowness and Nordic friluftsliv), (supra)nation (Nordicity and Northern Europe) and place (peripherality). The project works with the ideology of the slow movements, elevated from its initial geographical context and married with the place-bound concept of the Nordic friluftsliv, and further extends it to the larger geographical area of the peripheries of the European North, propagated by the NPA. This place branding process, however, is not free from inherent tensions and complexities. In this regard, Brown and Hall (2000) discuss the paradoxes of tourism in the peripheries, namely the use of tourism as a way to overcome the characteristics of peripherality that attract tourism in the first place, or the lure of remoteness resulting in overcrowding and 'touristification' and thus erosion of the 'classic' properties of peripherality. These contradictory developments can already be observed in many North European destinations, especially Iceland and Norway (e.g., Aanesen et al., 2018; Cságoly et al., 2017).

BRIEF OVERVIEW OF THE SAINT PROJECT RESULTS

The interregional slow adventure brand was developed during the three-year SAINT project, which involved tourism SMEs, destination management organizations and research institutions. The development process had the following stages: (a) the elements of the slow adventure experience (based on the criteria by Varley & Semple, 2015) were identified through SME workshops; (b) the criteria were tested and evaluated through an SME survey; (c) core criteria of slow adventure for the SAINT project area were identified; (d) guidelines for the slow adventure brand were developed; (e) marketing efforts were implemented.

In order to understand how the slow adventure tourism product can be defined and operationalized, a transnational survey was conducted that built upon the existing baseline of the nature-based tourism studies in the Nordic context (Fredman & Margaryan, 2014; Stensland et al., 2014). In total, 126 SMEs across the SAINT project area participated in the survey. Table 7.1 shows the common outdoor activities, typical for the northern periphery region,[6] that fit the ethos of slow adventure: (i) expeditions into nature; (ii) wildlife viewing and bird watching; (iii) cultural or heritage activities linked to nature; (iv) slow food cooking and outdoor cooking/dining experience; (v) hiking; (vi) recreational kayaking, canoeing and rowing; (vii) overnight stays combined with nature experience; (viii) fishing; (ix) outdoor photography; (x) wild foraging; and (xi) nature studies. These activities proved to be almost equally relevant for all partner countries with the exception of Iceland, which had a slightly different pattern (high importance of nature photography, as well as ice cave tours, glacier hiking, caving and ice hiking).

The project evaluated the relevance of the slow adventure experience criteria, collaboratively developed during partner meetings. The survey revealed the core pillars of slow adventure elements for the SAINT project area, i.e. human- and nature-powered slow journeys, inspiring connectedness with nature, wildlife watching, nature and culture interpretation, slow food, outdoor skills, health and wellness, and storytelling. These pillars were converted into the core criteria for SME eligibility. Based on

---

[6]   The activities were selected from a pool of Nordic friluftsliv activities previously identified by Fredman and Margaryan (2014) and Stensland et al. (2014).

Table 7.1   *The relevance of core slow adventure activities for generating annual sales in SMEs*

	Finland	Iceland	Ireland	Northern Ireland	Norway	Scotland	Sweden
Expeditions into nature	**2.8**	1.9	**2.6**	**2.3**	**2.0**	**2.6**	**2.2**
Wildlife viewing/bird watching	**2.1**	1.9	**2.3**	**2.0**	**2.0**	**2.6**	**2.0**
Cultural or heritage activities linked to nature	**2.4**	1.7	**2.6**	**2.5**	1.8	**2.3**	1.8
Slow food cooking, outdoor cooking/ dining experience	**2.5**	1.6	**2.2**	**2.1**	**2.0**	**2.3**	**2.2**
Hiking	**2.4**	**2.1**	**2.3**	**2.0**	1.8	**2.3**	**2.0**
Recreational kayaking, canoeing and rowing	**2.5**	1.7	**2.5**	1.8	**2.0**	**2.3**	1.8
Overnight stays combined with nature experience	**2.3**	1.6	1.9	**2.0**	**2.0**	**2.4**	**2.0**
Fishing	**2.0**	1.4	**2.3**	1.7	**2.5**	1.9	**2.3**
Outdoor photography	**2.2**	**2.6**	**2.2**	1.8	1.8	**2.3**	1.4
Wild foraging	**2.2**	1.5	**2.3**	2.2	**2.0**	**2.1**	1.8
Nature studies	1.8	1.9	**2.0**	**2.0**	1.6	**2.4**	1.4

Notes:
1: Not relevant at all
2: Somewhat relevant
3: Highly relevant
Values equal to 2 or above are in bold.

these, a set of guidelines was eventually developed for the use of the slow adventure brand and a trademarked logo. The logo incorporates a stylized image of a snail, which visually ties it to the global network of slow movements (see, e.g., the logo of the Cittàslow network). The project concluded with extensive marketing activities in all participant countries.

DISCUSSION AND CONCLUSION

As stated by Boisen (2015, p. 14) 'place branding refers to the conscious process of creating, gaining, enhancing, and reshaping the distinct presence of a place in the minds and hearts of people'. In this chapter, we discussed one example of utilizing Nordicity and, specifically, Nordic outdoor recreation in a tourism marketing-oriented project that aims to create an interregional slow adventure brand in the northern peripheral region of Europe. The process demonstrates what Giovanardi and Lucarelli (2018) call 'travelling', which refers to the transformation of the marketing constructs of slow, Nordic, northern and peripheral. High levels of flexibility and mobility of these concepts across cultures and geographies qualify them to be what Danson and de Souza (2012) call 'fuzzy concepts', meaning that they appear, and are recognized, described and experienced in constant flux. Thus, the Slow Food movement that originated in Italy has transformed into a global phenomenon beyond its initial geographic and cultural context. Similarly, the concept of Nordic outdoor recreation, at a confluence of the ideas of slowness and peripherality, is expanding across the North European region via the interregional slow adventure brand.

Overall, the attention to interregional place brands in the Nordic context and beyond is hardly accidental. Under the EU regionalization policy, transnational projects have been identifying interregional place branding as a key goal (Zenker & Jacobsen, 2015). The fundamental assumption behind this approach is that communicating the assets of a transnational region as a single offer makes the offer more attractive and competitive than the individual parts of the region (Braun, 2015; NPA, 2016). Here two points are especially noteworthy in relation to the SAINT project and the slow adventure brand: first, growing attention to place branding can be tied to an overarching belief that regions are in ongoing competition with each other in ever-expanding global markets, including those of tourism (Boisen, 2015; Lucarelli & Berg, 2011). In this context, slow adventure follows the logic of the Slow Food movement: regional competition and its undesired consequences, (e.g., loss of local authenticity, weakened social and ecological standards, etc.) can be countered through responsible production and branding principles. Through cross-regional cooperation, northern peripheral regions may be able to enhance their regional production cycles by using their natural, cultural and heritage assets. Thus, by protecting their socio-cultural diversity and plurality from global competition, these regions – perceived as collective projects or enterprises – may be better positioned to generate their unique value propositions (UVP) as communicated through branding efforts like slow adventure. Second, increased responsibilities of European regions, limited financial resources and strong incentives for higher functionality and cooperation to receive EU funding result in a proliferation of the so-called nonstandard regionalization phenomenon (i.e., regionalization outside more standardized spatial divisions) (Deas, 2006; Boisen, 2015). Among possible configurations, one is the 'nonstandard regionalization of project-based cross-border cooperation' (Boisen, 2015, p. 20), of which the SAINT project is a direct example. Through its cohesion policy, the EU provides strong incentives to develop cross-border cooperation, accompanied with ongoing efforts to gradually reduce legal, administrative and cultural-linguistic barriers along the internal borders of the EU, as well as continued investments into cross-border infrastructure (Braun, 2015; Witte & Braun, 2015). As a result, multiple new cross-border regions materialize with various life spans and levels of institutionalization. According to Witte and Braun (2015), cross-border place branding then emerges as a way to quickly give substance to cross-border cooperation on economic development. It is therefore not surprising that in the case of the SAINT project, branding has become its central output. Moreover, the initially explicit *Nordic* concept (as used by Varley & Semple, 2015) is giving way to a less defined notion of *northern territories*, following the incentive to adapt to a pre-existing nonstandard NPA region and, consequently, contributing to an essentially depoliticized and fuzzy regionalization.

The SAINT project highlights the growing attraction of the northern peripheries as tourism destinations as well as a growing tendency of these regions to consider tourism an important development avenue – a trend observed by tourism researchers over the last two decades (Brouder, 2013; Brown & Hall, 2000; Hall & Boyd, 2005; Kristjánsdóttir et al., 2018; Müller & Jansson, 2006). Tourism has become a go-to strategy for economic development in the peripheries since it holds promise for generating income under conditions when other sectors fail, while also being characterized by low skill requirements and low barrier to entry (Brouder, 2013; Müller & Jansson, 2006). At the same time, peripheral areas are imagined as places of alternative and exclusive tourism, rooted in the traditions of exoticization and romantization of these regions in Europe (Hall & Boyd, 2005; Gunnarsdóttir, 2011; Ísleifsson, 2011). In this sense, the slow adventure brand can be considered a successor of this tradition since it aligns peripherality with *slowness* (Clancy, 2018; Dickinson & Lumsdon, 2010; Fullagar et al., 2012; Honore, 2004) and *adventure* in recreation (Elmahdy et al., 2017; Fredman et al., 2014), both of which fit well within the classic discourses on tourism in peripheral areas (Brown & Hall, 2000; Danson & de Souza, 2012; Hall & Boyd, 2005; Müller & Jansson, 2006). At the same time, the brand capitalizes on notions of Nordic quality, as well as less traditional outdoor recreation activities involving high levels of comfort. This enables a departure from the typical *borealist* image of the north and has potential for attracting high-income, long-haul tourists.

The strong tourist image of Nordic outdoor recreation, along with 'wild' and Nordic nature, remains the backbone of the slow adventure brand, including the traditional philosophy of friluftsliv and environmental ethics (Booth, 2014; Gössling & Hultman, 2006; Partanen, 2017; Sandell & Sörlin, 2000). In addition, the Nordic image has been enriched with the contributions from a larger cultural pool of the European North and adapted specifically to the context of peripherality (Brown & Hall, 2000; Danson and de Souza, 2012; Hall & Boyd, 2005; Müller & Jansson, 2006). The contributions from the non-Nordic countries in terms of the outdoor recreation approaches can also be found, albeit in more implicit and informal ways (expressed, for example, in a stronger prioritization of storytelling, music, arts and crafts, and culinary traditions, as in the case of Ireland and the UK). The SAINT project, therefore, presents an example of extrapolating an initially Nordic-specific brand first to a larger region of European northern peripheries and, potentially, further internationally. Through conceptualization and formalization of slow adventure, with the help of official guidelines and a trademark, the brand itself becomes available for appropriation beyond its initial geographical and cultural context.

REFERENCES

Aanesen, M., Falk-Andersson, J., Vondolia, G. K., Borch, T., Navrud, S., & Tinch, D. (2018). Valuing coastal recreation and the visual intrusion from commercial activities in Arctic Norway. *Ocean & Coastal Management, 153*, 157–167.

Aasetre, J., & Gundersen, V. (2012). Outdoor recreation research: Different approaches, different values? *Norsk Geografisk Tidsskrift – Norwegian Journal of Geography, 66*(4), 193–203.

Alessio, D., & Jóhannsdóttir, A. L. (2011). Geysers and 'girls': Gender, power and colonialism in Icelandic tourist imagery. *European Journal of Women's Studies, 18*(1), 35–50.

Berglund, N. (2017, 15 May). Tourism booms in Norway's Arctic. *Views and*

News from Norway. http://www.newsinenglish.no/2017/05/15/tourism-booms-in-norways-arctic/ [Accessed 2 May 2018].

Boisen, M. (2015). Place branding and nonstandard regionalization in Europe. In S. Zenker & B. Jacobsen (Eds.). *Inter-regional place branding* (pp. 13–25). New York: Springer.

Boisen, M., Terlouw, K., & van Gorp, B. (2011). The selective nature of place branding and the layering of spatial identities. *Journal of Place Management and Development, 4*(2), 135–147.

Booth, M. (2014). *The almost nearly perfect people: Behind the myth of the Scandinavian utopia*. London: Jonathan Cape.

Braun, E. (2015). Foreword: Interregional place branding: A new frontier? In S. Zenker & B. Jacobsen (Eds.). *Inter-regional place branding* (pp. v–vi). New York: Springer.

Briedenhann, J., & Wickens, E. (2004). Tourism routes as a tool for the economic development of rural areas. Vibrant hope or impossible dream? *Tourism Management, 25*(1), 71–79.

Brouder, P. (2013). *Tourism development in peripheral areas: Processes of local innovation and change in Northern Sweden* (Unpublished doctoral dissertation). Mid Sweden University, Sweden.

Brown, F., & Hall, D. (2000). *Tourism in peripheral areas*. Clevedon: Channel View.

Cai, L. A. (2002). Cooperative branding for rural destinations. *Annals of Tourism Research, 29*(3), 720–742.

Clancy, M. (2018). Introduction. The rise of slow in a fast world. In M. Clancy (Ed.). *Slow tourism, food and cities: Pace and the search for the 'good life'* (pp. 21–38). Abingdon: Routledge.

Cságoly, Z., Sæþórsdóttir, A. D., & Ólafsdóttir, R. (2017). Tourism changing the edge of the wild. *Journal of Outdoor Recreation and Tourism, 17*, 1–8.

Danson, M., & de Souza, P. (Eds.) (2012). *Regional development in Northern Europe: Peripherality, marginality and border issues*. London: Routledge.

Deas, I. (2006). From a new regionalism to an unusual regionalism? The emergence of nonstandard regional spaces and lessons for the territorial reorganisation of the state. *Urban Studies, 43*(10), 1847–1877.

Dickinson, J., & Lumsdon, L. (2010). *Slow travel and tourism*. London: Earthscan.

Elmahdy, Y. M., Haukeland, J. V., & Fredman, P. (2017). *Tourism megatrends, a literature review focused on nature-based tourism*. MINA fagrapport 42. http://www.umb.no/statisk/ina/publikasjoner/fagrapport/if42.pdf [Accessed 2 May 2018].

Ermann, U., & Hermanik, K. J. (2017). Introduction: Branding the nation, the place, the product. In U. Ermann & K. Hermanik (Eds.). *Branding the nation, the place, the product* (pp. 11–24). Abingdon: Routledge.

Fredman, P., & Margaryan, L. (2014). *The supply of nature-based tourism in Sweden: A national inventory of service providers*. Report. Östersund: ETOUR.

Fredman, P., Stenseke, M., & Sandell, K. (2014). *Friluftsliv i förändring. Studier från svenska upplevelselandskap*. Stockholm: Carlsson.

Fredman, P., Wall-Reinius, S., & Grundén, A. (2012). The nature of nature in nature-based tourism. *Scandinavian Journal of Hospitality and Tourism, 12*(4), 289–309.

Fullagar, S., Markwell, K., & Wilson, E. (Eds.). (2012). *Slow tourism: Experiences and mobilities* (Vol. 54). Bristol: Channel View Publications.

Gelter, H. (2000). Friluftsliv: The Scandinavian philosophy of outdoor life. *Canadian Journal of Environmental Education*, *5*, 77–90.

Giovanardi, M., & Lucarelli, A. (2018). Sailing through marketing: A critical assessment of spatiality in marketing literature. *Journal of Business Research*, *82*, 149–159.

Gössling, S., & Hultman, J. (Eds.) (2006). *Ecotourism in Scandinavia: Lessons in theory and practice*. Wallingford: CABI.

Guide to Finland (n.d) Retrieved from http://guidetoiceland.is

Gunnarsdóttir, G. (2011). The front page of Icelandic tourism brochures. In S. R. Ísleifsson (Ed.). *Iceland and images of the North* (pp. 531–553). Quebec: Presses de l'Université du Quebec.

Hall, C. M., & Boyd, S. W. (2005). *Nature-based tourism in peripheral areas: Development or disaster?* Clevedon: Channel View.

Hall, C. M., Müller, D. K., & Saarinen, J. (2009). *Nordic tourism: Issues and cases*. Bristol: Channel View Publications.

Hermans, D. (2016). *Tourist images of Iceland: A regional comparison of tourism promotional material*. Akureyri: ITRC.

Honore, C. (2004). *In praise of slowness: How a worldwide movement is challenging the cult of speed*. New York: Harper Collins.

Hörnsten, L. (2000). *Outdoor recreation in Swedish forests* (Unpublished doctoral dissertation). Swedish University of Agricultural Sciences, Uppsala, Sweden.

Ísleifsson, S. R. (2011). Imaginations of national identity and the North. In S. R. Ísleifsson (Ed.). *Iceland and images of the North* (pp. 461–481). Quebec: Presses de l'Université du Quebec.

Kristjánsdóttir, K. R., Ólafsdóttir, R., & Ragnarsdóttir, K. V. (2018). Stakeholder participation in developing sustainability indicators for a European Northern periphery tourism system. *Journal of Rural and Community Development*, *12*(2–3), 210–235.

Lane, B. (1994). Sustainable rural tourism strategies: A tool for development and conservation. *Journal of Sustainable Tourism*, *2*(1–2), 102–111.

Lee, Y. S., Weaver, D., & Prebensen, N. K. (Eds.). (2017). *Arctic tourism experiences: Production, consumption and sustainability*. Wallingford: CABI.

Leirhaug, P. E. (2009). The role of friluftsliv in Henrik Ibsen's works. In *Proceedings from Ibsen Jubliee Friluftsliv Conference*, 14–19 September (pp. 1–12). North Trøndelag, Norway: University College, Levanger.

Lucarelli, A., & Berg, P. O. (2011). City branding: A state-of-the-art review of the research domain. *Journal of Place Management and Development*, *4*(1), 9–27.

Margaryan, L., & Zherdev, N. (2011). *Tourism development in North Iceland: The issues of seasonality and image production*. Akureyri: ITRC.

Müller, D. K., & Jansson, B. (Eds.). (2006). *Tourism in peripheries: Perspectives from the far north and south*. Wallingford: CABI.

NPA (2016). Northern Periphery and Arctic Cooperation Programme 2014–2020. http://www.interreg-npa.eu/fileadmin/Programme_Documents/Approved_Co operation_Programme_Jan2016.pdf [Accessed 2 May 2018].

OECD (2018). *Income inequality*. https://data.oecd.org/inequality/income-inequal ity.htm [Accessed 15 May 2018].

Partanen, A. (2017). *The Nordic theory of everything: In search of a better life*. London: Gerald Duckworth & Co.

Pritchard, A., & Morgan, N. J. (2000). Privileging the male gaze: Gendered tourism landscapes. *Annals of Tourism Research*, *27*(4), 884–905.

Rakić, T., & Chambers, D. (Eds.). (2011). *An introduction to visual research methods in tourism* (Vol. 9). London: Routledge.

Said, E. (1979). *Orientalism*. New York: Vintage.

Sandell, K., & Sörlin, S. (2000). *Friluftshistoria: från 'härdande friluftslif' till ekoturism och miljöpedagogik: Teman i det svenska friluftslivets historia*. Stockholm: Carlssons bokförlag.

Schram, K. (2011). Banking on Borealism: Eating, smelling and performing the North. In S. R. Ísleifsson (Ed.). *Iceland and Images of the North* (pp. 305–329). Quebec: Presses de l'Université du Quebec.

SDG (2017). *SDG index and dashboard report 2017*. http://www.sdgindex.org/assets/files/2017/2017-SDG-Index-and-Dashboards-Report--regions.pdf [Accessed 15 May 2018].

Stensland, S., Fossgaard, K., Apon, J., Baardesen, S., Fredman, P., Grubben, I., Haukeland, J. V., & Røren, E. A. M. (2014). Naturbaserte reiselivsbedrifter i Norge Frekvens-og metoderapport. *INA fragrapport, 25*, 1–136.

Sylvén, M. (2015). Rewilding Lapland. Creating a sustainable future for Europe's largest unspoiled natural and cultural treasure. Rewilding Europe project brochure. https://www.rewildingeurope.com/wp-content/uploads/2015/12/Rewilding-Lapland-EN.pdf [Accessed 2 May 2018].

Turner, L., & Ash, J. (1975). *The golden hordes*. London: Constable.

Varley, P., & Semple, T. (2015). Nordic slow adventure: Explorations in time and nature. *Scandinavian Journal of Hospitality and Tourism, 15*(1–2), 73–90.

Visit Sweden (2017). *Sweden on Airbnb*. https://www.youtube.com/watch?v=C6671CL5fFg [Accessed 5 May 2018].

Vuorinen, M., & Vos, M. (2013). Challenges in joint place branding in rural regions. *Place Branding and Public Diplomacy, 9*(3), 154–163.

Wall-Reinius, S., & Bäck, L. (2011). Changes in visitor demand: Inter-year comparisons of Swedish hikers' characteristics, preferences and experiences. *Scandinavian Journal of Hospitality and Tourism, 11*(sup1), 38–53.

Witte, J-J., & Braun, E. (2015). Cross-border place branding in Europe. In S. Zenker & B. Jacobsen (Eds.). *Inter-regional place branding* (pp. 87–98). New York: Springer.

World Bank (2018). *World Development Indicators: GDP per capita (current US dollars)*. http://databank.worldbank.org/data/reports.aspx?Code=NY.GDP.PCAP.CD&id=1ff4a498&report_name=Popular-Indicators&populartype=series&ispopular=y [Accessed 15 May 2018].

Zenker, S., & Jacobsen, B. P. (2015). *Inter-regional place branding*. New York: Springer.

8. Nordic landscapes in collaborative place-making interventions

Anne Marit Waade, Jens Christian Pasgaard, Mathias Meldgaard and Tom Nielsen

Source: Mathias Meldgaard, private photo.

Figure 8.1 *"Light sabre" design intervention in Hvide Sande, October 2017*

Hi Mathias. I'd like to start by praising you for the mooring posts on the central quay, and for the idea of illuminating the fishing net posts in the harbour. It's nice to gain a fresh perspective on Hvide Sande to highlight some of the details we typically overlook. BUT ... As a resident of the harbour area, I must insist that the practical design of the "light sabre" project (from Star Wars) is changed to stop us being blinded during the beautiful hours of dusk or when we take the dog for a walk in the evening. (There is a reason why we don't live in the neon hell of a big city, where people are constantly blinded by advertisements and LED lights). Is it possible to illuminate the fishing net posts from beneath with a golden, soft, warm kind of light? I have attached a couple of images of a quick mock-up I made with some neighbours, as an alternative. I think it is much more suitable. (e-mail received from a citizen of Ringkøbing-Skjern municipality, dated 10 October 2017)

This chapter presents two cases of bottom-up place-making practices which are characteristic of contemporary Nordic place-branding approaches. Both cases involve citizens, stakeholders and professionals in place making, without complying with an overall, unified and politically defined branding strategy. And they are both part of the research and innovation project called 'Rethinking Tourism in a Coastal City',[1] taking place in Ringkøbing-Skjern (RKS) municipality along the west coast of Denmark. This project is based on close collaboration between researchers from the fields of architecture, anthropology and culture/media studies on the one hand, and local institutions, entrepreneurs, citizens and the municipality on the other. The ambition is to develop tourism through site-specific interventions and new modes of cross-sectoral and co-creative collaboration. In this process, the coastal landscapes of the region characterised by hybridity and entanglement between natural, urban, leisure and infrastructural landscapes play a significant role.

Two of the cases developed in this context are (a) a collection of transformative architectural design interventions in Hvide Sande harbour (the "light sabre" project mentioned above is one of these interventions); and (b) the 'New Nordic noir screen tourism' project related to two television drama series which are being developed and which are to be shot on the west coast of Denmark. The examples represent two different modes of collaborative place-branding and place-intervention approaches in a Nordic rural branding context. The light sabre project illustrates an *on-site provotyping intervention* engaging citizens, stakeholders and professionals in the landscape planning; and the screen tourism model illustrates a *process intervention* aiming to develop cross-sectoral collaboration, co-creation and new windows for destination branding. The interventions are part of a tourism innovation project, and, as such, they are not part of a destination branding strategy.

RKS municipality is located on the west coast of Denmark. It is the largest municipality in Denmark (close to 1,500 square kilometres), but has a low population density (57,000 inhabitants). The town of Hvide

---

[1] 2016–2019, funded by the Danish Innovation Fund.

Sande is a key location in RKS, housing the lock between the North Sea and Ringkøbing Fjord. It is an active port in the Danish west coast region, traditionally living off fishing and farming. It has also been a prime tourist destination for many decades because of its wide, white beaches and coastal landscape. Development in RKS as a whole is an excellent example of a polarisation process in Denmark (just as in most other European countries), with jobs, people and economic growth being concentrated around the major towns – leaving a peripheral landscape characterised by a loss of population and jobs and a stagnating economy (Raugze, Daly & van Herwijnen, 2017). But within this overall quantitative and economic description of developments, the qualitative aspects of the transformation processes are overlooked. At present, the driving transformative forces for development in Hvide Sande are tourism-related investments and the continued, but changed, industrial use of the natural resources (wind farms and fishing). These two driving forces are often perceived to be in conflict (Urry & Larsen, 2011; Nielsen & Pasgaard, 2006).

Our main idea in this article is to chronicle a different way of developing and branding places. Rather than focusing on flagships, visual icons and brand values, our examples illustrate that creating artefacts and mobilising the local people through events, provotyping, workshops, informal discussions and experiences are good ways of creating a multifaceted and participatory-based place-making process, generating a strong sense of ownership as well as new ideas, new partnerships and collaborations, landscape imageries and new modes of tourism (Kavaratzis & Kalandides, 2015).

STRATEGIC PLACE MAKING THROUGH TACTICAL MANOEUVRES

Drawing on the distinction between place branding and place making, the two cases demonstrate how place making (in this case as collaborative place interventions initiated as respectively landscape design and screen production projects) includes the potential for place branding. While place branding is generally a top-down process led by the communication or tourism division within a municipality (Singh, 2010; Ooi, 2008; Anholt, 2010), place making is a bottom-up process of enhancing local place identity through a combination of community involvement and place-specific design (Richards, 2017). Place making is a philosophy and a process involving the planning, design, management and programming of public spaces which celebrate the local (Porter, 2017: 17). Thus, by presenting two illustrative cases, the article contributes to the recent discussions about inclusive and participatory-based place-branding practices (Kavaratzis & Kalandides, 2015; Bode & Kjeldgaard, 2017; Grönroos, 2012) that include complex processes interweaving tourism, culture, business and landscape planning understood as processual and performative branding practices (Giovanardi, Lichrou & Kavaratzis, 2018; Lucarelli & Hallin, 2015; Therkelsen & Halkier, 2008). As Giovanardi et al. (2018) conclude in their recent work, this particular form of *inclusive place branding* encompasses three significant dimensions: a strategic, a cultural and a political dimension (p. 182ff). The strategic dimension relates to the way in which participatory-based and co-creative place-branding practices are managed and governed; the cultural dimension reflects the specific cultural tensions and common ground that influence specific branding processes; and the political dimensions reflect the degree to which democratic values and citizenship are balanced and challenged by place-branding processes. The two cases that we present in this article illustrate these three dimensions in significant ways. Furthermore, the article contributes to Nordic place-branding research by focusing on a rural and coastal location (the town of Hvide Sande) which is archetypical of the majority of municipalities within the region. RKS follows the established branding rationale of rural and coastal locations by drawing on its landscapes and countryside as resources (Porter, 2017). This is clearly emphasised in the place-branding slogans for the area, respectively 'Sense the West Coast' (Hvide Sande Tourism) and 'The Kingdom of Nature' (RKS municipality).

We see this process as a form of strategic place making using tactical manoeuvres. Each of the design and collaborative process interventions is a tactical manoeuvre, and taken together they contribute to the long-term strategic development of locations, thereby branding the specific places involved through open-ended processes and citizen engagement. Based on our empirical studies, we contribute to the field by investigating place intervention, co-design, co-creation and cross-sectoral collaboration both as place-making processes and as a research design. With regard to the innovative aspect of the research, we also reflect on our own roles as researchers in these interventions and processes.

In the following, and as a theoretical framework for our case analyses, we will give a brief introduction to the way in which Nordic landscapes and the Nordic region are approached and considered within the two disciplines represented in this article: the landscape architecture tradition, and the Scandinavian crime series and media studies tradition, respectively (Pasgaard, 2012; Hansen & Waade, 2017; Porter, 2017). In the two cases below, we exemplify and discuss how this bottom-up strategy creates unpredictable, uncontrolled and complex processes of place making in the tourism-dominated landscape.

PART 1: RETHINKING NORDIC LANDSCAPES WITHIN THE FIELD OF ARCHITECTURE

The Nordic landscape (like the concept of 'Nordic' itself) can be defined in various ways. Architecture critic and historian Christian Norberg-Schulz (1996) describes the north and the Nordic landscape as being characterised by the low angle of the sun and the ever-changing weather (sun, shade, light, humidity). The atmosphere is ever changing (unlike the atmosphere of the south, which has a more stable climate with the sun exposing objects and landscapes in a clear light). The shifting moods and atmospheres define the Nordic region. The low angle of the sun means that things are hidden or blurred by semi-darkness. Everything is in flux, without any clear beginnings or ends. To understand the landscape, it is not sufficient to see it or understand it through representations. You need to engage in it, intrude in it (Norberg-Schulz, 1996: 9–17). This analysis has many limitations because of its obvious reductionist and idiosyncratic approach, based in an essentialist phenomenological tradition. Nevertheless, the reductionist approach points to some interesting characteristics of the concept of 'Nordic' based on architecture and the physical environment. According to Norberg-Schulz, the role of architecture is to help people inhabit the landscape by helping them to understand its specific affordances and qualities. This may involve topography, material, light, microclimate, etc. Architecture can communicate the qualitative aspects of the landscape. This conservative essentialist idea of '*the* landscape', building on Heidegger, is strange in relation to the idea that the Nordic landscape is subject to constant change. But it reflects the approach of recent tourism-related projects which use architecture as a way to convey specific landscape qualities to visitors (for example the Juvet Landscape Hotel in Norway by the architects Jensen & Skodvin or the new access ramps and viewing platforms at Kalø Castle Ruins in Denmark made by MAP Architects). In recent years, this approach has been used both implicitly and explicitly in strategic projects designed to enhance tourism, for example the 'Norwegian Tourist Routes' and 'Stedet tæller' (2013) ('The place matters') in Denmark. Such projects employ a strategy based on places and architecture, with certain locations and characteristic landscapes being chosen and enhanced using small but expertly designed architectural interventions placed as objects in the landscape. The thing that distinguishes this approach from more traditional approaches is the idea of making a small-scale contribution to an existing context instead of redefining this context by adding new, large-scale or very visible identity-bearing structures. In these cases the qualities of the place are boiled down to an essence that is easy to understand and easy to communicate through a single image. This approach is one of the archetypal approaches of the tourism industry to adjust to rather simple expectations (simple variations of the romantic or the collective gaze) (Urry & Larsen, 2011; Pasgaard, 2012: 18).

Mari Hvattum (2009) has criticised this geographical determinism and visual hegemony of the place-based regional approach both from a constructivist position in terms of identity construction, and from the perspective of relational aesthetics. She advocates a practice- and action-oriented approach to place making, inspired by cultural geography. The practice-based approach here could be understood as being different from (but not in opposition to) a strategic approach based on the idea of stable place values that can be communicated. This alternative can draw on a tactical approach and the ideas formulated as tactical urbanism. Tactical urbanism has emerged as a practice and then a theoretical field since around 2000 (see e.g. Bishop & Williams, 2012; Oswalt, Overmeyer & Misselwitz, 2013). Theoretically speaking, tactical urbanism has been inspired by mid-twentieth century thinkers like Henri Lefebvre, Michel de Certeau and to a certain extent Walter Benjamin. Common to all these scholars was that they were interested in the individual citizen and not least in everyday life "composed of a multiplicity of moments, such as games, love, work, rest, struggle, knowledge, poetry and justice, and links professional life, direct social life, leisure and culture" (Kofman and Lebas, 1996: 30). A tactical approach can be defined as a short-term approach based on existing resources and the engagement of locals and people who are present in the spaces and landscapes concerned. The strength of a tactical approach is that it reduces the distance between the user and the designer.

PLACE INTERVENTION 1: DESIGN INTERVENTIONS AS CO-CREATIVE PROVOTYPING AND TACTICAL URBANISM

The first case comprises a collection of transformative architectural design interventions in Hvide Sande harbour. A research group at The Aarhus School of Architecture (AAA) conducted the work, informed by input and feedback from many different local actors and tourists. In continuation of the overall project aims, it is important to outline that this group has an intensified focus on coastal cities as condensations in the hybrid coastal landscape (which has undergone urbanisation for a century, today dotted with an almost continuous structure of summer cottages). The key problem, from a tourism industry perspective, is that the Danish coastal towns, generally speaking, do not perform very well. RKS offers spectacular wide white beaches, but the coastal cities are challenged by lack of investment in the urban fabrics and key urban spaces. According to a survey conducted by Videncentret for Kystturisme (2013), tourists visiting coastal areas in Denmark are "unimpressed by the town-centres, shopping possibilities, restaurants, public toilets and the relationship between price and value" and maybe most challenging; they find the coastal cities "rather boring". Accordingly, the main task has been to rethink and redesign the coastal cities. In order to initiate a search for hidden potentials, the research group at AAA decided to let 21 students at the master's degree programme "Studio Urban Design | Landscape Architecture" conduct highly explorative mappings at preselected sites in the RKS. Based on the students' findings and resulting project ideas for tourism-related development, it was decided to use Hvide Sande as a testing ground for further exploration. The key reason for this is that Hvide Sande holds a sufficient mix of tourism-dominated and everyday-dominated spaces and activities. Simultaneous to the MA-students' analyses a doctoral student started to look for untapped potentials, new strategic locations and available materials throughout the town. A main agenda was to identify and highlight local qualities in order to inform a future urban planning process and thereby also inform a future site-based and site-specific branding of Hvide Sande.

One of the design interventions developed in this context was the "light sabre" intervention, for which LED lamps were installed in three stacks of fishing net posts in Hvide Sande harbour in Ringkøbing Fjord. The e-mail and picture (Figure 8.1) presented at the beginning of this article were received as a response to this intervention. The installation sought to establish a dialogue with local stakeholders as a qualitative inquiry of the place and the transformative process it undergoes and the conflicts this generates. As the e-mail correspondence indicates, a group of local citizens took action and established an alternative installation, using a "golden, soft and warm light" as a critical comment on the transformation caused by the design intervention and a physical testimony of their perception of the place. This critique was then incorporated into a third design iteration and on-site adjustment in collaboration with the author of the e-mail and a couple of other interested neighbours. The fishing posts are in constant use and are therefore regularly moved and relocated by the fishermen, so the local people are now active in adjusting the design intervention. Interestingly, the work with the light and the demand for a more subtle light effect as well as the users' wish to adjust the installation so it does not ruin the experience of the night skies, resonates well with Norberg-Schulz's ideas of Nordic Architecture as being determined by moods and atmospheres. The intervention with its clear purpose of marking a place becomes an example of a place-based development with no alignment with overall urban plans or branding strategies except for the very overall context of the research project in which the municipality is a collaborator, Four other design interventions have also been developed and implemented as provotypes in Hvide Sande, involving (a) relocating mooring lumber from a supply yard to a central quay; (b) mounting yellow IKEA chairs on pier stones; (c) placing saunas and hot tubs in the industrial harbour; and (d) suspending orange traffic cones from a disused conveyor belt which had once been used for loading ice onto fishing boats. "Provotyping" is a term used to describe "provocative prototyping", which is a method for gaining a rapid reaction to influence an ongoing design process (see e.g. Boer, Donovan & Buur, 2013). The actual provotyping process has its point of departure in the local context. In Hvide Sande, this is a context where the place (this part of the harbour) has gradually lost its functional significance as fishing harbour due to a series of economic and environmental circumstances, while a growing demand for authentic tourism experiences has started a gradual transformation of the characteristic fishing shacks into holiday cottages. The inception of ideas for the design interventions happens more or less coincidentally, but is always anchored in something experienced in the given context (based on mappings by students and Mathias Meldgaard). The people experiencing the provotypes are able to respond and engage in the development processes, as seen in the "light sabre" example. The process becomes more structured as attention is provoked through dissonance, for example suspending traffic cones from the disused conveyor belt, and as responses are systematically assessed through workshops with invited local actors. Here, an important discussion is the afterlife and potential up-scaling of the provotype, which could develop from a test site into a more permanent place re-shaped by the local users.

The provotypes should be seen as a way to test a tactical approach which exposes rather than hides antagonistic or differing ideas of use (industrial, inhabitants' everyday culture, recreational consumption, etc.), and builds from local culture by involving locals and users in the development of prototypes. The idea is to develop frameworks, places and spaces, which fluid or unstable in their character (more or less temporary structures), make a blend between different people with different "gazes", and different agendas possible (Pasgaard, 2012: 113). This way of approaching the test site, the coastal town of Hvide Sande, is based on the overall understanding that Hvide Sande is neither a tourist space nor an industrial space or urban space, but a space which is becoming increasingly dominated by tourism in a context where romantic and collective tourist gazes influence developments (Pasgaard, 2012: 114–124). Importantly, from a branding perspective, this approach creates visual and palpable brand articulations contesting the look and feel of traditional coastal cities and coastal landscapes. The advantage and appeal of such provoked dissonance or semantic confusion is that the coastal town advances its spatial complexity and can accommodate several cultural meanings rather than being degraded into a one-sided branding strategy. The coastal town thereby appeals to several tourist segments and can embrace multi-layered brandings strategies. As such, these cities are less likely to fall into stereotypical seaside categories. An interesting afterlife of the "light sabre" intervention so far is that the local brewery Mylius-Erichsen Bryghus (2018) used a photograph of this particular provotype in one of their recent advertisements.

PART 2: NORDIC NOIR SCREEN PRODUCTIONS AS TOURISM INNOVATION AND PLACE BRANDING

The *New Nordic noir* initiative was initiated by Filmby Aarhus in 2016 aiming to developing a site-specific crime series on the west coast of Denmark inclusive of an online playable platform and screen tourism. While the provotyping case was a small-scale, on-site intervention and bottom-up process coordinated by the researcher concerned, the New Nordic noir case was part of a top-down initiative and a long-term process in which the researcher's role involved following the process on the sidelines and facilitating cross-sectoral collaboration and knowledge exchange. The production is still under development, and the ambition is that two to three series will be shot and released within a period of five years, and the online platform as well as the screen tourism will be developed in relation to the series. The New Nordic noir initiative aims to utilise the international popularity of Nordic crime series and the particular cold, desolate and gloomy Nordic climate and landscapes. The west coast of Denmark is a good choice of location, with its harsh climate representing a different way of presenting the west coast as a tourist destination by contrast with the typical tourist marketing and destination branding campaigns. This way of creating site-specific culture productions is well known within art history, but is still relatively rare within television drama production (Kaye, 2000). Site-specific drama productions present new stories and images about a place, as well as bringing actors and film crews to the locations concerned – leading in turn to media coverage as well as local enthusiasm and a sense of identity. Each of these elements adds extra layers to the branding process.

In general, Nordic noir as trademark encompasses crime literature and crime series from the Nordic region (Stougaard-Nielsen, 2017). In Nordic noir the particular dark lightening, melancholic mood, the bleak Nordic landscapes and cold climate conditions, as well as the region's welfare state, gender equality and languages, have become significant production values that in turn have inspired crime series productions outside the Nordic region (Creeber, 2015; Hansen & Waade, 2017; Roberts, 2016). Recalling Norberg-Schulz's (1996) account of the specific Nordic in the region's architecture relates directly to the Nordic noir concept, in which darkness and the foggy, overcast and blurred light are significant elements. The notion that spaces, entrances, etc., are hidden in the shadows, which Norberg-Schulz describes as characteristic of Nordic building, is also obviously an aspect of Nordic noir. The international popularity of the Nordic crime stories is linked to the recent "Nordic wave" in which food, design, architecture, gender culture and "hygge" have achieved significant attention internationally (Syvertsen, Gunn Enli & Hallvard, 2014). Parallel to this, screen tourism has become an emerging industry internationally. Scandinavian crimes series, both in print and on screen, induce tourism, for example *Wallander* in Ystad, *Millennium* in Stockholm, *Fjällbacka* tourism based on Camilla Läckberg's crime novels and *Dicte* tourism in Aarhus based on Elsebeth Egholm's crime stories. Today, screen tourism is most typically a result of long-term, cross-sectoral collaboration and investments in which local authorities, tourism organisations and nations place their destination as a "product" in screen productions. Location placement can be used to boost tourism and destination branding, but it also has the potential to strengthen local creative industries, as well as attracting investors and new inhabitants (Paulsgaard, 2009; Waade, 2013).

In the New Nordic noir screen tourism intervention place branding takes place on several levels. First, the process of developing screen tourism and attracting screen productions has become part of the local cultural political strategy, and thus works as indirect place branding, since cultural vibrancy as such attracts visitors (Ooi & Ströber 2010). Second, both screen productions and screen tourism open up new ways of valuing and exploiting the coastal landscapes in small, provincial municipalities. For example, Nordic noir crime series include a particular landscape aesthetic and most typically fancy dark, cold, gloomy and winterly landscapes (Creeber, 2015; Jensen & Waade, 2013), in contrast with the obligatory glossy sun and summer features of tourism destination brands. The screen tourists want to experience the places as they know them from the television series and, as such, Nordic noir tourism comprises the potential for developing off-peak tourism. Third, and what we will emphasise in this context, is how locally based screen production encompasses the potential for a participatory-based process in which citizens, stakeholders and local enterprises engage in co-creative processes. As such, screen tourism has become a new rationale within screen production that requires cross-sectoral collaboration. Finally, and perhaps most important when it comes to place branding, is the fact, that when the television drama series will be released in few years, it will be a significant window for branding RKS as a tourist destination for both Danish and international viewers. What is interesting in this context is the fact that small, provincial Nordic municipalities such as RKS can attract international screen productions and develop screen tourism despite the fact that they have no local creative industry.

PLACE INTERVENTION 2: NEW NORDIC NOIR AS CROSS-SECTORAL COOPERATION

The main partners involved in the New Nordic noir screen tourism case are Filmby Aarhus and RKS. Filmby Aarhus set up a partnership with the municipality in RKS, and in the beginning they gained funding to develop their screen ideas from the organisation behind Aarhus 2017, the European Capital of Culture. Since the crime series and the screen tourism still is under development, this case study reflects the way in which the collaboration and co-creation takes place. The Rethinking Tourism innovation project has collaborated with key individuals in the New Nordic noir initiative with a view to developing screen tourism in partnership with RKS. Rather than on-site interventions as was the case for the landscape design example, this case illustrates process intervention, in which the role of the researcher has been to initiate, support and inspire key individuals in the municipality and give them access to research, expertise and practical knowledge. The overall ambition has been to develop a cross-sectoral collaboration within the municipality across the division for culture, tourism and strategic planning, as well as with external partners, stakeholders and experts. At this stage it is far too early to conclude anything about how the case impacts the place branding of RKS or how the coastal landscapes are re-framed and transformed through the screen productions. However, focusing on the process of intervention, the researcher's role has been to inspire, facilitate and initiate collaboration between the municipality's tourism and the culture departments and media players on a regional and national level; to exchange knowledge with and make contact with similar municipalities within the Nordic region that have been successful in developing local screen tourism; and to engage citizens as well as international PhD students in co-creative processes. In addition, the fact that RKS and the west coast are seen as attractive film locations among international television producers generates excitement and a particular way of seeing and valuing the landscapes among local citizens, politicians and local businesses. As such, screen tourism in RKS has the potential to change both the social and the affective dynamics of the place.

This is the first time the municipality has been involved in screen productions and screen tourism initiatives, so the first step has been to learn about and gain information from other similar location placement initiatives and screen tourism destinations. The place-branding challenges that RKS deals with in this context are not restricted to tourism, but involve a general need to attract young families as well as new inhabitants and investors to the area. When it comes to tourism, RKS's overall ambition is to attract tourists from countries other than Germany, to keep the number of Danish visitors, develop more wide-scaled "reasons to go", and develop better and more differentiated tourist experiences also outside the traditional seasons. Screen tourism is one among several initiatives that aim to meet these challenges. As such, fictive crime series can reframe the visual representations and traditional tourism imageries of sunny beaches.

So far, the New Nordic noir initiative has involved (a) on-location training events for scriptwriters and producers in Hvide Sande, with the participants developing ideas for the series; (b) a matchmaking event in Hamburg (spring 2017), in which pre-defined German–Danish co-producer teams were invited to pitch their ideas to the board; (c) workshops for stakeholders and creatives to develop the online *West Coast Universe*; and (d) starting to prepare for related screen tourism in RKS. In the first year (2017), two television drama projects were selected for further development, and at the time of writing (2018), the scriptwriting and funding processes are still ongoing. The ambition is that the television drama series will premiere in 2020. Simultaneously with the production of this drama series, the online platform *West Coast Universe* is being organised as creative workshops in which students, researchers and professional industry partners (museums, IT companies, architects and tourism organisations) have taken part. In August 2018, the politicians in RKS decided that film and television will be their focus area in the years to come, and they aim to attract film productions, engage children and young inhabitants in screen productions and screen-related activities, host an annual film festival and develop screen tourism. As the first steps in this direction, in 2018 a Danish film production has been shot in the area and the first Bunker film festival has been organised.

Following the three dimensions of inclusive place branding presented by Giovanardi et al. (2018: 182ff.), strategic, cultural and political respectively, the New Nordic noir screen tourism case illustrates how these dimensions are negotiated and practised side by side. It is important to take into account that New Nordic noir screen tourism has not been a place-branding initiative as such, but that it does involve additional branding value for the municipality. First, the strategic dimension is illustrated by the new cross-sectoral collaboration involving meetings and workshops with key individuals from the different divisions within the municipality (culture, tourism and strategic planning respectively), and the fact that the municipality hires a film advisor to develop location placement and screen tourism. Supplementary to this, and more as a co-creative strategy, in June 2018 RKS hosted an on-site PhD training camp in Hvide Sande in which the young researchers developed moodboards and audio-visual ideas for RKS's future place-branding strategies related to the New Nordic noir initiative. In relation to the cultural dimension, the New Nordic noir case demonstrates the importance of a common language and knowledge about screen production and screen tourism. To develop this common understanding and language across three sectors and divisions, the process has involved gaining knowledge and insights from other best-practice cases. In April 2018, the key members of staff from RKS went on a study trip to Ystad municipality in Sweden, which is known internationally for the *Wallander* series and recognised as a screen tourism destination. As an affiliated researcher, Anne Marit Waade organised this study trip alongside the new film advisor. To strengthen this common language and understanding of screen tourism as strategic potential, the key individuals from RKS were invited to take part in and present the 'New Nordic noir' at international research conferences ('Landscapes in television drama', Aarhus, September 2017, and 'Transnational television drama', Aarhus, June 2018). Furthermore, the film advisor and the researcher attended the PictureThis festival in Copenhagen (2018) to learn about new digital technology in screen tourism and screen productions, and the researcher was invited to take part in the *West Coast Universe* workshops with stakeholders and partners (April 2018). Regarding the political dimension in inclusive place branding, it is important to acknowledge the general interest in screen production and screen tourism and the fact that series shot locally have a particular appeal to and recognition among the locals (Waade, 2013). The New Nordic noir screen tourism case illustrates the way in which synergies between different initiatives and processes create a political momentum in which media cover the case, the local government invests in screen productions, and a degree of public attention is generated to which citizens, local stakeholders and businesses can relate. At this stage, the project is an open-ended process involving planning and developing ideas, synergies and collaboration, building networks and partnerships, gaining input and engaging stakeholders, commercial partners and citizens.

So what are the perspectives for this screen tourism project in relation to Nordic place branding? The overall lessons learned from this case are that Nordic noir offers a new grammar for touristic place making, and for rural destinations. The west coast of Denmark will be screened for and presented to an international market, making this production a significant marketing window for this particular destination. The rationale behind the RKS screen production strategy is to attract tourists in off-peak periods, create new and better experiences for the tourists who already visit RKS, and become an attractive location for other screen productions. A significant part of the New Nordic noir initiative was that the place itself (Hvide Sande) should play a crucial role: the creative work took place there, the stories were inspired by the place and the local history, the series will be shot and produced on location, it has been developed and will be produced in close collaboration with local partners, and it aims to generate value for the region. Site-specific television drama series represent extra narrative, aesthetic and funding values to the production, but the Nordic noir place identity also creates branding value and identification for citizens. As we know from participatory-based place-branding experiences, this strong and positive identification among the citizens is crucial (Kavaratzis & Kalandides, 2015; Bode & Kjeldgaard, 2017). Rather than developing the typical slogan, logos and marketing campaigns to brand a place, these dynamic processes are about strengthening the synergies, developing cross-sectoral and public–private collaborations, realising the brand values and opportunities in the process, and, not least, including different groups of people – citizens, students, producers, actors and researchers – to gain input and attract attention. This way of branding a place may also be hard to control: it is not so much a question of defining and managing the outcome, but more a question of stimulating processes and engagement locally.

CONCLUSION: INTERVENTIONAL PLACE MAKING AS PLACE BRANDING

There are some interesting differences between the two cases, mainly related to the different disciplines they represent: the "light sabre" intervention has grown out of a landscape design tradition, and the screen tourism intervention out of a screen production and media studies tradition. In relation to place making, there are some basic differences between the two fields: while the point of departure and main focus of landscape architecture is places, this is still new within screen productions; while the architect works with physical places, objects and material from the outset, the starting point for screen productions is most often imageries and ideas; while the architect is used to working closely together with local stakeholders and clients, this is not common in screen productions; and while the architect is used to working in open-ended planning processes, screen production is subject to time limits. Following the ideas of Avermaete and Teerds, the architect's practice is increasingly linked to the actions of multiple actors and involves local stakeholders and users, in which the urban territory "and the knowledge and skills of citizens are understood as immanent sources to be unlocked, activated, and managed by the architectural project" (Avermaete and Teerds, 2016: 11). By contrast, in screen productions the creative process and ideas are kept secret until the day of release, with only a limited number of key individuals from funding bodies and commissioning boards knowing about them. The approach in the provotypes described here is highly tactical, with a loose or vague link to overall strategies, and is based on minimal budgets. But it has the potential to affect the overall development and also the branding of the town involved. The Nordic noir projects, on the other hand, depend on large budgets and secrecy. So they can only move forward after being implemented in the overall branding strategies of the municipality concerned.

Despite these differences, there are some interesting similarities and potential when it comes to place branding. Both cases illustrate an *interventional place making* that carries potential for place branding as well as positive community dynamics. Since place branding is not the main objective but rather a result of the different interventions as multifaceted tactical manoeuvres, they represent an indirect mode of place branding. Both cases challenge the typical understanding of what a destination is, contributing and provotyping new stories and new ways of seeing and using places. Furthermore, both cases illustrate how place branding can be reflected and performed (both formally and informally and in close collaboration with citizens, tourists, stakeholders and students) to create local engagement and input – the fact that RKS has followed up on the New Nordic noir initiative by developing a local film policy reaching out to screen producers as well as citizens and local cultural institutions. The RKS cases differ from other participatory-based place-making processes by illustrating an explorative, interventional and open branding process. The two cases consist of more or less consciously organised interventions and function as tactical manoeuvres in the more general place-making process. Even though they focus on different ideas, people and events, together they bring extra layers of images, use and understanding to Hvide Sande as a hybrid place, a "spatial augmentation" (Sandvik, 2015: 97ff). Some of the ideas, events and objects may not be followed up on or realised, but they all function as tactical and iterative manoeuvres that ultimately transform places with new layers of meaning, use and imageries. In general, the different design and process interventions possess transformative potential and power.

The Nordic specificity in this context is linked to the hybrid landscapes in the means of being urban and rural at the same time, as well as the small communities and collaborative practices that characterise Nordic culture. In general, this way of practising place branding and destination development is reflected in a Nordic democratic culture, regional policy and citizen-based engagement that is a general condition that exists beyond place branding. As such, we can argue that there is a unique way of Nordic participatory place branding given the emphasis on collaboration and consensus making in the Nordic context (Syvertsen et al., 2014).

REFERENCES

Anholt, S. (2010), *Places: Identity, Image and Reputation*. Basingstoke: Palgrave Macmillan.

Avermaete, T. & Teerds, H. (2016), 'The roles of the architect: Toward a theory of practice'. In S. Frausto (Ed.) *On the Role of the Architect* (Lexicon no. 1, pp. 7–11). Delft: The Berlage Center for Advanced Studies in Architectural and Urban Design, Faculty of Architecture and the Build Environment, Delft University of Technology.

Bishop, P. & Williams, L. (2012), *The Temporary City*. London: Routledge.

Bode, M. & Kjeldgaard, D. (2017), 'Brand doings in a performative perspective: An analysis of conceptual brand discourses'. In J. F. Sherry & E. Fischer (Eds.), *Contemporary Consumer Culture Theory* (pp. 251–282). New York: Routledge.

Boer, L., Donovan, J. & Buur, J. (2013), 'Challenging industry conceptions with provotypes', *CoDesign*, **9** (2), 73–89.

Creeber, G. (2015), 'Killing us softly: Investigating the aesthetics, philosophy and influence of *Nordic Noir* television', *Journal of Popular Television*, **3** (1), 21–35.

Giovanardi, M., Lichrou, M. & Kavaratzis, M. (Eds.) (2018), *Inclusive Place Branding – Critical Perspectives on Theory and Practice*. Routledge Studies in Critical Marketing. Oxfordshire: Routledge.

Grönroos, C. (2012), 'Conceptualising value co-creation: A journey to the 1970s and back to the future', *Journal of Marketing Management*, **28** (13–14), 1520–1534.

Hansen, K. T. & Waade, A. M. (2017), *Locating Nordic Noir*. Basingstoke, Hampshire: Palgrave Macmillan.

Hvattum, M. (2009), 'Stedets Tyrani', *Arkitektur N*, (4), 40–51.

Kavaratzis, M. & Kalandides, A. (2015), 'Rethinking the place brand: The interactive formation of place brands and the role of participatory place branding', *Environment and Planning A*, **47**, 1368–1382.

Kaye, N. (2000), *Site-specific Art: Performance, Place, and Documentation*. London: Routledge.

Kofman, E. & Lebas, E. (1996), 'Introduction: Lost in transposition – time, space and the city'. In E. Kofman & E. Lebas (Eds.) *Henri Lefebvre, Writings on Cities*. Oxford: Blackwell, pp. 3–60.

Lucarelli, A. & Hallin, A. (2015), 'Brand transformation: A performative approach to brand regeneration', *Journal of Marketing Management*, **31** (1–2), 84–106.

Mylius-Erichsen Bryghus (2018), online advertisement, post on Facebook December 2017. https://www.facebook.com/search/str/mylius+erichsen+bryghus/photos-keyword (accessed 12 September 2018).

Nielsen, T. & Pasgaard, J. C. L. (2006), 'Turismen som forandringskraft', *Arkitekten*, **108–13**, 44–51.

Norberg-Schulz, C. (1996), *Nightlands: Nordic Building*. Cambridge, MA: MIT Press.

Ooi, C.-S., (2008), 'Reimagining Singapore as a creative nation: The politics of place branding', *Place Branding and Public Diplomacy*, **4** (4), 287–302.

Ooi, C.-S. & Ströber, B. (2010), 'Authenticity and place branding. The arts and culture in branding Berlin and Singapore'. In B. T. Knudsen & A. M. Waade (Eds.) *Re-Investing Authenticity* (pp. 66–79). Bristol/Buffalo/Toronto: Channel View Publications.

Oswalt, P., Overmeyer, K. & Misselwitz, P. (2013), *Urban Catalyst: The Power of Temporary Use*. Berlin: DOM Publishers.

Pasgaard, J. C. L. (2012), *Tourism and Strategic Planning* [PhD thesis]. Copenhagen: Det Kongelige Danske Kunstakademis Skoler for Arkitektur, Design og Konservering.

Paulsgaard, G. (2009), 'Cool & crazy – Place reinventing through filmmaking'. In T. Nyseth & A. Viken (Eds.) *Place Reinvention – Northern Perspectives* (pp. 145–164). Farnham: Ashgate Publishing.

Porter, N. (2017), *Landscape and Branding: The Promotion and Production of Place*. London, New York: Routledge.

Raugze, I., Daly, G. & van Herwijnen, M. (Eds.) (2017), *Shrinking Rural Regions in Europe: Towards Smart and Innovative Approaches to Regional Development Challenges in DEPOPULATING RURAL REGIONS*. Luxembourg: ESPON EGTC.

Richards, G. (2017), 'From place branding to placemaking: The role of events', *International Journal of Event and Festival Management*, **8** (1), 8–23.

Roberts, L. (2016), 'Landscapes in the frame: Exploring the hinterlands of the British procedural drama', *New Review of Film and Television Studies*, **14** (3), 364–385.

Sandvik, Kjetil (2015), *Plot til lyst – spilbare mordgåder på tværs af medier*. Aalborg: Aalborg University Press.

Singh, A. K. (Ed.) (2010), *Destination Branding: An Introduction*. Hyderabad, India: Icfai University Press.

Stædet Tæller (2013), Website. http://www.stedet-taeller.dk (accessed 18 November 2018). (See also the cross-Scandinavian project 'Via Nordica' website. http://www.cedr.eu/event/via-nordica-2020/ (accessed 18 November 2018).)

Stougaard-Nielsen, J. (2017), *Scandinavian Crime Fiction*. London, New York: Bloomsbury Academic.

Syvertsen, T., Gunn Enli, O. M. & Hallvard, M. (2014), *The Media Welfare State: Nordic Media in the Digital Era*. Ann Arbor, MI: The University of Michigan Press.

Therkelsen, A. & Halkier, H. (2008), 'Contemplating place branding umbrellas: The case of coordinated national tourism and business promotion in Denmark', *Scandinavian Journal of Hospitality and Tourism*, **8** (2), 159–175.

Urry, J. & Larsen, J. (2011), *The Tourist Gaze 3.0 – Leisure and Travel in Contemporary Societies*. Los Angeles, CA: Sage.

Videncentret for Kystturisme (2013), *Kystturisters tilfredshed med feriesteder i Danmark* (Coastal Tourists' satisfaction with holiday resorts in Denmark), a questionnaire survey conducted in 2013. https://www.kystognaturturisme.dk/media/1056/kystturisters-tilfredshed-med-feriesteder-i-danmark.pdf, (accessed 18 November 2018).

Waade, A. M. (2013), *Wallanderland: Skandinavisk krimi og filmturisme*. Aalborg: Aalborg University Press.

9. Translocal communities and their implications for place branding

Rikke Brandt Broegaard, Karin Topsø Larsen and Lene Havtorn Larsen

INTRODUCTION

This chapter studies today's increasingly translocal lives by analysing the opportunities and challenges that translocality creates for rural place branding. We explore the role of translocal actors in community development on four Nordic islands. After a long period of demographic and economic decline, several rural Nordic islands seem to be emerging as hotspots for attracting people from urban areas, many of whom engage in local island development projects even though they do not live there full time.[1] Taking translocal networks and engagements into account brings into view the flows of people and the resources they make available through translocal networks, relations and hubs of engagement (Greiner & Sakdapolrak, 2013), thereby highlighting a hitherto understudied aspect of development and branding potentials in rural places. Similarly, such translocal affiliations pose new challenges to place-branding theory and practice, as they highlight the connectivity between actors at different places and underline a translocal sense of place (Massey, 1994, 2005). They also stress the relational and ever-changing character of place identity understood as a process, which is influenced by both continuities and discontinuities, and shaped by power relations (Kalandides, 2011).

We observe two defining shifts: The first is a move away from a resident–visitor dichotomy towards an appreciation of an array of differentiated attachment modes (Giovanardi, Lucarelli, & Decosta, 2014; Milbourne, 2007; Milbourne & Kitchen, 2014). As mobility increases, translocal lifestyles with people being engaged in more than one place, become more common (Greiner & Sakdapolrak, 2013). Thus, the often used dichotomy

---

[1] For a similar observation on hotspots and uneven geographies of second homes in Sweden, see Back and Marjavaara (2017).

between residents and non-residents is of little utility (Halfacree, 2012). The second shift concerns a turn from differentiation to de-differentiation of everyday life and the touristic experiences, paving the way for leisure time being utilised as a continuum of interaction and engagement (Uriely, 2005). The chapter examines the implications of these two defining shifts for place branding and rural community development.

The objective of the chapter is to explore the opportunities and challenges that translocality creates for rural place branding by analysing translocal actors' involvement in place making on four Nordic islands. First, we argue for the relevance of including translocal actors in place-branding studies, while also drawing on literature from migration-development studies. Next, we introduce our research design, methodology and case study setting. After presenting our findings from the four studied islands, we discuss their implications for the development of rural places, place-branding processes and local governance of translocal engagement. We conclude by arguing for the importance of including translocal perspectives on rural development and place branding.

TRANSLOCAL ACTORS – AN UNDERSTUDIED ASPECT OF RURAL PLACE DEVELOPMENT

Translocality is a relevant concept to include when studying place development and place branding due to the increased connectedness of daily life involving different places. This interconnectedness is facilitated by increasing mobility, representing differences both in temporal and spatial terms, including everyday commuting, commuting between multiple homes, leisure-time travels as well as seasonal and long-term migration (Brickell & Datta, 2011; Milbourne, 2007; Milbourne & Kitchen, 2014; Rockenbauch & Sakdapolrak, 2017). The concept of translocality describes the 'socio-spatial dynamics and processes of simultaneity and identity formation that transcend boundaries' (Greiner & Sakdapolrak, 2013, p. 373), thereby highlighting connections between places (whether urban and rural, or home and second home, or origin and destination). Until recently, translocal approaches have mainly been prevalent within research on global migration and development studies focused on empirical cases from the Global South. Here it has widely been recognised that increased mobility and multi-local lives have generated multi-local attachments. These create new development opportunities for both the places of origin, and recipient residential places (see for example De Haas, 2010; Sørensen, 2012).

New development opportunities are created through feedback processes generated by the multi-local embeddedness of mobile social actors, through whom ideas, knowledge, practices and economic resources and values are circulated. This in turn generates circulation between places, as well as between mobile and non-mobile actors through translocal actors' networks (Agergaard & Broegger, 2016; Greiner & Sakdapolrak, 2013; Rockenbauch & Sakdapolrak, 2017). Within the context of rural studies, Milbourne called over a decade ago for an appreciation of the diverse spatial and temporal scales of rural mobility, including 'movements in to, out of, within and through rural places; [. . .], journeys of necessity and choice; economic and lifestyle-based movements; [. . .] and uneven power relations and processes of marginalization' (Milbourne, 2007, pp. 385– 386). By focusing on translocal actors in the development and branding of rural places, translocal networks and the connectedness between places are brought into focus, rather than seeing rural places as locally bound entities (Gallent, 2014; Greiner & Sakdapolrak, 2013; Kalandides, 2011; Milbourne & Kitchen, 2014; Rye, 2011).

We use the term *translocal actors* to denote people and communities of people who choose to engage in a rural place without having their permanent residence there, and who invest, build and draw upon networks in more than one place simultaneously. They may or may not have second homes in the area,[2] but they feel veneration and attachment to the place and/or people in that place. However, it is pertinent to stress that not all part-time dwellers or 'reiterative tourists' involve themselves in local development projects to a degree that may define them as engaged translocal actors.

They are driven by affective bonds to the place (Oliveira, Roca, & Leitão, 2010) and motivated by making the place they care for into not only a more attractive place for themselves, but also to help drive local development. The contributions of translocal actors are often embedded in a series of complex social practices (Gielis, 2009), which may be perceived as mooring points (Adey, 2006; Brickell & Datta, 2011; Milbourne & Kitchen, 2014), i.e. strings, anchors, relations, commitments, networks, nodes (there is no lack of attachment metaphors!) that connect the individual to a place through a community with which they engage. Our research explores how these translocal actors influence rural change and rural place brands, and whether and how translocal actors are taken into account in planning processes. We consider the potential for development that they bring through their resources and connectivity between places and networks, as well as the challenges that their engagement may imply for local community development and the contestation of place.

---

[2] For literature mentioning the interaction of second home owners with Nordic rural places, see Müller (2012), Back and Marjavaara (2017), Rye (2011) and Farstad (2013, 2016).

Following Braun, Kavaratzis and Zenker's (2013) call to pay more attention to the role of residents in place branding, we extend this to include translocal actors. We argue that a translocal lens is necessary for appreciating the multiple ways, and on multiple temporal and spatial scales, that people engage with place, regardless of their formal 'permanent' residence (Gallent, 2015; Halfacree, 2012; Müller, 2011; Müller & Hall, 2003; Rye, 2011). Finally, translocalism carries important implications for rethinking place-branding frameworks in order to address the full range of translocal place attachments. This chapter offers such a rethinking.

STUDYING TRANSLOCAL COMMUNITIES ON FOUR NORDIC ISLANDS

This chapter is based on an exploratory research project, which takes a translocal approach to enrich the understanding of rural development perspectives. Empirically, we have selected four rural Nordic islands with an enduring presence of translocal actors. While these islands are not representative of all Nordic rural islands, they illustrate the translocal actors' engagement in local development as well as their contribution to (rural) place branding and brand renewal. On the other hand, communitarian and self-organised bottom-up local development initiatives are typical for rural areas throughout the Nordic region.

Methodologically, the study combines desk-research with a qualitative interview-based analysis of selected 'communities of engagement' as well as place-branding policies in each island. Twenty-one semi-structured interviews have targeted two types of informants: (1) local development authorities, local tourism actors and Local Action Group (LAG) representatives; and (2) examples of translocal actors on each island in a small number of concrete 'communities of engagement'. Transcriptions and extensive notes based on interview recordings were coded in Nvivo, using both emergent and pre-defined categories.

The discussion is placed in a rural context, comparing four Nordic islands with similar regional potentials and challenges: Bornholm, Samsø and Fanø in Denmark, and Gotland in Sweden. All four islands struggle with limited education and labour market opportunities and low economic growth rates. The islands are all well-known tourism destinations with many visitors and large second-home communities. They also have active local foods and arts & crafts brands, as well as iconic natural landscapes.

STEREOTYPICAL FORMAL BRANDING MATERIALS AND ALTERNATIVE PLACE NARRATIVES

The official place-branding materials that promote the four islands for tourists display remarkable similarities. They focus on unique natural scenery, on access to sunny beaches, quality local foods, a rich cultural heritage including high quality arts & crafts and many outdoor activities for the entire family. In terms of attracting new residents, all four islands primarily target families with children. They offer a less stressful family life, a safe and active environment for children and inclusion in engaged communities.[3] Bornholm has a strong local foods brand, but also brands itself (with varying success) on other qualities under the slogan 'Bright Green Island'[4] (Hansen, 2010). Samsø's brand is very similar, with a strong emphasis on a sustainable 'good life on Samsø', simultaneously drawing on Samsø's transition into becoming a 'fully renewable energy island' while branding itself as a community strongly committed to engaging all residents in this process.[5] Fanø utilises its proximity to the provincial city of Esbjerg in branding itself as a place to live close to nature, while accessing all the amenities urban areas have to offer.[6] Gotland also brands itself on quality of life under the slogan 'Closer to life'. Gotland has been successful in attracting many affluent Stockholm residents as 'Summergotländders'. Direct access to rugged naturescapes, to 'New Nordic' local food products and Nordic cultural heritage based on a romanticised version of a frugal natural resource economy seem to be the common branding qualities – not only on the four case islands, but in many rural Nordic brands.[7] What makes these islands stand out compared to for example Northern Sweden and Norway, are their beaches and other 'southern' amenities. Yet, they have difficulty standing out from each other, and end up offering a generic rural island branding, resulting in non-distinctive brands (Andersen, Samson, & Winther, 2010).

Increasingly, alternative narratives about life on the islands are generated by local communities and translocal actors, contributing to the polyphony of voices that compete to define places (see also Ren &

---

[3]   https://bornholm.info/en/;   https://www.visitsamsoe.dk/en/;   http://visitfanoe.dk/da/home/; http://gotland.com/en/ (all accessed 12 May 2018).

[4]   http://www.brightgreenisland.dk/Sider/In-English.aspx (accessed 12 May 2018).

[5]   https://www.samsoe.dk/kommunen/flyt-til-samsoe/velkommen-til-samsoe (accessed 12 May 2018).

[6]   http://reader.livedition.dk/fanoe/158/html5/ (accessed 12 May 2018).

[7]   See for example Vesterålen (https://visitvesteralen.com/en) and East Iceland (https://www.east.is/) (accessed 12 May 2018).

Blichfeldt, 2011). The community engagement and involvement of trans-local actors contribute to brand renewal. Local firms and projects tell the story about their involvement in the local community to investors and customers. Through their successful engagement of 'outside' people and resources, they become engagement hubs, places that interconnect extra-local resources and a global outlook with the ultra-local engagement and development of the place. The relational character of this place branding gives it authenticity at first sight (Hankinson, 2004; Szondi, 2010), but depending on the degree of involvement of locals, or their agreement with the communicated image, the authenticity may be only a glossy selling point of a narrative promoted mainly by others (Aitken & Campelo, 2011; Askegaard & Kjeldgaard, 2007; Holt, 2002).

COMMUNITIES OF TRANSLOCAL ACTORS AND THEIR INVOLVEMENT IN PLACE MAKING

Our study shows that the translocal actors are not a homogenous group, although they are clearly distinguishable as a separate group of actors on the islands. Development actors and local authorities on all four islands immediately recognise translocal actors and translocal communities of engagement. Each described several local projects or events that drew upon translocal actors' resources, but also expressed a general appreciation for especially summerhouse owners, who are extremely loyal consumers of local products and function as island ambassadors. Based on our interviews, we have identified five sub-categories of translocal actors and the communities through which they engage themselves, which we present below.

The first type we have dubbed the 'translocal cultural heritage revitalisers'. They are deeply attached to a particular place and embedded in local social and cultural practices. Frequently, they have owned their summer residence over several generations, and they involve themselves in cultural heritage projects that are particular to the small towns in which their summerhouses are located. An example is from Sønderho on Fanø, where a project focuses on dredging Wadden Sea sand from the blocked Sønderho Harbour as well as reconstructing a lost sailing ship that was a renowned part of local maritime history. A core group of translocal residents, consisting of recently retired lawyers, university directors and other academics, drives the project. The translocal actors are motivated by a desire to contribute positively to local development but are also deeply attached to the qualities that define the particularity of the place. This is combined with their own personal interests – in this case, an interest in sailing and the Wadden Sea. Although received positively by the full-time residents and the municipality, cultural heritage revitalisation projects run the risk of romanticising the past and curbing development.

The second type we call 'translocal entrepreneurs', as they involve themselves in the development of local businesses. We have found examples of these on both Bornholm and Samsø, most visibly within the quality food sectors. There are essentially two types of entrepreneurial communities – one concerns translocal investment communities and the other summer lifestyle entrepreneurs. On Bornholm, a local farmer and cured meats producer has successfully engaged a translocal group in financing the creation of a local specialty meats slaughterhouse. By approaching prestigious members of different translocal communities, from visiting performing artists to renowned restaurant owners, the local entrepreneur was able to brand the shares in the company as exclusive, well-sought-after products. Engagement in this project was not only motivated by the wish to support the development of local foods, but also by investors' wish to be a part of an exclusive 'club'. The translocal lifestyle entrepreneurs – again primarily witnessed within the quality food sector – start up new businesses during the summer months in order to test their business concept. They keep their place of residence elsewhere, and are not solely interested in profit, but are drawn to the excitement of experimenting with new food products in an innovative environment. The engagement of both investors and lifestyle entrepreneurs relies profoundly on the strong food brands that are associated with both Bornholm and Samsø.

A third type consists of translocals who engage themselves in resource transition projects, be they towards more sustainable energy or food production and consumption. We call them 'translocal idealists'. Again, examples are from Samsø and Bornholm. On Samsø, a local organic farm production company has sold a large number of non-profit shares in a transition project that acquires farmlands and turns them into organic-based farms. Translocals are strongly represented among the shareholders. Likewise, the Samsø Energy Academy has sold individual shares to translocal investors in a sea-based windmill park. Both projects simultaneously draw upon and strengthen Samsø's sustainable island brand. This type of translocal actor is motivated by a desire to contribute to projects that pull 'in the right direction' and the values expressed in Samsø Energy Academy's slogan of 'communal governing of the commons', where commons are defined as the earth's resources, is an important motivator.

A fourth type we dub 'translocal place developers'. The clearest example is from Gotland, where a community of engaged local citizens strategised to develop their local town, and as part of this 'recruited' selected summerhouse owners with specific competencies networks or other resources into an exclusive working group around the Vamlingbo Rectory. This led to the establishment of a cooperative company, which has sold not-for-profit shares to a large number of full-time and part-time residents. The cooperative company has a professional board that engages translocal actors and has completely refurbished the rectory with an art gallery, a café and historical gardens, while turning two historical buildings into modern conference and exhibition facilities. These buildings are presently on sale in order to invest the profit into a new project to bring the harbour and pier back to life. These translocal actors are primarily motivated by a desire to develop vibrant and active local villages, but also the socially prestigious status of many of the summer residents in the area makes the community highly attractive to engage oneself in.

A fifth type engages in translocal communities of shared interests related to leisure time and the cultural sphere. Examples from our empirical study include the kite festival on Fanø and the Bergman film festival on Fårö, off Gotland. Here, translocal kite flying communities as well as Bergman and film 'aficionados' return year after year to practise their interests, for some as a leisure time interest, for others a life-long passion or livelihood. They are motivated by their interest in, and profound knowledge of, a specific activity around which an informal community has formed (see also Fisker, 2016). They are not anchored to the locality and do not have cause to interact with locals, yet they are often keen place ambassadors.

Although translocal actors may be driven by an affective bond to the place and a sincere wish to contribute to its positive development, their deep commitment to the projects is often not purely altruistic. Self-interest also often plays a role, whether it concerns cultural heritage or entre-preneurial projects. In several of the studied places, the translocal com-munity can be characterised as an 'elite', a highly resourceful community where access cannot be bought, but is gained through a combination of social status, and level of engagement. The members gain status through a complex internal social positioning process. Recognition within these groups seems to be an important driver. The implication, as seen from a local development perspective, is that these resources cannot be harnessed from outside – for example by local governance actors.

TRANSLOCAL ACTORS: RURAL DEVELOPMENT POTENTIALS AND CHALLENGES

Overall, our empirical findings show important development potentials based on the engagement of translocal actors and their application of diverse resources in local development projects. Some of the projects mentioned above, like the Sønderho Harbour project, would not have been instigated without the initiative of translocal actors. Others relied on financial capital invested by translocal actors, like the Bornholm slaughterhouse and the sustainable farming project on Samsø. Still others would not have had the scope and the scale that they have, such as the Vamlingbo Rectory project, without the aid of project participants with professional leadership experience, management backgrounds and access to capital funding.

However, the engagement of translocal actors in local development also has more indirect and subtle effects that influence both place-making processes and brand development. When development projects are widely recognised by the local population as relevant and important, translocal actors' project participation has the potential to create new and alternative narratives about the place. When 'outsiders' choose to engage themselves in local development projects, the value of the place is re-assessed and can potentially shift from a narrative of decline into much more positive and complex place understandings (see also Hansen, 2010). Employing progressive nostalgia, the cultural heritage projects simultaneously refurbish and renew local landmarks and buildings, taking place in collaboration between full-time local residents and translocal actors, thereby forming important co-creative arenas for place making and branding (Aitken & Campelo, 2011; Braun et al., 2013; Giovanardi et al., 2014; Kavaratzis, 2012; Kavaratzis & Kalandides, 2015; Lichrou, O'Malley, & Patterson, 2010).

Additionally, collaboration between locals and translocals through engagement in entrepreneurial projects can create new translocal communities. Contributions to the Bornholm slaughterhouse were partly motivated by participants' positioning themselves socially in relation to each other not only among local and translocal communities tied to Bornholm, but also related to social positions within entrepreneurial and artistic communities in Copenhagen. In this way, the translocal engagement geographies are multi-scalar (in the sense of Brickell & Datta, 2011). This function of 'transcending scale' (Smith, 1992) is visible in all community types described above. Translocal actors often use themselves as 'interconnectors' between the rural place they feel attached to and wider networks beyond (Gallent, 2014; Müller & Hall, 2003; Rye, 2011). Furthermore, projects may function as gateways for translocal actors to become part of a community.

Another important contribution by translocal communities of engagement relates to self-governance or engagement forms. This is most clearly visible in the group we dub 'translocal idealists', but is also an integral part of the place development project in Vamlingbo on Gotland. Several interviewees expressed that they saw a connection between investment, ownership (of shares), trust and engagement. This may be perceived as a type of 'Capitalism 2.0', with roots in the Nordic tradition of cooperatives, where collective ownership generates engagement, and where formal opportunity to influence democratic processes is equally distributed between members, independent of their economic resources. The cooperative organisation defines the relation between actors, and both *requires* and *fosters* long-term commitment and reciprocity. An important aspect of this is that such communities should not be perceived to be local or exclusive. Their core characteristics of collectiveness must essentially be inclusive and open, rendering them multi-scalar and multi-local.

Overall, these communities of engagement challenge the conceptualisation that part-time visitors are just consumers of rural places, as suggested by Scott's characterisation of rural districts as mere 'recreational landscapes' (Scott, 2010) for urban residents. Instead, we can conceptualise these engaged communities as producers and co-producers of rural places through their contributions to local heritage projects, entrepreneurial businesses – not only as new sites of transformative resource use, but also offering new sites of innovative communities of commons governance (see also Giovanardi, 2012; and Lichrou et al., 2010 for similar arguments in non-rural settings).

A striking feature about the involvement of translocal actors is that their engagement tends to be anchored in specific locations. Namely, they do not engage in general development projects targeting the entire island. Rather, they engage in specific thematic projects, place-bound and thereby localised, resulting in uneven geographies of engagement (Back & Marjavaara, 2017). Yet, as translocal engagement is by definition multi-scalar (Brickell & Datta, 2011), the relational branding effect of even highly localised projects can be valuable, both socially and spatially.

LOCAL GOVERNANCE OF TRANSLOCAL ENGAGEMENT?

Across all four islands, our interviews with planning and branding authorities showed that, although the local development planners immediately recognise translocal actors, they do not address them directly in any planning or branding processes. Local governments seem to suffer from a 'blind spot' concerning the translocal actors, as they have a hard time spotting them in more systematic ways. Translocal actors can thus be characterised as an 'invisible population' (Back & Marjavaara, 2017). They are statistically invisible, as they hardly figure in any register data, beyond possibly as second home owners (Back & Marjavaara, 2017; Müller, 2011), a consequence of the administrative practices allowing only for one place of residence (Müller & Hall, 2003). According to Müller (2011, p. 140), this administrative practice leads to 'systematic disadvantages for rural communities' due to the foregone (income) tax revenues to which the second home owners could otherwise contribute.

However, the presence and agency of translocal actors have implications for branding through alternative place-branding platforms, such as private or community-initiated book projects or TV programmes, or the use of localities of the islands in private firm branding materials. The translocals both build on and develop the place brand, simultaneously consuming and producing place images (Pasquinelli, 2015). However, the translocal actors are neither represented, or taken into account in local government's place-branding processes due to their lack of resident status (Braun et al., 2013). Yet, as we have shown, they are highly resourceful actors – culturally, socially and not least financially – offering network resources that extend across multiple localities, often at high levels of society, whether politically, economically or in specific niche professions. As stakeholders, they participate strongly in place making and, according to Kavaratzis (2012), their role should be considered in a participatory place branding.

Translocal communities of engagement are not without challenges. While contributing with place-making resources to rural areas, the agency of translocal communities also raises questions about the right to define places, particularly between interests in conserving a perceived 'authentic' or static version of a place vis-à-vis change (Zwiers, Markantoni, & Strijker, 2016). Place-branding processes are also an arena for contestation of place and what 'the good island life' is, we argue.

In a critical light, translocal place-producing activities may be understood as gentrification processes, threatening to displace less resourceful residents (Slater, 2009). According to Ronström (2013), this goes on in Visby on Gotland, which is becoming a 'playground' for the rich. Perhaps we can develop the concept of gentrification and talk about *creatification* by conceptualising Florida's (2004) creative class as moving out to engaged communities on certain islands during the weekends and 'playing' with likeminded (both local and non-local) friends in a non-committal environment, while displacing a number of non-invited locals in the process.

As mentioned, many translocal actors are very resourceful: They are highly educated and connected with both public and private decision-makers. It may be potentially challenging for rural civil servants to meet them at eye level. It is relevant for planning authorities to consider issues of unequal power in cases where local, potentially less articulated place-making initiatives come into competition with these new actors. In our interviews with local government representatives, translocal actors are highly appreciated for their engagement in and contribution to local development causes. At the same time, the local governments see themselves as having a primarily symbolic supportive function in these projects and are hesitant to consider regulatory measures, lacking critical reflection on potential gentrification or displacement challenges. Yet, we argue that translocal community engagement processes call for particular attention to power asymmetries in contestations, negotiations and definitions of what 'desired' places are (Kalandides, 2011; Milbourne, 2007; Rockenbauch & Sakdapolrak, 2017).[8]

CONCLUSION

Translocal actors shape rural development and place-branding processes in the four studied Nordic islands by contributing in differentiated ways to place-based development projects. In some cases, the agency is instigated by the translocal actors, whereas at other times, the translocal community becomes engaged in response to an invitation from local entrepreneurs or other community members. The translocal actors contribute as 'connectors' between the local community and multiple places and actors, thus transcending scales of engagement. They also contribute with social remittances through knowledge, networks and finance, among other resources. Multi-local attachments seem strong and are thus an important part of the motivation behind many translocals' vibrant engagement. The translocal actors contribute to branding and brand renewal vis-à-vis the official brand strategies that all look very similar.

An entrepreneurial local government is fundamental for receiving and engaging translocal actors and their resources, as our examples have found. However, we found no examples of local governments actively involving or shaping translocal resource engagement, probably as a consequence of the 'statistically' invisibility of the population of translocal actors. However, the resourcefulness and agency of some translocal actors may highlight the need for local governments' attention to power inequalities, as these may lead to *creatification* and displacement. We question whether the local governments' passive appreciation expresses a fear of

---

[8] Rye (2011) interestingly found a strong heterogeneity in rural locals' view on second home developments in Norway, with the most positive attitudes among the local elite, as well as among people who had friends or acquaintances among the second homers.

inhibiting translocals' enthusiasm, or whether local governments experience translocals' engagement potentials as 'a 'giant' that must be governed lightly' (Rantanen, 2018, p. 8).

Acknowledgement of the presence and influence of translocal actors urges an adjustment of place-branding frameworks to embrace this group of 'interconnectors' between residents and visitors; realising that the resident–visitor dichotomy used in place brand policies – and studies – is too simplistic, considering contemporary (rural) mobility patterns, spatially and temporally. Understanding rural places as part of local, regional, national and global processes of community engagement opens up multiscalar and dynamic understandings of rural places and their resources. We argue that this is an often neglected, but necessary, approach to the study of processes of change and branding in rural places (see Kalandides, 2011 for a similar argument in an urban setting). Based on our pilot study, we see a need to explore alternatives to the current administrative practice of limiting residence to one place, thereby creating a dwelling hierarchy, which systematically places the rural municipalities at a disadvantage, as argued by Müller (2011). We recommend further exploration of the complex relationship between residency dichotomies, tax issues, lack of visibility vis-à-vis governance systems and translocals' opportunities for participation – as (part-time) residents with both rights and obligations.

REFERENCES

Adey, P. (2006). If mobility is everything then it is nothing: Towards a relational politics of (im)mobilities. *Mobilities*, *1*(1), 75–94. https://doi.org/10.1080/17450100500489080.

Agergaard, J., & Broegger, D. (2016). Returning home: Migrant connections and visions for local development in rural Nepal. *Geografisk Tidsskrift – Danish Journal of Geography*, *116*(1), 71–81.

Aitken, R., & Campelo, A. (2011). The four rs of place branding. *Journal of Marketing Management*, *27*(9–10), 913–933.

Andersen, H. T., Samson, J., & Winther, L. (2010). Kunsten at sælge et sted – stedsidentitet og branding. *Samfundsøkonomen*, *2010*(6), 28–32.

Askegaard, S., & Kjeldgaard, D. (2007). Here, there, and everywhere: Place branding and gastronomical globalization in a macromarketing perspective. *Journal of Macromarketing*, *27*(2), 138–147.

Back, A., & Marjavaara, R. (2017). Mapping an invisible population: The uneven geography of second-home tourism. *Tourism Geographies*, *19*(4), 595–611.

Braun, E., Kavaratzis, M., & Zenker, S. (2013). My city – my brand: The different roles of residents in place branding. *Journal of Place Management and Development*, *6*(1), 18–28.

Brickell, K., & Datta, A. (2011). *Translocal geographies: Spaces, places, connections*. Farnham: Ashgate Publishing.

De Haas, H. (2010). Migration and development: A theoretical perspective. *International Migration Review*, 44(1), 227–264.

Farstad, M. (2013). Local residents' valuation of second home owners' presence in a sparsely inhabited area. *Scandinavian Journal of Hospitality and Tourism*, 13(4), 317–331.

Farstad, M. (2016). Worthy of recognition? How second home owners understand their own group's moral worth in rural host communities. *Sociologia Ruralis*, 56(3), 408–426.

Fisker, J. K. (2016). *Interessebaserede fællesskaber som grundlag for FRITIDSKLYNGER*. Esbjerg: Danish Centre for Rural Research (CLF), University of Southern Denmark.

Florida, R. (2004). *The rise of the creative class: And how it's transforming work, leisure, community and everyday life*. New York: Basic Books.

Gallent, N. (2014). The social value of second homes in rural communities. *Housing, Theory and Society*, 31(2), 174–191.

Gallent, N. (2015). Bridging social capital and the resource potential of second homes: The case of Stintino, Sardinia. *Journal of Rural Studies*, 38, 99–108.

Gielis, R. (2009). A global sense of migrant places: Towards a place perspective in the study of migrant transnationalism. *Global Networks*, 9(2), 271–287.

Giovanardi, M. (2012). Haft and sord factors in place branding: Between functionalism and representationalism. *Place Branding and Public Diplomacy*, 8(1), 30–45.

Giovanardi, M., Lucarelli, A., & Decosta, P. L. E. (2014). Co-performing tourism places: The 'Pink Night' festival. *Annals of Tourism Research*, 44(1), 102–115.

Greiner, C., & Sakdapolrak, P. (2013). Translocality: Concepts, applications and emerging research perspectives. *Geography Compass*, 7(5), 373–384.

Halfacree, K. (2012). Heterolocal identities? Counter-urbanisation, second homes, and rural consumption in the era of mobilities. *Population, Space and Place*, 18(2), 209–224.

Hankinson, G. (2004). Relational network brands: Towards a conceptual model of place brands. *Journal of Vacation Marketing*, 10(2), 109–121.

Hansen, R. H. (2010). The narrative nature of place branding. *Place Branding and Public Diplomacy*, 6(4), 268–279.

Holt, D. B. (2002). Why do brands cause trouble? A dialectical theory of consumer culture and branding. *Journal of Consumer Research*, 29(1), 70–90.

Kalandides, A. (2011). The problem with spatial identity: Revisiting the 'sense of place'. *Journal of Place Management and Development*, 4(1), 28–39.

Kavaratzis, M. (2012). From 'necessary evil' to necessity: Stakeholders' involvement in place branding. *Journal of Place Management and Development*, 5(1), 7–19.

Kavaratzis, M., & Kalandides, A. (2015). Rethinking the place brand: The interactive formation of place brands and the role of participatory place branding. *Environment and Planning A*, 47(6), 1368–1382.

Lichrou, M., O'Malley, L., & Patterson, M. (2010). Narratives of a tourism destination: Local particularities and their implications for place marketing and branding. *Place Branding and Public Diplomacy*, 6(2), 134–144.

Massey, D. (1994). A global sense of place. In D. Massey (Ed.), *Space, place and gender* (pp. 146–156). Cambridge: Polity Press.

Massey, D. (2005). The event of place. In D. Massey (Ed.), *For space* (2005 ed., pp. 138–142). London: Sage.

Milbourne, P. (2007). Re-populating rural studies: Migrations, movements and mobilities. *Journal of Rural Studies*, *23*(3), 381–386. https://doi.org/10.1016/j.jrurstud.2007.04.002.

Milbourne, P., & Kitchen, L. (2014). Rural mobilities: Connecting movement and fixity in rural places. *Journal of Rural Studies*, *34*, 326–336.

Müller, D. K. (2011). Second homes in rural areas: Reflections on a troubled history. *Norsk Geografisk Tidsskrift – Norwegian Journal of Geography*, *65*(3), 137–143.

Müller, D. K., & Hall, C. M. (2003). Second homes and regional population distribution: On administrative practices and failures in Sweden. *Espace, Populations, Sociétés*, *2*, 251–261.

Oliveira, J., Roca, Z., & Leitão, N. (2010). Territorial identity and development: From topophilia to terraphilia. *Land Use Policy*, *27*(3), 801–814.

Pasquinelli, C. (2015). City branding and local SME: A smart specialisation perspective. *Symphonya. Emerging Issues in Management*, *1*, 64–77.

Rantanen, M. (2018). Controversial expectations for the roles of multiple dwellers in local development. Unpublished Paper. Presented at the 5th Nordic Rural Research Conference: Challenged Ruralities: Welfare States Under Pressure. Vingsted, 14–16 May 2018. Ruralia Institute, University of Helsinki.

Ren, C., & Blichfeldt, B. S. (2011). One clear image? Challenging simplicity in place branding. *Scandinavian Journal of Hospitality and Tourism*, *11*(4), 416–434.

Rockenbauch, T., & Sakdapolrak, P. (2017). Social networks and the resilience of rural communities in the Global South. *Ecology and Society*, *22*(1), art.10.

Ronström, O. (2013). Gute, gotlänning, fastlänning, svensk. Etonymer och social kategorisering på Gotland. *Tidskrift för kulturforskning*, *12*(2), 39–53.

Rye, J. F. (2011). Conflicts and contestations. Rural populations' perspectives on the second homes phenomenon. *Journal of Rural Studies*, *27*(3), 263–274.

Scott, A. J. (2010). The cultural economy of landscape and prospects for peripheral development in the twenty-first century: The case of the English Lake District. *European Planning Studies*, *18*(10), 1567–1589.

Slater, T. (2009). Missing marcuse: On gentrification and displacement. *City*, *13*(2–3), 292–311.

Smith, N. (1992). Contours of a spatialized politics: Homeless vehicles and the production of geographical scale. *Social Text*, *33*, 55–81.

Sørensen, N. N. (2012). Revisiting the migration–development nexus: From social networks and remittances to markets of migration control. *International Migration*, *50*, 60–75.

Szondi, G. (2010). From image management to relationship building: A public relations approach to nation branding. *Place Branding and Public Diplomacy*, *6*(4), 333–343.

Uriely, N. (2005). The tourist experience: Conceptual developments. *Annals of Tourism Research*, *32*(1), 199–216.

Zwiers, S., Markantoni, M., & Strijker, D. (2016). The role of change- and stability-oriented place attachment in rural community resilience: A case study in south-west Scotland. *Community Development Journal*, *53*(2), 281–300.

10. THE PRISON: from liability to asset in branding of the Danish city Horsens

Ole Have Jørgensen

INTRODUCTION

When the author moved to the Danish city of Horsens many years ago, a colleague of his wife working in another city asked: "How do you dare move to Horsens with all the crime?" The image of Horsens (90,000 inhabitants in the municipality, budget 950 million euro) was for years dominated by Horsens State Prison, in operation between 1853 and 2006 (Jørgensen 2014). The prison may be described as a non-iconic signature institution with a 20,000 square meter complex of buildings, situated in a 12 hectare fenced area on a small hill on the outskirts of Horsens. Horsens was earlier perceived as violent and criminal, described in the media as the "Chicago of the North" and "The City of Fear" (Jørgensen 2017), and, as the quote above illustrates, this perception still lingers among Danes. All of this in spite of the fact that the local crime rate was documented as being lower than in comparable sized cities (Jørgensen 2005), and all prisoners left the prison in 2006.

The abandoned buildings give home to a collection of 15,000 prison and prisoner artifacts (the largest collection of its kind in the world), which was seen as a potential foundation for a prison museum. After a period of significant political and local discussion and resistance to municipal involvement, the city council finally decided to purchase the empty institution from the state in 2015 and turned it into a flagship project named THE PRISON. At the present stage THE PRISON entails different business areas: the Prison Museum (owned and run by the city), events (where THE PRISON serves as venue), landlord for an incubator house for small and medium-sized enterprises (SMEs) and entrepreneurs, SleepIn (a hostel), and meetings and conferences. Since 2012 THE PRISON has had between 60,000 and 160,000 annual visitors, (excluding the Prison Museum with a total of 280,000 visitors from 2012 to 2017).

A number of old and non-operational prisons all over the world have been converted to condominiums, hotels, museums and tourist sites (Taylor 1994, Strange and Kempa 2003, Wilson 2008, Flynn 2011, Swensen 2014), and prison tourism has become a popular tourist experience in a number of countries (Walby and Piché 2011, Wilson 2004, Hartmann 2014, Swensen 2014, Barton and Brown 2015). Such contested heritage sites may be associated with a negative or predominantly negative image (as illustrated in Horsens) that may affect citizen attitudes toward the place. There is ample research on branding strategies to restore negative place image (Gertner and Kotler 2004, Baker 2007, Avraham 2013), and Avraham (2014) has even conceptualized various approaches of turning a place's liability into an asset. Yet, these processes are not described in a longitudinal manner and little is known about situated practices of regeneration interventions, where a contested local feature constitutes the center of the re-imagineering.

The aim of this study is to present an empirical case of Nordic local place branding and heritage governance in a development context. The chapter chronicles the image regeneration of Horsens throughout the past decade and analyzes the factors influencing the political decisions behind the acquisition of the prison. The first section describes the image transformation based on a longer time series of data showing the stability in cognitive evaluation of the prison element in the city image, while the affective evaluation is changed during the regeneration process. Key information sources for this process are discussed. The second section focuses on the political navigation through local dispute and conflict up until a final decision to turn the prison into a flagship project. The analysis is based on data derived from the municipality's annual Top of Mind Awareness Analyses (TOMA), information from the city's administration, local media monitoring data, citizen surveys in relation to the prison, and semi-structured interviews with THE PRISON's CEO and the chairman of the board.

THE IMAGE TRANSFORMATIONS OF HORSENS

Horsens has conducted aided TOMA analysis annually since 1997 (missing out 1998, 1999 and 2006). This analysis is based on telephone interviews with 500 citizens representative of the national population in age, gender and geography but all living outside Horsens. The annual TOMA is reported to the council and published and commented upon by the mayor in the local media. Figure 10.1 depicts the 'prison' response in the annual TOMA since 2000 illustrating how people living outside

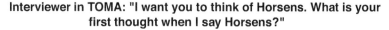

Interviewer in TOMA: "I want you to think of Horsens. What is your first thought when I say Horsens?"

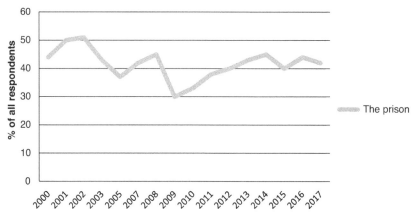

Notes: This figure illustrates how people living outside Horsens still remember the prison despite the fact that the last prisoner left in 2006.
Annual sample size is 500 with minor variation between years. The 95 percent confidence interval on annual numbers is +/– 4.2. In short this illustrates how cognitive evaluation may be stable over a long period of time.

Figure 10.1   The "prison" response in the annual aided TOMA since 2000

Horsens still remember the prison despite the fact that the last prisoner left in 2006, supporting the point made by Fakeye and Crompton (1991, p. 12) that "An image, whether positive or negative, may continue long after the factors that molded it have changed." There is some variation between years but, since the 95 percent confidence interval on annual figures is +/– 4.2, it is difficult to draw a final conclusion on statistical changes over time from Figure 10.1. From 2010 all respondents who mentioned the prison were then asked: "You have answered that you think of the prison. Is this in a positive or a negative sense?" Table 10.1 also shows that there is a major change in citizens' attitude to the prison. Over the period citizens' perceptions have grown significantly positive, while the share of neutral/don't know shows a significant decline. The proportion of negative attitudes is statistically unchanged over the period. The change in affective evaluation of the prison (Table 10.1) has had significant influence on politicians' later decision to buy the prison.

The image source analyses of 2016 and 2018 kindly provided by THE PRISON's management provide some indications about how people know THE PRISON and its experience offerings. Analyses are based on elaborate questionnaires using the Analyse Danmark online DK-panel

Table 10.1   Aided TOMA analysis among people living outside Horsens

Based on responses about the prison, see Figure 10.1, the interviewer continued: "You have answered the prison, is this negative or positive?" Percentage responses in each category, 95 percent confidence interval max. +/− 5.5

Year	2010	2011	2012	2013	2014	2015	2016	2017
Positive	23	36	44	53	52	56	49	60
Negative	16	11	14	9	11	9	13	13
Don't know/neutral	60	53	41	37	37	35	38	27

Note: The growth in "positive" and the decline in "negative/don't know" are both statistically significant at p less than 0.0001. In short this illustrates the change in affective evaluation over time.

with 30,000 citizens. Responses were collected from a web panel including 1026/1004 (2016 and 2018 respectively) representatively selected respondents at national level and 1043/1011 representatively selected respondents from the eastern part of Jutland at regional level. The results are weighted according to gender, age, municipality and region to match Statistic Denmark's relative national distribution intending to give a representative picture of the population in Denmark (5.7 million) and in the region (1.3 million).

As seen from Table 10.2, there are three main sources of citizens' knowledge about THE PRISON, both nationally and regionally: "From friends who have visited prison", "from television" and "from the press". Social media and web image sources are getting surprisingly few responses bearing in mind that all respondents are members of an online panel. Besides, there seems to be a regional as well as national development where influence from friends is increasing while influence from especially the newspapers and printed media is decreasing. Geographical proximity conditions a higher knowledge of the museum and previous participation in events.

Image Impact Factors

Boisen et al. (2017) refer to the task of place branding as reputation management, while Cleave and Arku (2017) point to the awareness of a place brand and that it needs to create a positive image in the minds of those the brand interacts with to create a strong sense of place. It is generally accepted that perceived place image is formed by two distinctly different but hierarchically interrelated components, the cognitive and the affective

Table 10.2   Data from "Familiarity Analysis" 2016 and 2018

Question: Do you know that Horsens State Prison is closed down as a prison and today is used as a culture, conference and event venue named THE PRISON?	National response, 2016/2018 in % of total number of respondents	Regional response, 2016/2018 in % of total number of regional respondents
	77/83*	95/96
From above followed by:	National respondents	Regional respondents
How did you learn about THE PRISON?	2016/2018 in % of total respondents	2016/2018 in % of total respondents
From friends who have visited "The Prison"	31/36*	38/42*
From TV	37/36	32/29
From printed press and newspapers	37/29*	33/28*
I know "The Prison" because of the museum	14/18*	26/31*
From postings on Facebook including shared or sponsored postings	14/14	13/16
I have been to a concert at "The Prison"	11/11	14/16
I have been to a cultural event at "The Prison"	6/8	15/18
From a search on the internet	12/12	10/12
I have been to a meeting or a conference	2/2	4/4
I know people working at "The Prison"	4/1	4/4
Something else	9/8	8/6
Don't remember	5/5	3/4

Notes: Responses to the general question about knowledge of THE PRISON followed by responses to the close end multiple choice question: "How did you learn about THE PRISON?" National respondents (*n* = 1026/1004) and regional respondents (*n* = 1043/1011).
* Indicates a statistically significant difference (95 percent probability) between years.

component (Baloglu and McCleary 1999). Cognitive evaluation refers to beliefs or knowledge about place attributes, the brand awareness, whereas affective evaluation refers to feelings toward or attachment to the place, the brand image. Image and reputation are influenced through several channels of image formation agents (Gartner 1993) and it is believed that actual visitation creates an image more realistic than the image existing prior to visitation (Gunn 1972). In addition, the so-called solicited and unsolicited organic images are the stories that people share with each other either face-to-face or, increasingly, online on request or spontaneously (Tasci and Gartner 2007). While satisfied tourists are more likely to recommend a destination to others (see further references in Prayag et al. 2017), dissatisfied tourists are likely to engage in negative word-of-mouth (Chen and Chen 2010).

There are very few examples of time series data that illustrate image change over time but in her study on the European Capital of Culture culture-led regeneration of Glasgow and Liverpool Garcia (2017, p. 3183) has made an in-depth media content analysis of three decades of press data. The findings led her to the assumption that "Evidenceable and sustained change in media representations of place can be taken as tantamount to image change", but she found little evidence of a long-term sustained image change.

The present case illustrates a situation where the cognitive component, the awareness, is stable at a high level (see Figure 10.1), but the affective component, the image, has changed over time. The negative response remains at the same level, the indifferent response is reduced significantly and the number of positive respondents is growing significantly. The prison-part of the city's brand has been changed and the most natural explanation would be that people already knowing the prison, are informed about the new activities from one or several information sources. But this question was never posed to the respondents in TOMA. Instead the two Familiarity Analyses (see Table 10.2) may be consulted. These surveys reflect statistically representative samples of the national (and regional) population, and may be used to deduce the key sources of information leading to the changed attitude to the prison (and consequently to the city).

The change from prison to cultural conference and event venue is nationally well known and regionally extremely well known (see Table 10.2). Three main sources of this information dominate in both measurements at the same level and are markedly higher than all other sources: "Information from friends who have visited THE PRISON", "TV", and "Printed press/newspapers".

The first source illustrates the importance of word-of-mouth (and mouse), the solicited and unsolicited organic images, the stories people share with each other (Gartner 1993). Del Bosque and Martin (2008) showed that affective images influence word-of-mouth as an outcome of brand loyalty to a destination suggesting a direct connection between affective image and word-of-mouth which might be supported by the Horsens case. The Prison Museum in a prison, metal music and the annual Medieval Festival are all well synchronized with a prison atmosphere leaning against "dark tourism", and appeal to cognitive as well as affective senses with potential photo and sound opportunities to be distributed on social media. THE PRISON pays attention to elaborate storytelling and untraditional initiatives to achieve editorial attention instead of spending money on traditional marketing and communication, according to Henning Nørbæk and Astrid Søes Poulsen. They also pointed to situations where THE PRISON is a venue and where the organizers of the event in question are responsible for marketing the event. Thus, a large part of the information from TV and printed press/newspapers originates from the event organizers. Even though the media monitoring may be inadequate at the moment, the analysis above shows how significant events (concerts) as well as permanent offers (the museum) are significant contributors to the overall media coverage, but also that there are a large number of other sources.

TV, printed press and newspapers play an equally important role originating from secondary communication from THE PRISON or the event managers taking advantage of the high national level of knowledge of the venue. It is a well-known fact that newspaper circulation is diminishing (national and regional newspaper circulation dropped 42 percent from 2005 to 2015 in Denmark (Albrecht 2015)) and the drop continues. TV is also an important secondary communication where the visual identity of THE PRISON is repeated again and again.

At a reasonably lower level we find knowledge of the Prison Museum and the organic images from visits and personal participation in concerts and other cultural events are more important as a regional than as a national information source which is understandable because of the distance. Shared or sponsored postings on Facebook and searching on the internet indicate a surprisingly low impact from these sources.

Monitoring Impact

Examples of documented systematic impact monitoring are scarce in spite of the findings of Anselmsson and Bondesson (2013, p. 1615), where "The systematic monitoring and follow-up of brand performance separate high-performing brands from their low-performing counterparts". Klijn et al. (2012, p. 505) analyzed data from 274 Dutch respondents involved in city marketing, but the study did not measure "hard" objective effects. The evidence of how flagship projects and major cultural projects contribute to a range of regeneration projects is also limited (Evans 2005). Bell and Jayne (2006), Richards and Palmer (2010) and Smith (2012) mention no examples of well-documented brand impacts in relation to events and urban regeneration. The European Capital of Culture (ECoC) program is often seen as a leading example of culture-led regeneration intervention of host cities, but little evidence has been gathered to determine long-term sustained image change in these cities (Garcia 2017). In his study on actual campaign components and marketing initiatives used for "turning a place's liability into an asset", Avraham (2014, p. 1356) emphasizes that his study is pure content analysis research and "there is no way to know if the use of this strategy was successful or not". In their meta-analysis of quantifying the effectiveness of place branding, Cleave and Arku (2017) mention a number of potential measurement strategies but report no time series and do not refer to any examples of quantitative documentation of a qualitative affective evaluation. On the other hand, Jørgensen (2014) illustrated how the Danish city Horsens, through a systematic effort with regard to concerts and cultural events has changed its image so that about 50 percent of the citizens of the country today connect the city's name with concerts and cultural events (compared to 2 percent when the project started in 2000).

A CONTESTED RE-IMAGINEERING PROCESS: NORDIC BRAND GOVERNANCE PRACTICES

In a recent review of place branding and urban policy cases across Europe, Lucarelli (2018) identifies two different governance approaches: (i) Branding embedded in a participatory process where citizens are seen as co-owners (Dutch cases, Eshuis and Edwards 2013); and (ii) a more performative view where the brand regeneration process always is a matter of power and politics (Swedish cases, Lucarelli and Hallin 2017, Danish cases, Jørgensen 2015, Lundholt et al. forthcoming). A third, comparative aspect (fundamental national differences in government structures) has barely been touched upon, as mentioned by Braun et al. (2017). They found that German and Dutch assessments of conflicts among brand stakeholders vary and suggested that fundamental international differences in regional and local political structure and culture may be of significant importance when governance approaches to branding are discussed.

The present case addresses this empirical flaw and puts it into perspective in the light of the Nordic model of local governance. A number of books and papers have commented upon and analyzed the Scandinavian or, as later expressed, "The Nordic" model, including recent books like Knutsen (2017), Bendixen et al. (2018) and Witoszek and Midttun (2018). The local political leadership in the Nordic countries has a strong tradition of a consensual, corporatist style of decision making (Goldsmith and Larsen

2004), recently described by Pedersen and Kuhnle (2017) as consensual governance or by Knutsen (2017) as decentralized co-operative governance. In a specific Danish context Klausen (2009) sees the city council as a shareholder in the city's development on behalf of the citizen, and Jørgensen (2015) has illustrated how Danish city branding projects are managed by communication officers with direct access to and sometimes sitting next door to the mayor and/or the city manager. Nine out of 25 cities in his study had experience with aborted branding projects due to a change in political leadership, political conflicts and/or a general loss of political support. A study of intra-organizational counter-narratives in Danish city branding (Lundholt et al. (forthcoming)) found that mayors are aware of the need for continued political support for branding projects, but projects are nonetheless realized in spite of resistance if there is political support to them.

The council and the citizens of Horsens were very concerned about the future of the old prison. The council saw housing potential in the open space around the prison but had no interest in getting involved with the significant building stock. Eventually this view changed over time and was influenced by a number of factors. In 2006 the city's public relations (PR) group (financed by the council and working from city hall) proposed to transform the old prison into an attraction named "World of Crime" where the collection of prison and prisoner artifacts and the high national level of knowledge could be the setting for a potential and unique flagship project for the city (interview with Henning Nørbæk, at the time chairman of the city's PR group, now chairman of the board of THE PRISON Foundation). In contrast to the "World of Crime", the editor of the local liberal newspaper argued in 2007 for dismantling the prison to bring an end to the prison image. Also in 2007 the newspaper carried out a survey among citizens from Horsens, where 77 percent supported the idea of an attraction like "World of Crime", while only 12 percent were against it. But the idea of "World of Crime" triggered at least 79 different letters to the editor over the years 2006–2011: 61 were critical of any future use of the prison while 18 were positive and supported ideas for how the prison could be developed as an attraction. Thirty-one of the critical letters were written by the same person and when he passed away in 2010 the overall production of letters ended. Interviews in the newspaper with ten different council members in 2010 revealed that there was no political agreement about the prison's future, and some argued that the city should in no way be involved in any project. The controversial concept "World of Crime" was officially abandoned in 2008 because it could be seen as a "Tivolization" or "Disneyfication" of the prisoners as well as their victims.

Due to the financial crisis the sale project failed in 2008 and, in the limbo that followed, the council accepted and partly financed continued work by the city's PR group to develop potential project ideas in an iterative process similar to skunk work, well known in organizational theory as an "enriched environment that is intended to help a small group of individuals design a new idea by escaping routine organizational procedures" (Rogers 2003, p. 10). The present chairman of the board, Henning Nørbæk, was responsible for the process and activities with full support from the mayor even though the mayor himself was very skeptical about the potential. The prison was then opened for visitor groups and different activities to make local citizens acquainted with the place and to adjust their traditional pre-understanding. This method had been used successfully by the council some years before when the city financed a new arena for sports and events. At that time there were local protests, but, as literally thousands of citizens were taken through the building site and the unfinished constructions to create a form of sense making (Weick 1995) for the future perspective, many developed into ambassadors for the arena (personal observation by the author who served as city manager in Horsens at the time). In cooperation with the property owner (the state company Freja Ejendomme A/S), small companies were invited in as tenants, the museum concept was developed and the process stepped up in the autumn of 2011 (as illustrated in the budgetary agreement for 2012). Horsens had in cooperation with Copenhagen won the prestigious tender to host part of the Danish Presidency of the Council of the European Union in 2012, 40,000 tickets were sold for a Metallica concert at the prison in the summer of 2012 and Horsens hosted the third stage of the Giro d'Italia 2012. A well-known strategy for urban revitalization is to organize different types of events (Richards and Palmer 2010, Smith 2012) and this strategy had been used successfully in Horsens since 2000 (Jørgensen 2014). The three abovementioned initiatives were in a planning phase in 2011 and inevitably produced an open window for investments. Especially the Metallica concert within the prison walls opened local eyes to the potential of the buildings and structures. Eventually a large majority of the city council decided to see the prison as the key to a future focus on tourism and events and to work with the state owner to open the prison, including the Prison Museum in 2012. During budget negotiations in the autumn of 2011 1 million euros was set aside for necessary structural changes, and the council decided to establish a commercial foundation "Fonden FÆNGSLET" (THE PRISON Foundation) with a long-term perspective to develop a sustainable private company. In 2013 the annual Medieval Festival was moved from the city center to the prison and, in the autumn of 2014, the council almost unanimously decided to buy the buildings and the land for nearly 4 million euros and hand the buildings over to the commercial foundation FÆNGSLET. The initial focus on housing potential survives and still serves as a fallback position, securing the city's investment if THE PRISON project fails in the long run.

The political process and decisions behind initiatives of this character are hardly dealt with in literature. In Horsens the city council played a crucial role moving from positive, dubious or critical and negative atti- tudes to any municipal involvement at the beginning of the process in 2006 to see the future potential of the prison and to reach a unanimous decision to buy the prison in 2014. The first key decision was quickly to abandon the "World of Crime" concept, and it was also essential that the council, in spite of the political differences of opinion, accepted civil servant skunk work going on for years at a time full of uncertainty. As such, the process illustrates the Nordic model for consensual governance (Pedersen and Kuhnle 2017) at work.

The first and very successful initiative in the skunk work was to open the prison for visitor groups and organize different smaller activities to make them ambassadors for the potential of the prison. Another important ini- tiative was the lasting interest in creating a prison museum using the objects from the prison. These activities can all be described as an important "pre- branding" exploratory phase, targeting local citizens and potential custom- ers. Timing was also crucial. Preparations for large events may represent an open window of opportunity for other activities in the political sphere – and can be very efficiently used, but are usually very difficult to plan for. Undoubtedly the routinely collected data from TOMA where the positive affective evaluation of the prison increased over time (Table 10.1) and a growing number of visitors developed a data-driven reciprocity between project and council. Finally, this study illustrates that turning a liability into an asset may be a long-term project, in this case an eight-year project, where the first results documented by data showed up after five years.

CONCLUSION

This case represents a brand governance situation where the citizens as well as the politicians are well aware of the problem (the negative image effect of the prison) but disagree on solutions. At the end of the day it is the local consensual democracy within the council that decide, with or without citizens' acceptance, supporting the view of Lucarelli and Hallin (2017) and Lundholt et al. (forthcoming). THE PRISON is a dominant element of the brand of Horsens among local citizens as well as in the outside world, and this element has now changed from a liability into an asset. The change was brought about in a number of steps including "Nordic-style" consensual governance by the city council, a "pre-branding" explorative process to build local support, skunk work on content, timing, systematic documentation – and time. The case illustrates the importance of a branding process involving communication on all available media platforms. Still, it should be borne in mind that the data in this case represent a "communication snapshot" at a time where the media world is changing (printed media dropping, TV developing and social media growing) making any comparison with older studies very difficult. Finally, this case illustrates one of the extremely few examples from literature where the change of the affective evaluation of a city brand is well documented over time.

REFERENCES

Albrecht, J. (2015), 'De magiske 42 %'. *Journalisten*, 2015, **8**, 1–6.

Anselmsson, J. and Bondesson, N.L.A. (2013), 'What successful brands looks like: A managerial perspective'. *British Food Journal*, **115** (11), 1612–1627.

Avraham, E. (2013), 'Battling stereotypes of terror and wars: Media strategies for marketing tourism to Middle Eastern countries'. *American Behavioral Scientist*, **57**(9), 1350–1367.

Avraham, E. (2014), 'Spinning liabilities into assets in place marketing: Toward a new typology'. *Place Branding and Public Diplomacy*, **10** (3), 174–185.

Baker, B. (2007), *Destination Branding for Small Cities*. Portland, OH: Creative Leap Books.

Baloglu, S. and McCleary, K.W. (1999), 'A model of destination image formation'. *Annals of Tourism Research*, **26** (4), 868–897.

Barton, A. and Brown, A. (2015), 'Show me the prison! The development of prison tourism in the UK'. *Crime Media Culture*, **11** (3), 237–258.

Bell, D. and Jayne, M. (eds.) (2006), *Small Cities. Urban Experience beyond the Metropol*. London and New York: Routledge.

Bendixen, S., Bringslid, M.B. and Vike, H. (2018), *Egalitarianism in Scandinavia*. Cham: Palgrave Macmillan.

Boisen, M., Terlouw, K., Groote, P. and Zouwenberg, O. (2017), 'Reframing place promotion, place marketing, and place branding – *moving beyond conceptual confusion*'. *Cities*, **80**, 4–11.

Braun, E., Eshuis, J., Klijn, H.-E. and Zenker, S. (2017), 'Improving place reputation: Do an open place brand process and an identity-image match pay off?' *Cities*, **80**, 22–28.

Chen, C.-F. and Chen, F.S. (2010), 'Experience quality, perceived value, satisfaction and behavioral intentions for heritage tourists'. *Tourism Management*, **31** (1), 29–35.

Cleave, E. and Arku, G. (2017), 'Putting a number on place: A systematic review of place branding influence'. *Journal of Place Management and Development*, **10** (5), 425–446.

del Bosque, I.R. and Martin, H.S. (2008), 'Tourist satisfaction: A cognitive–affective model'. *Annals of Tourism Research*, **35**, 551–573.

Eshuis, J. and Edwards, A. (2013), 'Branding the city: The democratic legitimacy of a new mode of governance'. *Urban Studies*, **50** (5), 1066–1082.

Evans, G. (2005), 'Measure for measure: Evaluating the evidence of culture's contribution to regeneration'. *Urban Studies*, **42** (5/6), 959–983.

Fakeye, P.C. and Crompton, J.L. (1991), 'Image differences between prospective, first-time and repeat visitors to the lower Rio Grande Valley'. *Journal of Travel Research*, **30** (2), 10–16.

Flynn, M.K. (2011), 'Decision-making and contested heritage in Northern Ireland: The former Maze Prison/Long Kesh'. *Irish Political Studies*, **26** (3), 383–401.

Garcia, B. (2017), 'If everyone says so . . . press narratives and image change in major event host cities'. *Urban Studies*, **54** (14), 3178–3198.

Gartner, W.C. (1993), 'Image formation process'. *Journal of Travel and Tourism Marketing*, **2** (2/3), 191–215.

Gertner, D. and Kotler, P. (2004), 'How can a place correct a negative image?' *Place Branding*, **1** (1), 50–57.

Goldsmith, M. and Larsen, H. (2004), 'Local political leadership: Nordic style'. *International Journal of Urban and Regional Research*. Doi: https://doi.org/ 10.1111/j.0309-1317.2004.00506.x (accessed 10 July 2019).

Gunn, C. (1972), *Vacationscape, Designing Tourist Regions*. Austin: University of Texas.

Hartmann, R. (2014), 'Dark tourism, thanatourism, and dissonance in heritage tourism management: New directions in contemporary tourism research'. *Journal of Heritage Tourism*, **9** (2), 166–182.

Jørgensen, O.H. (2005), 'Branding', in F. Frandsen, L. Bøgh Olsen, J. Ole Amstrup and C. Sørensen (eds), *Den kommunikerende kommune*. København, Denmark: Børsens Forlag A/S, pp. 146–165.

Jørgensen, O.H. (2014), 'Developing a city brand balance sheet – using the case of Horsens, Denmark'. *Place Branding and Public Diplomacy*, **11** (2), 148–160.

Jørgensen, O.H. (2015), 'Place and city branding in Danish municipalities with focus on political involvement and leadership'. *Place Branding and Public Diplomacy*, **12** (68). Doi: https://doi.org/10.1057/pb.2015.18.

Jørgensen, O.H. (2017), *18 år for Horsens*. Horsens: Spökebacken, DK.

Klausen, K. (2009), *Strategisk ledelse – de mange arenaer*. Odense: Syddansk Universitetsforlag.

Klijn, E.H., Eshuis, J. and Braun, E. (2012), 'The influence of stakeholder involvement on the effectiveness of place branding'. *Public Management Review*, **14** (4), 499–519.

Knutsen, O. (2017), 'Introduction: The Nordic Models', in O. Knutsen (ed.), *The Nordic Models in Political Science. Challenged, but Still Viable?* Norway: Fakbokforlaget, pp. 9–18.

Lucarelli, A. (2018), 'Place branding as urban policy: The (im)political place branding'. *Cities*, **80**, 12–21.

Lucarelli, A. and Hallin, A. (2017), 'Brand transformation: A performative approach to brand regeneration'. *Journal of Marketing Management*, **31** (1–2), 84–106.

Lundholt, M., Jørgensen, O.H. and Blichfeld, M.S. (forthcoming), 'Intra-organizational brand resistance and counter-narratives in city branding and their influence on top management – a comparative study of three Danish cities'. *Qualitative Market Research*.

Pedersen, A.W. and Kuhnle, S. (2017), 'The Nordic welfare state model', in

O. Knutsen (ed.), *The Nordic Models in Political Science. Challenged, but Still Viable?* Norway: Fakbokforlaget, pp. 219–238.

Prayag, G., Hosany, S., Muskat, B. and Del Chiappa, G. (2017), 'Understanding the relationships between, tourists' emotional experiences, perceived overall image, satisfaction, and intention to recommend'. *Journal of Travel Research*, **56** (1), 41–54.

Richards, G. and Palmer, R. (2010), *Eventful Cities: Cultural Management and Urban Revitalization*. Oxford: Butterworth-Heinemann.

Rogers, E.M. (2003), *Diffusion of Innovations* (5th ed.). New York: Simon and Schuster.

Smith, A. (2012), *Events and Urban Regeration: The Strategic Use of Events to Revitalize Cities*. New York, NY: Routledge.

Strange, C. and Kempa, M. (2003), 'Shades of dark tourism, Alcatraz and Robben Island'. *Annals of Tourism Research*, **30** (2), 386–405.

Swensen, G. (2014), 'From bastions of justice to sites of adventure'. *Folklore: Electronic Journal of Folklore*, **57**, 101–116.

Tasci, A.D.A. and Gartner, W.C. (2007), 'Destination image and its functional relationships'. *Journal of Travel Research*, **45** (4), 413–425.

Taylor, B. (1994), *From Penitentiary to 'Temple of Art': Early Metaphors of Improvement at the Milbank*. Manchester and New York: Manchester University Press.

Walby, K. and Piché, J. (2011), 'The polysemy of punishment momorialization: Dark tourism and Ontario's penal history museums'. *Punishment & Society*, **13** (4), 451–472.

Weick, M. (1995), *Sensemaking in Organizations*. London: Sage.

Wilson, J.Z. (2004), 'Dark tourism and the celebrity prisoner: Front and back regions in representations of an Australian historical prison', *Journal of Australian Studies*, **28** (82), 1–13. Doi: 10.1080/14443050409387951.

Wilson, J.Z. (2008), *Prison: Cultural Memory and Dark Tourism*. New York, NY: Peter Lang.

Witoszek, N. and Midttun, A. (eds) (2018), *Sustainable Modernity: The Nordic Model and Beyond*. Oxford and New York: Routledge.

Additional Sources

During this study the author has had access to the following additional information:

- **The city council's signed annual budgetary agreements (Budgetaftaler) for the years 2007–2018.**
- **The administration's subscription to media search from the company Retriever (for 1 January 2010 to 31 August 2018):** Search on "Horsens, Fængslet" (THE PRISON) gave 944 hits from printed media and 976 hits on edited webpages. Two concerts with Metallica (11 percent and 14 percent respectively of all hits), concerts with Rammstein, Volbeat and Aerosmith (concert visitors totaling 150,000), and the Prison Museum, total 33 percent of hits on print

and 38 percent of hits on the web. TV and radio is not monitored (Henning Nørbæk).

- **The electronic archive of *Horsens Folkeblad* (the local newspaper):** All issues of the newspaper covering 2007 were searched for letters to the editor concerning the future of the prison in order to find relevant keywords for a further electronic search. The words "World of Crime", Fængslet (the prison) and slottet (the castle, the local nickname for the prison) turned out to be key words and were used in an electronic survey from 2006 to 2011 leading to 79 letters.

- **Interviews with the CEO and the chairman of the board of THE PRISON:** The author carried out a semi-structured interview in April 2018 with the chairman of the board, Mr Hennning Nørbæk, and the CEO of the prison, Mrs Astrid Søes Poulsen. The CEO was appointed in 2016, while the chairman of the board has been cultural consultant and head of culture in the city since 1987, and has chaired the board since 2017. The interview followed a questionnaire with a focus on process, strategy and narratives in relation to THE PRISON.

- **The present situation for THE PRISON (September 2018, Astrid Søes Poulsen):** THE PRISON communicates through the following channels with http://www.faengslet.dk as the center: Facebook (18,000 followers), LinkedIn (1200 connections), Instagram (low priority) and monthly newsletters to 5000 subscribers. PR also includes some press releases and contacts to regional TV while national media are hard to reach. Some events do, however, hit the national media (like the concerts with Metallica and Ramstein).

11. Branding Sámi tourism: practices of indigenous participation and place-making

Susanna Heldt Cassel

INTRODUCTION

The indigenous Sámi people of the Nordic countries have recently become more involved in tourism activities and are more engaged in branding Sámi culture in tourism (Fonneland, 2017). The Sámi are not a homogenous group. Their status as indigenous people, including institutionalized practices of reindeer herding, is somewhat different within Sápmi (the land of the Sámi), which stretches over northern Norway, Sweden, Finland and northwest Russia (Sametinget, 2018). These differences also partly influence participation in tourism and the possibilities of developing Sámi tourism as either a side activity from reindeer herding or as a main occupation and income source (Viken and Müller, 2017).

How actors participate in branding Sámi tourism destinations varies, from bottom-up initiatives controlled by Sámi entrepreneurs, such as labelling and constructing Sámi brands (de Bernardi et al., 2017; Keskitalo and Schilar, 2017) to branding regions and places using Sámi culture and heritage from a top-down policy perspective. Sámi tourism, as with other forms of indigenous tourism, may be described as a double-edged sword. While it may increase commercial opportunities and economic benefits, it may also re-colonize indigenous people (Butler and Hinch, 2007; Fonneland, 2017).

Indigenous tourism with limited indigenous control reinforces the othering of indigenous people and subordinates them (in relation to the majority population) in ways that reinforces colonial relationships (Silver, 1993; Bunten, 2008). In urban tourism, ethnic minorities and their connection to specific places are similarly used as attractions and as a part of branding places in cities, such as ethnic districts (Diekmann and Smith, 2015). However, a growing awareness is possible in relation to using indigenous and ethnic culture and heritage in branding tourism places.

In the Nordic countries, ethical concern has been an important aspect in discussing de-colonizing the Sápmi, even though cases of violations of the right to self-representation and indigenous cultural expressions have been noticed (Fonneland, 2017).

This chapter deals with how indigenous tourism development may be controlled through bottom-up initiatives, such as labelling and local tourism investments, as well as how these indigenous engagements in tourism branding paradoxically draw on traditional and sometimes stereotypical representations. Through two examples of practices in the Nordic region, one in Sweden and one across the Sápmi region, this chapter illustrates and discusses how issues of authenticity and indigenous control are negotiated through the participation of Sámi interests and entrepreneurs in the branding of tourism destinations.

Indigenous tourism, such as Sámi tourism, may be conceptualized as tourism involving indigenous culture and heritage in different ways. Most of it relies on the conceptualization of indigenous as different, distant and exotic in relation to the non-indigenous. Indigenous people represented in tourism contexts are often portrayed in line with commercial opportunities and portrayed as attractive from a visitor's perspective, which also reproduces stereotypes (Viken and Müller, 2017; Heldt Cassel and Miranda Maureira, 2017; Tuulentie, 2006). This is a general process in all tourism and in branding places for visitors, in which places are constructed and communicated through narratives that make them stand out as special, authentic and interesting.

This chapter's purpose is to analyse branding processes regarding the Sámi culture and heritage in a Nordic tourism context. The concepts of *participation* and *participatory place-branding* are discussed in relation to making tourism places by emphasizing heritage and culture. The chapter also highlights the role of power relations and indigenous control in tourism development. The chapter's relevance is to highlight a wider discussion on how branding tourism destinations and places is complex and controversial. This form of branding involves power to represent and co-construct culture and heritage of people and places (not least, minority groups and peripheral areas) by critically examining the concepts of participation in destination branding, particularly in a Nordic context.

The chapter begins by reviewing the academic debate and literature regarding place-branding and participatory approaches, and then discusses the particular challenges necessary to address participatory branding of places, cultures and heritage within indigenous tourism. The chapter then presents a few examples of recent developments within Sámi tourism and discusses how the Sámi can influence and control tourism development and branding of tourism places. Two cases, the Sápmi Lodge and the

Slow Food Sápmi network, were studied by analysing marketing material, websites and social media, as well as strategies, plans, and policy documents. The cases represent different ways in which the indigenous culture and heritage are promoted, expressed and performed in tourism, which links tourism development to issues of power relations and contested place identities. A critical approach, including postcolonial perspectives on indigenous tourism, highlights the contested and central concepts of authenticity and othering of indigenous people in the analysis of the texts and images. Specific emphasis was placed on the different articulations that resulted from branding practices.

PLACE-BRANDING AS A WAY OF MAKING PLACES

A place brand may be conceptualized as a mixture of different elements that creates a whole, through notions of location and geographical borders, landscape features, social relationships and the relationship between people and places (Campelo et al., 2011). According to Campelo et al., place brands are mainly driven by people's identity, so creating brands is a matter of determining this identity. For example, a nation's brand image, defined as the sum of beliefs and impressions people hold about a country, plays a significant role in the tourist's choice of destination (Martín-Santana et al., 2017).

The demand for more participatory approaches in place-branding activities is put forth in the literature as a way to make place branding more effective and achieve local engagement (Kavaratzis, 2012). As Eshuis and Klijn (2012) note, local stakeholders feel more committed and loyal to a brand when they have taken active part in the process of defining it and filling it with content. However, actually participating in place branding takes time and effort, and requires a structured and well-thought-out process. Such participation also requires policy-makers to let go of some of their power in decision-making (Zenker and Erfgen, 2014). Discussing ways to strategically implement participatory approaches implies a top-down perspective, in which local residents or interest groups are external stakeholders that should be included, but not drivers or those in control of the process itself.

As tourism becomes more important to the economic livelihood and quality of life in a place, intangible traditions are more likely to be managed and politicized in a more top-down manner. The degree to which a community intentionally manages intangible place-branding tools will vary, along with the mechanisms it uses to do so (Lew, 2017). Processes of place-branding, in terms of making of tourism places, are quite often a mix of bottom-up, participatory approaches and top-down, policy- or market-driven approaches. If an indigenous, tourism-development process becomes successful, it will likely attract external interests pushing (or pulling) it into increasing levels of top-down initiatives to increase tourism and take advantage of new market niches (Lew, 2017).

BRANDING INDIGENOUS TOURISM

The concept of *indigenous* has many layers of meaning in different political, social and cultural contexts (Keskitalo, 2017). Indigenous representations often aim to provide exotic, out-of-the-ordinary images of products and places that are necessary for attracting tourists (Pashkevich and Keskitalo, 2017; Viken, 2006). Indigenous tourism generally tends to portray indigenous groups and cultures as different by staging heritage and practices as authentic (MacCannell, 1989). This is done by focusing on traditional costumes, old rituals and religion, dance and handicrafts to please tourist desire for the exotic other (Bunten, 2008). In addition, indigenous groups, such as the Sámi, are often linked to nature, remoteness, and the Arctic in tourist representations and literature. This association distinguishes what is seen as peripheral within advanced industrial states from non-Sampi parts of the Nordic countries and northwest Russia (Heldt Cassel and Pashkevich, 2018; Keskitalo et al., 2013). By attaching notions of distance, difference, authenticity, peripheral or wilderness to places, in the process of marketing and promoting tourism, the people that live in these places are also portrayed as different and separated from the modern or the urban, in the context of tourism in northern territories (Heldt Cassel and Pashkevich, 2018). This construction of otherness through representing people and places is particularly obvious in defining and delineating indigenous people as different from the non-indigenous (Keskitalo, 2017).

Indigenous tourism can not only produce stereotypes of people and places, but also influence how individuals see themselves and perceive their identity and culture as related to places in a more complex way (Pashkevich and Keskitalo, 2017). In developing indigenous tourism destinations involving the interpretation of cultural practices in commercial contexts, the notion of authenticity can also be challenged and co-constructed in ways that benefit contemporary life within communities (Heldt Cassel and Miranda Maureira, 2017). The degree of control over the tourism products, and the level of participation in branding indigenous tourism destinations vary in an international perspective. This can range from no control and total exploitation of the indigenous populations to tourism driven by actors defining themselves and their tourism product, and controlling business opportunities and economic benefits (Hinch and Butler, 1996).

In branding indigenous tourism destinations, the Sámi are usually represented using certain defining cultural markers, such as traditional activities, tents (*lavvu*), clothing, and reindeer herding (Viken and Müller, 2017). These kinds of representations contribute to the notion that indigenous populations are different and exotic, and also commoditized for tourist consumption (Silver, 1993). However, tourism is also mostly welcome in most Sámi communities and seen as a means to economic development (Viken and Müller, 2017) and a way for the Sámi to re-negotiate their identities (Tuulentie, 2006). According to Tuulentie (2006), *exoticism, naturalness* and *colourfulness* are representations the Sámi use to brand tourism places, showing that this type of imagery is conjured up by both locals and tourists, that Sámi entrepreneurs and local organizations are active agents in creating place identities and brands. Keskitalo and Schilar (2017) show that how indigenous culture and heritage are represented and communicated in Sámi tourism discourses are not particularly different in terms of content, whether or not the organization or entrepreneur that contributes to the representation is indigenous.

Previous research on tourism marketing and promotional messages of Sámi cultures and heritage have studied website content and meaning of representations of the Sámi (de Bernardi, 2019; Olsen, 2008). Studies on how the discourse of the Sámi culture and heritage is produced through branding Sámi tourism places show how conflicting and paradoxical images of the Sámi people emerge (de Bernardi, 2019). The double identity constructions in branding Sámi tourism places and products may be reflected in the practical situation of many Sámi tourism entrepreneurs, who constantly struggle with conflicts and paradoxes when trying to combine tourism with reindeer herding (Tuulentie, 2006; Viken, 2006). These discourses connect to the everyday struggles of Sámi life, the ongoing political struggle for rights to be acknowledged as indigenous and as a separate nation from the Nordic nation states, and the struggle against colonial stereotypes.

In the case of the Sápmi region in the northern Nordic countries, there are different branding activities related to geographical divisions and identities that are not related to tourism, as branding the countries in international tourism contexts and branding of the northern regions as part of national and regional tourism policy began in the 2000s (e.g. Swedish Lapland; Visit Sweden, 2018).

The images of destinations in northern or Arctic places, circulated through websites and social media to promote tourism, mix representations of nature, connoting wilderness and frontier, with features of outdoor tourism activities and indigenous cultural practices. By doing this, the indigenous heritage and culture of the northern Nordic regions are discursively constructed as closely connected to nature and symbolically related to tourism as a cultural asset and adding to the construction of authenticity and exotification of Arctic destinations. These narratives and making of places in the Arctic region and the northern Nordic countries are particularly constructed and circulated as part of regional tourism policy documents and municipal tourism promotion of northern destinations (e.g. Kiruna Lapland, 2018; Swedish Lapland, 2018; Visit Finland, 2018).

EXAMPLES OF BRANDING IN SÁMI TOURISM DEVELOPMENT

In terms of branding Sámi culture and heritage, there are not only general regional or national tourism destination marketing initiatives, but several other examples of different initiatives and projects that also involve participatory practices and Sámi actors in bottom-up making of places. The following sections provide examples of branding the region of Sápmi and Sámi tourism through initiatives managed by Sámi entrepreneurs and stakeholders: The Sápmi Lodge and the Slow Food Sápmi branding initiative.

Sápmi Lodge

The Sápmi Lodge is an ongoing project to rebrand the mountain resort of Idre in northern Dalarna, Sweden. The project also brands Sámi tourism and Sápmi by introducing the culture and heritage in a concept hotel. This project highlights the ambiguities and paradoxes of branding Sámi culture and heritage as different and increasing local control of the tourism industry and participation in tourism development.

The Sápmi Lodge initiative, in the municipality of Älvdalen, aims to develop a tourism facility run by the Sámi community. The Lodge is developed in close proximity to the large mountain tourism destination of Idre, with two major skiing facilities. Sápmi Lodge serves as a unique example of how the Sámi community has been involved in a new type of collaborative and participatory process to develop tourism and brand Sámi culture and heritage (Sápmi Lodge project, application documents, 2017; Idre Sápmi Lodge, 2018). The project has been supported by the municipality, the Swedish regional and national governments, as well as European Union (EU)-funded projects for rural development and restructuring. The vision for the Sápmi Lodge, as presented on its website, highlights the importance of a deeper knowledge and understanding of the Sámi culture, education about the indigenous people, and sustainability and protection of nature and cultural practices (Idre Sápmi Lodge, 2018):

> Idre Sápmi Lodge should be a living and learning South Sámi venue. The area shall be characterized by an iconic architecture and a strong language and cultural appearance based on unique Sámi experiences. On the basis of this, Idre Sámi association will along with other land users and actors work for the sustainable development of the reindeer herding activity, and to protect the environment through information and activities that increase knowledge and understanding of Sámi culture, reindeer husbandry and the living conditions of people in sparsely populated areas . . .

The Sámi community has been herding reindeer along the border between Sweden and Norway for centuries. Since the 1970s, the tourism industry has taken over parts of this land for large-scale skiing facilities and accommodation. The resorts of Idre Fjäll and Himmelfjäll are developed around two mountains focused on downhill skiing, with recent massive expansion. With municipal support, the business managers of the tourism facilities in Idre made attempts to exploit more land and expand the resorts with more skiing slopes in protected areas. However, the industry stakeholders were not successful in convincing regional and national authorities of the sustainability of the projects and the efforts to protect natural resources in the area. Previous planning projects in the area, such as the Three Peaks project, were discursively constructed and communicated within a framework driven by the tourism industry (Engström and Boluk, 2012). This development initiative, which evolved into a major planning issue, left unresolved and latent conflicts between the reindeer herding association and the major tourism stakeholders. Therefore, the issue of the possibilities for the Sámi community to be engaged in, or resist tourism development in the Idre area has been under discussion for a long time. Some of the Sámi reindeer herders and entrepreneurs in the area are running tourism businesses, whereas others have resisted involvement in tourism, due to the belief that tourism interferes with the practices of reindeer herding (Interviews with reindeer herders, 2012 to 2014).

The purpose of the Sápmi Lodge project is different from previous projects to expand the tourism activities in the area. According to Sámi community representatives, its main purpose is to protect and preserve Sámi culture in the village of Idre, while informing and educating visitors about the Sámi population. The Lodge plans to open in 2019 and have a hotel, self-catering accommodation cabins designed as *lavus* (traditional

Sámi tents), a conference centre, a restaurant, and a shop where arts and crafts will be displayed and sold. A large tourism company is the main investor, but a board controls Lodge management, where a representative from the local Sámi community (the reindeer herding association in Idre) will hold the position of chairman. Representatives from the local Sámi association point out that the Sápmi Lodge will engage the young Sámi population in the area in entrepreneurship related to activities and employment at the Lodge. The Sápmi Lodge is an income opportunity and a way to (re)brand the Sámi culture and Sápmi in a way that is more authentic in terms of cultural expressions. It also involves the Sámi as managers and active stakeholders, rather than passive 'touristified' objects.

The Sápmi Lodge is an example of how Sámi culture and heritage in Sápmi are branded through participation of indigenous actors that decide what should be shown and how, and how the narrative about Sápmi and its people should be communicated in a contemporary context. The information on the website about the Sápmi Lodge describes the important aspects of the brand as authentic, genuine and 'the real Sápmi experience', by actively involving Sámi actors not only in design and display of culture, arts and food, but also as part of the management running the venue. The quote below from the website highlights the importance of constructing a brand for Sámi experiences that are genuine and credible:

> We are proud of being able to offer genuine Sámi experiences with Sámi hosts of entrepreneurs who work long-term . . .
>   They will respect the integrity of the culture and counteract that it is used for tourism objectification and they will have high standards of quality, safety and credibility. (Idre Sápmi Lodge, 2018)

This construction of a brand relies on the indigenous culture as being different, other and authentic, as well as controlled by the indigenous population in which the self is represented in a tourism context (Heldt Cassel and Miranda Maureira, 2017). This ambiguity makes branding Sámi culture and heritage through the Sápmi Lodge full of contradictions and possible underlying conflicts between the tourist gaze/outside perspective and the local and indigenous view. Using stereotypical cultural markers, as well as talking about local and indigenous control might seem contradictory, but could be interpreted as a way for the Sámi community to take control of interpretations and representations of people and places. On the Sámi Lodge website (Idre Sápmi Lodge, 2018), information about how the project is part of a broader, participatory, branding initiative of Sámi culture and heritage at large defines and constructs the role of Sámi tourism:

To be real Sámi tourism, the activities should be conducted under Sámi management. The services and products should be produced in a way that creates an understanding of the importance of the cultural landscape and Sámi core values. Tourism products should have a cultural and social anchorage within the Sámi community.

At the same time, as it is important to differentiate this establishment and brand from other kinds of Sámi tourism that are not authentic, the cultural practices and objects within the Sápmi Lodge that are important for this distinction are quite similar to the ways in which Sámi culture is typically represented in tourism contexts, such as a strong focus on the *lavvu* (Viken and Müller, 2017). This finding resonates with previous studies that show how the indigenous culture and heritage are represented and communicated in Sámi tourism discourses are not particularly different in terms of content, whether the organization or entrepreneur contributing to the representation is indigenous or not (Keskitalo and Schilar, 2017; Tuulentie, 2006).

Slow Food Sápmi

Slow Food Sápmi is an initiative initiated by Sámi entrepreneurs that connects the Sámi culture and heritage in the Sápmi region to the modern crossover culinary experience. By offering specific principles and interpretations of the content of the Slow Food Sápmi brand, the initiative raises questions of authenticity and the values and meaning constructed in culinary tourism.

Slow Food Sápmi has evolved from a broader tourism initiative, called Visit Sápmi, which was controlled by a network of indigenous entrepreneurs. It introduced a labelling system for real Sápmi experiences. Visit Sápmi was based on specific guiding principles and a set of criteria that aimed at delineating authentic Sámi products from those offered by external, non-Sámi actors. The goal was to brand Sámi culture and heritage through businesses using common standards regarding the indigenous component and the guiding principles of the experience (Visit Sápmi, 2017; Slow Food Sápmi Facebook pages, 2018). The Slow Food Sápmi network operates in the entire Sápmi region and is presented on its website (2018) as:

> Slow Food Sàpmi is a Sámi business organization that works for sustainable resource consumption focusing on developing and utilizing Sámi food and the Sámis' right to produce their own food. We represent Sámi food artisans and Sámi people interested in Sámi food crafts. The organization covers the whole of Sápmi, the Sámi areas in Sweden, Norway, Finland and Russia.

Slow Food Sápmi has member businesses that may use the Slow Food Sápmi label, and raise awareness and expand knowledge on traditional cooking in a tourism context. The Slow Food Sápmi organization is run by Sámi entrepreneurs through a steering committee of members, which ensures that Sámi community interests are taken care of and that the Slow Food Sápmi concept benefits the production of local food and promotes Sámi culinary cultures.

One of Slow Food Sápmi's subprojects is the food-truck project, which aims at raising awareness of traditional cooking and how it may be designed as a Slow Food experience. This is done through storytelling, experience design and food-related activities that may attract guests (Slow Food Sápmi, 2018). The project will also connect businesses and create a larger network of food entrepreneurs to be part of the Slow Food movement (Slow Food Sápmi, 2018). Representing the Sámi culture and heritage in terms of food and cooking that may be experienced in a tourism setting promotes a commodification of the Sámi culture, which could be problematic in a similar way to the Sápmi Lodge. However, the promoted culinary culture is only partly related to traditional cooking. It is refined to suit the modern tourist, who may request authenticity, but not too much (in terms of ingredients and cooking methods).

The branding connects the food experience with nature, mountain landscapes, purity, sustainability, authenticity and tradition. The cooking style draws on the principles of nose-to-tail, which is also found today in trendy cooking at high-end urban restaurants, in which little is wasted.

In this way, traditional knowledge is depicted as something valuable and important for the identity of the Sámi people, but also a possible asset in the commercialization of tourism products. In this example, the authenticity of the Sámi heritage, expressed through tourism, is a combination of something original and true. There is a clear notion of how this heritage could and should be interpreted and consumed by tourists, according to the producers of the brand and the tourism products, who stay in charge of and control the content. In this initiative, Sámi entrepreneurs may present selected cultural elements in a tourism context, which enhances local control in terms of defining the products as real and authentic in relation to other attempts to promote Sámi culture. At the same time, the culinary experiences themselves are staged by presenting new and innovative dishes that are not really related to everyday or traditional culinary practices.

CONCLUDING DISCUSSION

The Sámi culture and heritage presented in tourism branding are important parts of branding the Nordic countries in general, and the northern/Arctic areas in particular. The cross-border Sápmi region is branded through reference to outdoor adventures, snow, the northern lights and authentic indigenous experiences. These experiences are nationally promoted in branding Sweden, Norway and Finland as attractive, exotic products (used as 'spice' in top-down nation branding), and are also now commonly staged in local settings with indigenous control. The examples in the previous section illustrate that the question of what *indigenous* represents within tourism, and how the indigenous experience should be packaged and sold, is a matter of separating the real indigenous from commodified, objectified versions of the Sámi culture and heritage. Through the branding processes of Sápmi as a place where visitors may experience authentic Sámi culture and heritage (MacCannell, 1989), how Sámi culture and heritage should be represented are also constructed through negotiations within the networks and labelling systems (see also de Bernardi, 2019). Therefore, the defining features of the authentic Sámi experience, in relation to the natural, traditional and locally owned representation, are also a way of exercising power and excluding unwanted representations and entrepreneurs by engaging indigenous groups in labelling practices (such as Slow Food Sápmi) and local development projects (such as the Sápmi Lodge project). See also Heldt Cassel and Miranda Maureira (2017) for a similar discussion with examples from Canada.

The making of Sápmi as a place for tourism, as in the examples of the Sápmi Lodge and of Slow Food Sápmi, means not just attaching symbols and meaning to the place in terms of symbolic and cultural boundaries, but also specifically interpreting what the Sámi culture and heritage means (see also Tuulentie, 2006: Olsen, 2008; de Bernardi, 2019). In these place-making (or even world-making) processes (Lew, 2017), participation of the Sámi stakeholders and entrepreneurs is at the centre of defining authenticity (also see de Bernardi, 2019). In this process, authenticity is not defined by tourists or commercialized, market-driven practices, but by bottom-up initiatives of place-making. By controlling labels and being active partners in developing projects and deciding on ethical guidelines and principles for Sámi tourism brands, the content of the brand is also in the hands of Sámi entrepreneurs and communities. However, this is not to say that the content of the brand, in terms of representations and cultural elements that define what is or isn't Sámi, is completely different from previous, colonial, stereotypical representations. The authenticity, colourfulness and typical elements of traditional clothing and references to the reindeer are also used in local and indigenous representations. This makes indigenous tourism representations full of ambiguities and potential contradictions (Keskitalo and Schilar, 2017; Tuulentie, 2006).

Sámi entrepreneurs and stakeholders involved in planning and managing the Sápmi Lodge describe the establishment not only as a way of accessing a larger share of the tourism revenues in the area (Idre Sápmi Lodge, 2018), but also as a way of educating tourists about Sámi culture and the history of its people. This highlights the importance of participatory practices and place-branding as place-making, when the alternative would have been externally, top-down driven projects that use indigenous culture and practices as cultural assets for commercial or strategic purposes, which is still often the case when branding indigenous places in tourism (Fonneland, 2017; Bunten, 2008; Olsen, 2008). However, the bottom-up participatory place-making practices discussed in this chapter paradoxically still draw on specific articulations of Sámi place and culture in a way that does not really challenge the dominant stereotypes and the othering of indigenous people in society.

REFERENCES

Bunten, A. C. (2008), 'Sharing culture or selling out? Developing the commodified persona in the heritage industry', *American Ethnologist*, **35**, 3, 380–395. DOI: 10.1111/j.1548-1425.2008.00041.x.

Butler, R. and T. Hinch (eds.), (2007), *Tourism and Indigenous Peoples' Issues and Implications*, London: Butterworth-Heinemann Ltd.

Campelo, A., R. Aitken and J. Gnoth (2011), 'Visual rhetoric and ethics in marketing of destinations', *Journal of Travel Research*, **50**, 1, 3–14.

de Bernardi, C. (2019), 'Authenticity as a compromise: A critical discourse analysis of Sámi tourism websites', *Journal of Heritage Tourism*, **14**, 3, 249–262.

de Bernardi, C., O. Kugapi and M. Lüthje (2017), 'Sami indigenous tourism empowerment in the Nordic countries through labelling systems: Strengthening ethnic enterprises and activities', in I. B. de Lima and V. T. King (eds.), *Tourism and Ethnodevelopment Inclusion, Empowerment and Self Determination*, New York: Routledge, 200–212.

Diekmann, A. and M. K. Smith (eds.). (2015), *Ethnic and Minority Cultures as Tourist Attractions* (Vol. 65). Bristol: Channel View Publications.

Engström, C. and K. Boluk (2012), 'The battlefield of the mountain: Exploring the conflict of tourism development on the Three Peaks in Idre, Sweden', *Tourism Planning & Development*. DOI: 10.1080/21568316.2012.726261.

Eshuis, J. and E.-H. Klijn (2012), *Branding in Governance and Public Management*, New York: Routledge.

Fonneland, T. (2017), 'Sami tourism in Northern Norway: Indigenous spirituality and processes of cultural branding', in A. Viken and D. K. Müller (eds.), *Tourism and Indigeneity in the Arctic*, Bristol: Channel View Publications, pp. 205–220.

Heldt Cassel, S. and T. Miranda Maureira (2017), 'Performing identity and culture in indigenous tourism: A study of Indigenous communities in Québec, Canada', *Journal of Tourism and Cultural Change*, **30**, 12, 1–14. DOI: org/10.1080/ 14766825.2015.1125910.

Heldt Cassel, S. and A. Pashkevich (2018), 'Tourism development in the Russian Arctic: Reproducing or challenging the hegemonic masculinities of the frontier', *Tourism, Culture and Communication*, **18**, 1, 67–80. DOI: 10.3727/ 109830418X15180180585176.

Hinch, T. and R. W. Butler (eds.). (1996), *Tourism and Indigenous Peoples*, London: International Thomson Business Press.

Idre Sápmi Lodge (n.d.). Retrieved from https:// idresapmilodge.se/

Kavaratzis, M. (2012), 'From necessary evil to necessity: Stakeholders' involvement in place branding', *Journal of Place Management and Development*, **15**, 1, 7–19.

Keskitalo, E. C. H. (2017), 'Images of the North and Arctic in tourism and regional literature', in A. Viken and D. K. Müller (eds.), *Tourism and Indigeneity in the Arctic*, Bristol: Channel View Publications, 36–49.

Keskitalo, E. C. H. and H. Schilar (2017), 'Co-constructing Northern tourism representations among tourism companies, DMOs and tourists. An example from Jukkasjärvi, Sweden', *Scandinavian Journal of Hospitality and Tourism*, **17**, 4, 406. DOI: 10.1080/15022250.2016.1230517.

Keskitalo, E. C. H., G. Malmberg, K. Westin, U. Wiberg, D. K. Müller and Ö. Pettersson (2013), 'Contrasting Arctic and mainstream Swedish descriptions of northern Sweden: The view from established domestic research', *Arctic*, **66**, 3, 351–365. DOI: 10.2307/23594636.

Kiruna Lapland (n.d). Retrieved from http:// www.kirunalapland.se/

Lew, A. (2017), 'Tourism planning and place making: Place-making or placemaking?' *Tourism Geographies*, **19**, 3, 448–466. DOI: 10.1080/14616688.2017.1282007.

MacCannell, D. (1989), *The Tourist: A New Theory of the Leisure Class*, New York: Shocken Books.

Martín-Santana, J. D., A. Beerli-Palacio and P. A. Nazzareno (2017), 'Antecedents and consequences of destination image gap', *Annals of Tourism Research*, **62**, 13–25. DOI: 10.1016/j.annals.2016.11.001.

Olsen, K. (2008), 'The Maori of tourist brochures representing indigenousness', *Journal of Tourism and Cultural Change*, **6**, 3, 161–184. DOI: 10.1080/ 14766820802553152.

Pashkevich, A. and E. C. H. Keskitalo (2017), 'Representations and uses of indigenous areas in tourism experiences in the Russian Arctic', *Polar Geography*, **40**, 2, 85–101. DOI: 10.1080/1088937X.2017.130375.

Sametinget (2018), The official website of the Sami Parliament and the administration of related affairs in Sweden, http://www.sametinget.se (accessed May 2018).

Silver, I. (1993), 'Marketing authenticity in third-world countries', *Annals of Tourism Research*, **20**, 2, 302–318.

Slow Food Sápmi (n.d). Retrieved from http:// en.slowfoodsapmi.com/

Slow Food Sápmi Facebook pages (2019, June 28). Retrieved from https://www. facebook.com/SlowFoodSapmi/

Swedish Lapland (n.d). Retrieved from https:// www.swedishlapland.com/

Tuulentie, S. (2006), 'The dialectic of identities in the field of tourism. The discourses of the indigenous Sámi in defining their own and the tourists' identities', *Scandinavian Journal of Hospitality and Tourism*, **6**, 1, 25–36. DOI: 10.1080/ 15022250600560596.

Viken, A. (2006), 'Tourism and Sámi identity – an analysis of the tourism–identity nexus in a Sámi community', *Scandinavian Journal of Hospitality and Tourism*, **6**, 1, 7–24. DOI: 10.1080/15022250600560604.

Viken, A. and D. K. Müller (2017), *Tourism and Indigeneity in the Arctic*, Bristol: Channel View Publications.

Visit Finland (n.d). Retrieved from https:// www.visitfinland.com/ lapland/

Visit Sápmi (n.d). Retrieved from https:// visitsweden.com/ sapmi-and-sami/

Visit Sweden (n.d). Retrieved from http:// www.visitsweden.se/

Zenker, S. and C. Erfgen (2014), 'Let them do the work: A participatory place branding approach', *Journal of Place Management and Development*, **7**, 3, 225–234.

12. Tactical ruralism: a commentary on Nordic place-making practices

Szilvia Gyimóthy

The second part of this volume deals with Nordic branding in the making. It is a kaleidoscopic collection of Nordic place-making cases, each highlighting the practice of re-enchanting unknown, secluded, depopulated, marginalised or otherwise subaltern place brands on high latitudes. At first glance, these contemporary snapshots contribute with mere illustrations of bringing Nordic peripheries to the fore on global markets and consumption. Such is the conception and consolidation of a pan-Nordic adventure label (Laven, Chekalina, Fuchs, Margaryan, Varley & Taylor), the bottom-up transformation of a remote community on the Danish west coast (Waade, Pasgaard, Meldgaard & Nielsen), the insourcing of translocal communities to brand distant islands (Broegaard, Larsen & Larsen), the experience innovations of a former prison (Jørgensen), and the commoditisation of Sámi culture in tourism (Cassel).

Apart from illustrations, the chapters also address the mission impossible of unfixing (or rather, liquefying) the rigid frames determining contemporary regional brand conceptions – such as secluded geographical location, dark heritage, industrial decline, or marginalised indigenous populations. One might wonder about the novelty of such a descriptive endeavour in the Nordic context. Place-branding scholars have already dealt with a diversity of reframing practices; for instance, Avraham (2014) created a typology of game-changer scenarios for turning enduring liabilities into assets. These earlier contributions identified archetypal situations or problems; and, in so doing, attempted to distil the essence of place-branding challenges and effective communicative solutions *within* well-articulated frames. In contrast to reactionary and conformist performances, the chronicled Nordic practices are challenging and transgressing the conventional frames of place branding. Furthermore, the chapters explore the processes entangled with Nordic place brand transformations, highlighting the inclusive and networked character of evolving interactions between various actors. In this commentary, I will synthesise these common denominators of emergent Nordic place-making practices, as well as discuss distinct tactical, strategic and aesthetic approaches.

PLACE-MAKING UNCHAINED

Branding scholars and practitioners are in general preoccupied with the confines of place brands. These are essentialised as a particular configuration of favourable or unfavourable topographical, climatical, historical givens, which will subsequently determine potential place-making tactics and strategies. By fixing place brands in terms of their site of production, administrative boundaries and cartographical coordinates, place-making is reduced to a limited number of normative scenarios and aesthetic strategies perceived as appropriate in a given territorial context. Such contextual confines allow only for a limited number of appropriate place narratives. Traditionally, place-making in rural areas is conformed to retrospective patrimonialisation of the assets at hand (Frigolé, 2010), for instance, marketising "local" folklore or revalorising "typical" dishes or culinary practices in a particular region. Packaging localities into nostalgic and ethnocentric rhetoric is a mainstream commodification strategy in the cultural economy and has paradoxically resulted in similar place narratives across rural Europe. However, in the age of global mobilities and increasingly hybrid cultural manifests, the conservation (freezing) and radical particularisation of place brands is neither unique, nor possible.

In contrast, the chapters in this section highlight an extroverted and multi-scalar branding practice, which unfreezes or liquefies the rigid frames within which place-makers operate. Instead of clearly demarcated borders and locations, Nordic brands are constituted and constantly reframed along social, cultural and economic connections between the local and the global, which enables a creative and multi-sited approach to place branding. During this continuous negotiating, translating and reordering process, place meanings are de/respatialised and de/repoliticised. The cases of the Nordic adventure label and the Sápmi Lodge are not simple demonstrations of preservation and subsequent mercantilisation of traditional lifeways, but also illustrate that the enchantment of seductive Nordic utopias deploys the conception of new, more advantageous competitive frames. Subaltern Nordic "underdogs" explicitly adopt contemporary market ideologies (responsible consumption, sustainability, diversity) and product-branding tactics (designing recognisable labels and distinct appellations) to turn the odds in their own favour with legitimate or legible narrative constructions. This echoes the notion of a *reversely engineered* terroir (Paxson, 2010), in which exclusive place narratives are underpinned by moral, ethical and health rationales, rather than measurable quality claims based on traditions and history. Short of regular, documented tourist attractions, exogenous (market) agendas are adopted to generate innovative alternatives as well as new toponyms.

Manipulative rhetoric approaches are well described in organisation studies (Suchman, 1995) and in tourism (Elbe & Emmoth, 2014). The latter highlight destination management organisations' propensity to stick to pathos-driven persuasion in legitimising their actions, when they were unable to adapt to the dominant institutional logic. Clearly, the invention of the nebulous Nordic terroir is an example of such manipulative "liquefying" strategy, since the boundaries of the Nordic are ideological rather than cartographical (Lucarelli, in this volume). While provenance-labels and traceability certificates are the *sine qua non* of terroir-specific products, their Nordic counterparts are mostly promoted along eccentric narratives of sensuous exoticism (harsh climate, peculiar palate) and artisanal venture entrepreneurs (Gyimóthy, 2017). When Nordic place brands experiment with anthropomorphic identity constructions, they no longer settle for a proven underdog (or dare I say, "ugly duckling") self-image, but increasingly flirt with becoming a more self-conscious, unruly and bold *enfant terrible*.

BRANDSCAPING WITH TACTICAL RURALISM

The manipulative approach also permeates the aesthetic and material dimension of Nordic brandscapes. Place-making on the peripheries is practice and action oriented, as the lightsabre provotype on the Danish west coast demonstrates. Such bottom-up design interventions to contest the "boring" coastal townscape could be labelled *tactical ruralism* (inspired by the notion of tactical urbanism) to designate immediate and affordable adjustments of rural livelihoods and landscapes. Temporary architectural installations, co-designed and refined with local residents have the ability to change the affective vibrancy of rural places and, thus, offer viable alternatives to costly architectural icons known from urban contexts. If we adhere to the wave analogy, tactical ruralism has the capacity to change the resonance of place brands, also by very modest investments.

Provocative imageering, interventions and hybrid experiencescapes are cross-appropriating diverse contexts (illustrated in Part II of this volume by Sápmi Lodge, rural noir, and THE PRISON) and are creating semantic as well as sensuous confusions. The Nordic periphery, once framed as remote, inaccessible, or utterly trivial, is now boasting competitive cosmopolitan features (upmarket gastronomy, design, and fashion opportunities) without trading off essential countryside values. This hybridity is further augmented with an equally complex affective register, where tranquility and melancholy are exchanged for mystical, gloomy, and sometimes unsettling atmospheres. Drawing upon André Jansson's (2007) conceptual work, tactical ruralism (even in its most incremental form) produces textural transformations with eventually major repercussions in the way we talk about places, desire them, and consume and embody them. New citizen and visitor performances may trigger a chain reaction of alternative representations, which may, in the long term, further consolidate the reframing of Nordic brands.

NETWORKED PLATFORMS OF PLACE-MAKING: "IT TAKES A VILLAGE . . ."

Finally, let's address the organisational aspects of building Nordic place brand equities. To some extent, the chapters in this section address the question: how are Nordic place brands organised? Prominent scholars (Kavaratzis et al., 2017) have already highlighted the importance of inclusive and communitarian approaches to consolidating robust place branding; however, these were more focused on engaging residents and other local stakeholders to gain goodwill and credibility for brand transformations. As the Danish and Sámi cases show, the mobilisation of local support is not limited to the recruitment of trusted ambassadors (brand soldiers/champions), but also entails resource optimising and crowdsourcing of labour, ideas and immaterial property. The governance of Nordic rural brands is a light and economical construction, which emulates the organisational setup of tactical urbanism – it is characterised by short-term, concrete projects and the insourcing of diverse capacities and competences.

At first sight, these projects (inclusive of the skunk work of the Horsens Prison) seem to reproduce democratic governance structures characteristic to Nordic countries, where communities for centuries experimented with creating novel platforms to meet and exchange knowledge on an equitable, bottom-up basis. However, I would argue that fair Nordic structures are imposed by pragmatic reasons, rather than the ethos of inclusiveness. On the peripheries where collective and economic subsistence is at stake, communitarian models are essential to counterwork resource scarcity. In order to make a difference from scratch, all available resources are considered valuable and vital. Contrasted to prosperous urban contexts, where place branding is undertaken by professionals (municipality planners and promotional agencies), less resourceful place-makers are highly dependent on a diverse and unconventional group of actors and residents, such as kindergarten children, retired fishermen, indigenous artists or lifestyle entrepreneurs.

Although other researchers have already recognised the significance of collaborative endeavours in enabling spatial transformations, most studies have exclusively focused on the mobilisation of *local patriotism* and *local resources*. This is often grounded in a crude juxtaposition between residents vs. visitors as respective producers vs. consumers of locality. Broegaard, Larsen and Larsen contest this dichotomy and provide compelling evidence of contemporary mooring and dwelling practices that create multiple place attachments on Nordic and Baltic islands. Temporary citizen-visitors (translocal entrepreneurs, cottage owners, serious leisure communities) may develop affective bonds and longitudinal commitment to the places they visit or live on a part-time basis. They are effective part-time place marketers, who not only consume the pleasure periphery, but actively tame and colonise it to feel at home. As such, translocal actors and communities are important cultural, social and economic brokers, who (through creating closer ties, relations and commitments to urban and international centres) have the ability to change the positionality (competitive situatedness) of remote areas. Translocal mobility is reminiscent to Sheppard's (2002) notion of "wormholes", which captures random and asymmetric interdependencies of places connected in the global economy:

> Like networks, wormholes leapfrog across space, creating topological connections that reduce the separation between distant places and reshape their positionality. The presence and frequency of wormholes is then a measure of the degree to which positionality stretches selectively across geographic space. (Sheppard, 2002: 324)

The empirical and conceptual insights of translocalism advance the networked logic of branding, and may further sharpen our understanding of how place brands travel.

CONCLUSIONS: MAKING NORDIC PLACE BRANDS TRAVEL

Contrasted with the cool and cosmopolitan vibrancy of Nordic urban centres, most regional brands in the Nordic periphery are remarkably insignificant. This is partially attributable to their blurred contours, vast administrative territories, unclear or illegible narratives, and scarcity of designated products or conventional flagship icons. From a touristic and investment point-of-view, they could be quickly written off as "places that don't matter". However, Hvide Sande, Bornholm, Samsø, Fanø, Gotland, Idre, Horsens, and the emergent slow adventure label prove otherwise. Taken together, these cases share the tactical, strategic and aesthetic approaches in their striving for becoming "places that matter". Through the use of manipulative rhetoric, provocative design interventions, communitarian resource optimising, and translocal ambassadors they accommodate the making of vibrant D-I-Y brandscapes. Not only have they resisted conforming disadvantageous hegemonic images of the rural, but they aspire to set the standards and grammar of place-making along which they can be in their own league.

REFERENCES

Avraham, E. (2014). Spinning liabilities into assets in place marketing: Towards a new typology. *Place Branding and Public Diplomacy*, 10 (3), 174–185.
Elbe, J., & Emmoth, A. (2014). The use of rhetoric in legitimation strategies when mobilizing destination stakeholders. *Journal of Destination Marketing and Management*, 3 (4), 210–217. DOI: 10.1016/j.jdmm.2014.08.001.
Frigolé, J. (2010). Patrimonialization and mercantilization of the authentic: Two fundamental strategies in a tertiary economy. In X. Roigé, & J. Frigolé (Eds.), *Constructing cultural and natural heritage: Parks, museums and rural heritage* (pp. 13–24). Barcelona: Institut de Recerca en Patrimoni Cultural de la Universitat de Girona.
Gyimóthy, S. (2017). The reinvention of terroir in Danish food place promotion, *European Planning Studies*, 25 (7), 1200–1216.
Jansson, A. (2007). Texture: A key concept for communication geography. *European Journal of Cultural Studies*, 10 (2), 185–202.
Kavaratzis, M., Giovanardi, M., & Lichrou, M. (Eds.). (2017). *Inclusive place branding: Critical perspectives on theory and practice*. Abingdon: Routledge.
Paxson, H. (2010). Locating value in artisan cheese: Reverse engineering terroir for new-world landscapes. *American Anthropologist*, 112 (3), 444–457. DOI: 10.1111/j.1548-1433.2010.01251.x.
Sheppard, E. (2002). The spaces and times of globalization: Place, scale, networks, and positionality. *Economic Geography*, 78 (3), 307–330.
Suchman, M. C. (1995). Managing legitimacy: Strategic and institutional approaches. *The Academy of Management Review*, 20 (3), 571–610. DOI: 10.2307/258788.

PART III

Politics of disruptive Nordic place branding

13. Branding on the Nordic margins: Greenland brand configurations

Carina Ren, Ulrik Pram Gad and Lill Rastad Bjørst

INTRODUCTION: THE UNRULY BRANDING OF A NATION STATE UNDER CONSTRUCTION

In this chapter we take a look at how branding unfolds in Greenland, situated at the Arctic margins of the Nordic. According to Kirsten Thisted (2015) we are currently witnessing a transition to more self-representation in the Arctic: "While the Arctic has for generations been described and represented by people living in the South, the peoples of the Arctic are now to a much larger degree representing themselves, both on the political stage and in the media, art, literature and film" (p. 23). While Thisted's observation may hold true if we consider a very long time-perspective, the conditions for and distribution of agency are still skewed and much more complicated if observed up close, particularly, perhaps, if we include commerce on the list of actors to represent yourself. In the current chapter we take a closer look at Arctic representations in place branding as we investigate branding initiatives and enactments *in and of* Greenland.

Since 1996, when the brand consultant Simon Anholt coined the term nation branding, we have witnessed a growing awareness of the political and economic necessity to distinguish one place from another. This has gone hand in hand with a similarly global concern to engage in crafting stories of differentiation about the nation (Olins 2002, Hankinson 2007). While Anholt encouraged simplification of the legibility of a geographical area, creating a holistic narrative with streamlined territorial symbols and ideas, later brand researchers have argued – and lamented – that the many different institutions undertaking, often independently of each other, the role of cultural or commercial ambassadors for the nation brand, impede the ability to create coherent brand narrative, making national brands far more un-manageable than ordinary brands (Blichfeldt 2005). In this article, we take the unmanageability of brands, a certain desynchronization of branding activities and a resulting "polyphonic divergence" (Ren & Blichfeldt 2011) as a starting point in a situated account of how different Greenlandic nation brands are enacted into being at state, corporate and market level.

In the light of ongoing discussions on Greenlandic futures with or without Denmark (Gad 2016), the branding campaign of "Pioneering Nation" is a suitable starting point for our analysis. With the support of a new coalition government taking over after the introduction of an enhanced autonomy arrangement in 2009, the Pioneering Nation campaign was conceived as a coordinated branding effort to put Greenland on the map as it was launched in 2010. In the material, the brand is supported by two narratives: one that draws on traditional imagery of powerful nature, and another focusing on the pioneering spirit of the people of Greenland. In the visual identity of the brand, traditional as well as modern elements are mixed to reflect traditional "cool" references to Arctic wilderness and "hot" imaginaries of modernity, industriousness and development (Ren 2012, Bjørst & Ren 2015). The brand supports hybrid as well "modernistic" narratives of the Greenland of today in which Greenland is defined by a close (and ingenious) relationship to nature as well as a modern economy on the rise. Thus, the Pioneering Nation campaign is not merely an outside-directed marketing "coat hook", but is intrinsically linked to larger internal discussions about where Greenland is going and how. Already before the launch of the brand, Greenland's main export sector – fisheries, dominated by the publicly owned Royal Greenland A/S – decided to withdraw its support, since inclusion of industrialization (miners in hard hats, etc.), was believed to disturb its own brand, where only pristine nature and small-scale fishing vessels are allowed. In 2012, only a few years after the Pioneering Nation brand was conceived, the Greenland Tourism and Business Council was split up. The Pioneering Nation campaign followed the tourism portfolio, leaving other sectors even greater leeway to pursue their own branding efforts.

In the following, we explore how these efforts unfold when Greenland is branded for consumption, for investment and for politics. We focus our analysis on Greenlandic brand configurations in these distinct areas, asking our cases: Who gets to brand Greenland? What different narratives emerge in different sectors? To answer of these questions, we provide three case narratives, experienced through fieldwork and participant observations at a series of events created or utilized to brand Greenland. Following Ren and Blichfeldt (2011) we understand these place branding instances not as events which "just reflect a place, but actively takes part in creating what it is – and is not" (p. 430). We explore this further in our analysis by looking at how the Nordic is appropriated, constructed and incorporated in the branding of a nation under construction, namely Greenland.

BRANDING GREENLAND FOR CONSUMPTION

One example of how the combined hybrid and modern ideas of Pioneering Nation unfold could be captured during the Arctic Winter Games (AWG) 2016 hosted in Nuuk, Greenland, set to be the largest event of its kind in the nation's history. While this week-long event could and has been seen as a branding platform in itself (Ren & Thomsen 2016; Ren & Rasmussen 2017), we here explore in more depth a specific sub-event related to the daily press breakout sessions, as an instance of nation branding. All press-related activities during AWG were organized by the local AWG secretariat but in close collaboration with staff from VisitGreenland, the national tourist board, many of which were present in the press room and to accompany participants to the breakout sessions in town.

The breakouts were VIP media events working as extensions to the daily press conferences during which sports related content was supplemented by "a non-AWG2016 theme pertinent to Greenland".[1] Each morning, "A topic in ten minutes" selected by the local AWG secretariat would highlight "hand-picked individuals from all walks of life in Greenland to speak about a topic pertinent to them and of interest to the outside world".

Following the introductory presentation at the daily press briefing, journalists and other VIPs could "break out" of the sports program and have all the ingredients of a feature presented on a plate. As explained by the local AWG organizers:

> As hosted international media, you have exclusive complimentary access to several special events, both before and during the Games, which are not open to circumpolar media or to the general public. The pre-Games events will help acquaint you with the city of Nuuk, the various Games venues, classic themes and new trends in Greenland, and the beautiful Greenlandic nature. The events during the Games will get you closer to influential people in Nuuk and give you the chance to dig deeper into the themes and stories about which you are especially interested.[2]

These events offered journalists an opportunity to get "behind the scenes" of the AWG, but also, at least in the words of the organizers, to get close

---

[1] Printed media kit provided for AWG2016, p. 6.
[2] AWG2016 printed media kit, p. 7.

and dig deeper into the stories about Greenland briefly presented in the program.

The breakout sessions featured sailing trips, backcountry tours on snowmobile and exclusive dining as well as more intimate encounters with local musicians and artists in their homes. An example of such a staged encounter featured under the heading "Seafood Gastronomy". To the interested journalist, it promised "Cooking demonstration and tasting at the private home of Anne Nivíka Grødem, a food entrepreneur that goes by name *The Greenlandic Food Lover*. Anne Nivíka focuses on the love of good food and recipes using items available in Greenland."[3] On the website of this food entrepreneur, she explains her vision to: "Show the rest of the world what potential Greenland has as a food destination, and make Greenlandic food culture a 'reason-to-go'." Following this, her mission is to "Collaborate and be the initiator on projects and events based on promoting the Greenlandic food culture and Greenlandic produce."[4]

Journalists and media from Denmark, France, the USA, Australia, Belgium and Germany and "cross-country" media such as Al Jazeera and National Geographic joined the breakout to visit Anne Nivíka Grødem at her house. The typical Greenlandic wooden and colorfully painted house where the creative entrepreneur and social media "food influencer" lives with her husband and two children is located a short walk from downtown Nuuk, the capital city where AWG was held. Arriving at the house, journalists are greeted in a casual but hospitable manner. Wearing a red apron with white stylized ulus (traditional Inuit women's knife) and indigenous art work, Nivíka guides visitors into the heart of the house, a modern open kitchen and living space offering an awe-inspiring view to the waters surrounding Nuuk. The feel of the house is light, relaxed, but stylish. Wood, stone, fur and antlers work as striking elements in the simple, but tasteful interior decoration (Figure 13.1).

As guests are installed by the kitchen counter, Anne begins her personal story, explaining her upbringing by Danish parents in the North of Greenland. Anne Nivíka, or simply Nivíka – the preferred and Greenlandic name she uses in a business context – is herself a product of a hybrid and pioneering Greenland. Born of Danish parents, raised in Greenland and married to a Greenlander, Anne embodies an entrepreneurial pioneer. She gradually weaves her story into the topic of the breakout session, seafood, as she starts pulling fresh produce out of the fridge.

During the tasting, photographers take pictures of the food displayed while journalists ask questions about food and produce. The presented

---

[3]   AWG2016 printed media kit, p. 8.
[4]   https://nivika.gl/about.html (accessed 8 May 2018).

Figure 13.1   Anne Nivíka Grødem featuring a Nordic-style, post-modern
re-circulation of an ulu-style knife and traditional Inuit male
and female figurines

food is a combination of traditional Greenlandic servings such as mattak (raw hide and blubber of narwhal or white whale) and dried stockfish and more well-known produce such as lumpfish roe and scallop. The tasters are displayed and served on raw hand-made ceramic plates, of uneven sizes and colors, and is casually shared and consumed around the counter.

In spite of the informal feel in the kitchen, not much seems left to chance, with many hybrid cultural references to Nordic design, indigenous ethno-symbolism and Greenlandic fashion and produce, but also to cosmopolitanism, as ingredients from around the world – capers, olive oil, dried spices, fresh fruit – are used in the cooking in an explicit but unproblematic way. Ingredients bear reference to the current development in New Nordic cooking with the emphasis on freshness and locally sourced products, but in a more mundane and pragmatic Arctic version, where seasonality is supplemented with accessibility in the form of frozen and canned foods. After a few more bites of the lovely food, the visitors start wrapping themselves up in jackets, scarfs and hats as they prepare to exit into the snow of early Arctic spring.

BRANDING GREENLAND FOR INVESTMENT

Another prospective business sector, mining, exhibits a quite different take on pioneering. While mineral extraction has been conducted in Greenland since the 1840s, the idea that extraction of natural resources could make Greenland (more) independent was introduced by the time of the Second

Figure 13.2   The roll-ups at the Government of Greenland's official exhibition at Prospectors & Developers Association of Canada (PDAC) convention: "Greenland. Be an explorer. Be a pioneer"

World War (Rosing 2014, p. 6). A new Mineral Resources Act was introduced following the 2009 upgrade of Greenland's autonomy arrangement and, since then, the nation-building and development discourse promoted by Greenlandic politicians has pushed a positive spin towards a future with extractive industries. Together with industry representatives, politicians have advocated for a discursive shift from mining *in* Greenland towards mining *for* Greenland (Bjørst 2016). Because of the political will to "bet" on mining and make investments, branding initiatives have intensified and Greenland's official brand as a Pioneering Nation has found its way to the mining sector (Figure 13.2).

The message of "being a pioneer" speaks to the image of Greenland as a frontier but also to moving into the future where somebody (local people, investors or prospectors) can be the first to pioneer and explore. It also links to the dominant mining discourse at conventions like that of Prospectors & Developers Association of Canada (PDAC), where development in mining is understood as positive and desirable development, not only for Greenland but also for somebody who would like to do business with Greenland for personal gain. Mark Nuttall (2017) has questioned the effect of the Pioneering Nation brand when it comes to mining.

The brand might contain characteristics considered central to the nation's self-image and to how it wants to been seen by others, but "It nonetheless still positions Greenland as a place on the edge of the world, a place apart and somewhere different" (Nuttall 2017, p. 29). Additionally, pioneering in mining could imply that it is also risky business to take a chance with Greenland . . . since you might be one of the first doing what you do, and there is not a lot of good business cases to learn from.

While possibilities do exist for mining in Greenland, a concern is the fact that investors are still absent in greater scale. In effect, delegations have been sent to international mining conferences in places such as Canada, China and Australia, and several business2business events have been hosted in Greenland and in Denmark. The mining industry has taken an active part in co-branding and spelling out "opportunities" *for* Greenland as a place of mining. Hence the industry is struggling in its branding efforts, when enacting the brand to both Greenlanders and investors.

The managing director of the Australian company Greenland Minerals and Energy (GME), John Mair, is currently developing a mining project at Kuannersuit (Kvanefjeld) in South Greenland. On a panel during Greenland Day at PDAC 2016, Mair stated his surprise and regret of the lack of knowledge about mining in Greenland: "It is an evolving program . . . developing the Greenland brand for people outside, especially for the investment communities. To understand [in Greenland] that it requires clarity around timeline, clarity around the regulatory framework." According to him, the collaboration with the local communities was also important and "all about navigating and finding a common path". In other words, branding initiatives to frame Greenland as a place of mining was understood as both an internal and external exercise. Asked how he sees the development of extractive industries in Greenland compared to other places where he had operated, Mair (2016) replied:

> It is still developing the brand. A lot of us come from the Canadian industry or the Australian industry and experience where mining is a part of a common vocabulary. There is an understanding and mining is such a part of the economy. An awareness that really is not present in Greenland in any way to that extent. There is a much bigger accruement for that engagement. You start talking at stakeholder meetings [and] you really have to explain a lot of context.

The industry, here represented by GME, see themselves as a legitimate (and necessary) partner creating and crafting the brand, targeting not only the investors but also locals in Greenland.

Another institution engaged in the branding of Greenland as a place of mining is the Arctic Cluster of Raw Material (ACRM), founded by the Confederation of Danish Industry, Technical University of Denmark and Greenland Business (Sulisitsisut). Apart from the cooperation with Sulisitsisut, ACRM is a primarily Danish initiative and is economically supported by the Danish Industry Foundation. ACRM's branding exercises aim to "strengthen the competitiveness in Greenland and Denmark in the industry and contribute to sustainable growth and employment in both countries" (ACRM 2018, p. 3). In the welcoming introduction to its 2017 Conference, the head of the ACRM stated: "we want and need to do more to enlighten investors and foreign companies on the possibilities in Greenland" (Frederiksen 2017, p. 1). The "we" introduced by ACRM in the quote was somewhat ambivalent, as its exclusion of "investors and foreign companies" left it to include a club of mostly Danish partners.

This Danish–Greenlandic industry-driven initiative has met criticism from Greenland. "Why not partner up with somebody who knows something about mining", said Jørgen Hammeken-Holm, deputy minister for Mineral Resources at the conference. As Greenland's top representative, he challenged the legitimacy and initiatives of ACRM and Denmark as the venue to brand and attract investors to Arctic mining. Pointing at how investment funding from Danish and EU partners is lacking, he continued: "So, come on Denmark and the EU. If you want to be part of the game – join in" (Hammeken-Holm 2017). Despite ACRM's efforts to create a strong "we", its agency and legitimacy was contested by the Greenlandic representatives, as successful investment efforts in the mining of Greenland's mineral was lacking.

Following the debate and reading the conference program it seemed that, even if Denmark is less relevant as part of the branding of Greenland, the "Nordic" was an asset. In a project overview from 2018 published by ACRM it is stated that; "On a global comparison, Greenland presents a stable political and legislative system with a general low risk business environment on par with other developed Western and Nordic countries" (ACRM 2018, p. 15). In this quote, Greenland is identified as not just a developed Western but a Nordic country. This Nordic reference returns as Greenland is presented as an interesting place for extractive industries, where Greenlandic politicians highlight how they work with "Nordic standards". Again, the stable political and legislative system (as in the Nordic countries) is part of the sales pitch and branding of Greenland as an emergent Nordic welfare state with a low risk business environment when it comes to developing a mining sector. This passage is an example of how the Nordic dimension is enhanced to advocate for the trustworthiness of Greenland and that describing Greenland as part of the Nordic family is a strategic position.

BRANDING GREENLAND FOR GLOBAL POLITICS

Denmark and the Nordic also play important roles when Greenland is represented as a nation in global politics, whereas "pioneering" seems to have only an implicit role. The most recent global installation of sustainability – a United Nations (UN) affirmed Agenda 2030 promoting 17 Sustainable Development Goals (SDGs) and 169 targets – has now reached the Arctic. The program for the Finnish chairmanship of the Arctic Council 2017–2019, first, promises to "explore how the Agenda 2030 framework can be used in Arctic cooperation for the benefit of humans and nature" (Finland 2017, p. 5), before turning to the Arctic tradition of stressing the "development" aspect (Gad et al. 2018) by mentioning the SDGs as a possible tool in "strengthening the economic and social progress and cultural self-expression of Arctic communities" (Finland 2017, p. 14). On 1 December 2017, the Kingdom of Denmark organized a "High-Level International Conference on SDGs in the Arctic" as a contribution to these explorations of the Finnish Chairmanship. The incident made explicit how the preferred images of Greenland as decolonizing country and of Denmark as a particularly benevolent colonial power (Thisted 2014; Gad 2016) are always at stake when its diplomats engage the Arctic stage.

At the conference, the Government of Greenland had ample opportunity to brand its nation as preferred. The holistic embrace of the SDGs excluded few topics, and the program granted high-level representatives generous speaking time: The Greenlandic minister for independence and foreign affairs spoke as part of the welcoming ministerial session. The minister for finance was a prominent part of the frame setting session, generically labelled "The SDGs & the Arctic". The minister for social affairs, etc., was as part of the audience called upon by the moderator to comment on the proceedings as part of the concluding discussions. Particularly the minister for finance took the opportunity to present a coherent narrative of Greenland, its move towards sustainability, and key challenges and opportunities along the way.

His intervention began with a story of indigenous tradition and peoples affected by climate change, turning pioneers into victims:[5] "The sea ice that previously allowed for people to take the dog sled out on to it and fish is now gone in many places. In a lot of places, the hunters have had to abandon their traditional occupation, buy a dinghy and become fishermen instead" (Egede 2017), The near future was equally clear – that of a sovereign, Nordic-style welfare state:

---

[5]　For more nuanced analyses of the complex negotiations of positions on the way to this Greenlandic climate change narrative, cf. Bjørst 2012, 2018.

[W]hen we are talking about growth in a sustainable development context, then it is because we want a development that can ensure that our citizens have food on their tables, roofs over their heads and that all age groups have a social and cultural life in a safe society. I would like to see that we in Greenland can continue to develop our version of the Nordic welfare model towards becoming an Arctic welfare society that can form the basis of our independence. (Egede 2017)

Towards this aim, climate change – even if challenging for traditional ways of life – was not only a bad thing: "The particular climatic and geographical conditions in Greenland also allow for some new investment and business opportunities" (Egede 2017). In other words, Greenland is greening and is open for business (Nuttall 2017).

So Greenlandic Government representatives communicated their preferred brand for their island explicitly. In contrast, post-colonial sensitivity relegated officials of the Danish state to promoting their version of Greenland in more subtle ways. As it is always important to signal "equality" when communicating the relation between Denmark and Greenland, the electronic and printed invitations and documents for the event bore the insignia of the three polities in equal stature (Ministry for Foreign Affairs (MFA) 2017): the printed version of the program for the welcoming ministerial session featured a Danish, a Greenlandic and a Faroese minister.[6] The Danish MFA spent considerable time on explaining this aspect of status and process: "It is a key priority for the Danish government to cooperate closely with Greenland, the Faroe Islands and international partners to secure sustainable economic development in the Arctic. That's why we are here today as co-hosts and partners" (Samuelsen 2017).

However, diplomatic minutiae, subtle priorities of the issues discussed, and low-key practicalities contributed to re-installing the formal hierarchy. First, the ample speaking time reserved for the Greenlandic representatives was awarded them on a distinctly Danish platform. Before the equality signaled by the tripartite ministerial welcoming session, Fredrik, the Crown Prince of Denmark spoke, elevating Denmark from equality: "The Arctic part of the Kingdom of Denmark has always been very close to my heart" (Kongehuset 2017). Greenland's Department of Foreign Affairs (DFA) acknowledged submission to this most eminent representative of Danish sovereignty in a tweet exclaiming that the "@Naalakkersuisut [the

---

6   In contrast to Greenland, the Faroese Minister for Foreign Affairs (having less substantial stakes in the Arctic, and politically with a secessionist agenda) chose to actively undermine the brand promoted by Denmark of the "Community of the Realm" as an ideal – Nordic style – peaceful post-colonial community, by bailing from his prominent slot in the program in protest against Denmark (Michelsen 2017).

Government of Greenland] is honoured that the Crown Prince Frederik of Denmark [is] opening the SDGs in the Arctic conference" (DFA 2017). The emotional appeal of His Royal Highness's intervention left no-one in doubt about his reverence and respect for Greenlandic communities and nature:

> 17 years ago, I ventured out on a four month long journey along the coast of North and North East Greenland – one of the most isolated and remote areas in the world. . . . During my four months of isolation I learned . . . that nature is your master and to survive you must adapt to the environment. The indigenous Arctic population, have done so for centuries and I have the deepest respect for their traditional ways and customs" (Kongehuset, 2017).

His stories from Greenland (and his title) legitimated him speaking about Arctic issues and on behalf of the Greenlandic hunters, who he considers his friends. The conclusion of his anecdote indirectly reminded the audience that today, it is Danish servicemen – among whom most of his "travelling companions" were found – who master even Inuit technology to the defense of Danish sovereignty over Greenland: "For me it was a unique experience, but the expedition is not unique – every year the borders of Greenland are patrolled by such dog sleigh expeditions. It is, despite technology, still the only feasible way to be present in the vast and isolated parts of Greenland" (Fredriksen 2017).

In continuation, the Danish Minister for Foreign Affairs reminded the audience of the wider context in the form of the burden shouldered by Denmark for the benefit of Greenland: "[T]he pre-requisite for sustainable development is a peaceful and stable Arctic. Exactly for this reason, Denmark and Greenland will be hosting an inclusive meeting in May next year to mark the 10th anniversary of the Ilulissat Declaration about peaceful and responsible cooperation in the Arctic" (Samuelsen 2017). In other words, without Danish diplomacy and the Danish Defense Forces, Greenland would be but a pawn in the intensified great power rivalry of the Arctic thaw.

Finally, particularly the Greenlandic Minister for Finance stood out visibly and audibly, wearing the national *anoraq* costume among the suits filling the podium, and addressing the audience in Greenlandic via an interpreter. The brand effectively communicated, rather than the preferred narrative version, was one of a people less-than-capable of relating internationally on its own. Against this background, Denmark could stand out as the benevolent post-colonial caretaker of the natives (cf. Adler-Nissen 2014). When the Danish Arctic Ambassador, recently arrived in the region from a posting in Bangladesh, tweeted "Strong voices and ideas from ⌂┿╋▇" (Eskjær 2017), neither specific voices nor explicit ideas needed to be included: the Danish diplomatic platform as such was the message demonstrating Danish benevolence and indispensability as a reliable custodian of sovereignty over Greenland.

CONCLUDING DISCUSSION: THE "NORDIC" IN GREENLANDIC BRAND CONFIGURATIONS

Our cases demonstrate that place branding is undertaken very differently on the platforms of tourism, mining and diplomacy, and thus exemplifies the unruliness of place brands and their multiple sites of enactment (Ren & Blichfeldt 2011). As part of numerous activities of a nation still under construction, we see the branding of Greenland as an exercise in identity politics, in which independence from the Danish Commonwealth plays a crucial part. While Greenlanders largely agree that Greenland ought to be an independent nation state, the speed of the process is very much contended. Moreover, disagreement exists on what kind of nation Greenland should be, and on what roles and importance should be awarded to what elements of "traditional" and modern Greenlandic culture (Gad 2016). This brand multiplicity unravels itself as we turn towards the three cases, where different actors draw on various and often diverging discourses, aesthetics and narratives to enact the Greenlandic brand.

The culinary event "Home cooking with Anne Nivíka Grødem" exemplifies a hybrid narrative emerging from the hybrid Pioneering Nation mindset where Danish–Greenlandic heritage, locally sourced foods, and Nordic food and design trends are effortlessly styled and presented on a highly visual, digitally mediated global stage. Promising a unique and authentic glimpse "behind the scenes" of a Greenlandic home, the media event showcases Greenlandic everyday through food, but also links it, as we saw, to design and to an Nordic aesthetics of the home which might not be recognizable to the average Greenlander. The "Greenlandic" is mixed with cosmopolitan and Nordic tendencies as Greenlandic, colonial and pop cultural references are woven into a coherent and seemingly uncontested narrative.

However, the Pioneering Nation brand statement that "the population of Greenland is manifold and many different hands lift the country . . . – but everyone has a place and a significance" (VisitGreenland 2017, p. 11) is not only directed towards an international consumer market. It is simultaneously an intervention in a domestic identity politics that does not always value diversity (Gad 2018a, 2018b).

The brand of Greenland as a place of mining is still in the making and, in this sector, the *Pioneering* label core to the official branding strategy seems to be applied to the companies coming in, rather than to the nation. At present it is not so much Greenlandic actors who are pioneering and who brand Greenland, but rather a bunch of different actors trying with more or less successful endeavors and interactions. In this context, politicians refer to Greenland as part of the Nordic and as working with Nordic standards related to a "we" that sticks together. Within this logic, Greenland is identified as part of a "softer" capitalism than the one you would expect to find in Anglo-Saxon economies, and politically more stable than your standard developing country (cf. Gad 2016, p. 76). Both insiders (the Government of Greenland) and outsiders (the Danish-led ACRM initiative) use the Nordic relation ad hoc to strengthen the brand and create legitimacy.

On the diplomatic stage, Greenlandic and Danish officials promote different "Greenland" brands, both informed by specific aspects of an overall Nordic brand: while picking up the legitimacy flowing from the indigenous brand – having lived sustainably in peace with Arctic nature – Greenland presents itself as a prospective sovereign nation state. This future state is to be distinctively Nordic, first, because of its welfare system; second, because of its responsible way of taking part in important agendas of the international society, particularly by promoting and implementing green, sustainable solutions to ameliorate climate change. Denmark works to promote a "Greenland", which is the exemplar of a benevolent, Nordic way of decolonizing responsibly and harmoniously. When discussing how to import the UN SDGs to the Arctic, a division of labor relieves the tension between these two brands: Denmark promotes its preferred brand by providing a formal platform for Greenlandic officials to perform the presentation of substantial policy to support their preferred brand.

Branding Greenland is not just an effort negotiated between insiders and outsiders; it is simultaneously a negotiation about who may legitimately get away with talking on behalf of Greenland. In these negotiations, the "Nordic" may in certain instances come in handy, acting ad hoc as a strategic tool.

Seeing an aspect of a brand as "Nordic" serves as a way of normalizing what would else have to be excluded as "Danish", as the Other, which corrupted indigenous Greenlandic culture and identity. If modernity (or even better: post-modernity) can be draped in Nordic robes rather than Danish, a modern Greenland can be more at ease when branding itself towards resurrecting as an independent nation state.

REFERENCES

ACRM (2018). Business Opportunities in Greenland. http://acrm.dk/wp-content/uploads/2016/11/Business-Opportunities-in-Greenland-WEB.pdf (accessed 24 April 2018).

Adler-Nissen, R. (2014). The Faroe Islands: Independence dreams, globalist separatism and the Europeanization of postcolonial home rule. *Cooperation and Conflict, 49*(1), 55–79.

Bjørst, L. R. (2012). Climate testimonies and climate-crisis narratives. Inuit delegated to speak on behalf of the climate. *Acta Borealia, 29*(1), 98–113.

Bjørst, L. R. (2016). Saving or destroying the local community? Conflicting spatial storylines in the Greenlandic debate on uranium. *The Extractive Industries and Society, 3*(1), 34–40.

Bjørst, L. R. (2018). The right to "sustainable development" and Greenland's lack of a climate policy, in Gad, U. P., & Strandsbjerg J. (eds) *Politics of sustainability: Reconfiguring identity, space, and time in the Arctic* (pp. 121–135). Routledge Studies in Sustainability. New York: Routledge.

Bjørst, L. R., & Ren, C. (2015). Steaming up or staying cool? Tourism development and Greenlandic futures in the light of climate change. *Arctic Anthropology, 52*(1), 91–101.

Blichfeldt, B. S. (2005). Unmanageable place brands? *Place Branding, 1*(4), 388–401.

DFA (2017). https://twitter.com/GreenlandDFA/status/936870760005517312 (accessed 24 April 2018).

Egede, A. (2017). http://um.dk/en/foreign-policy/the-arctic/the-sdgs-in-the-arctic/speeches/aqqaluaq-egede/ (accessed 24 April 2018).

Eskjær, H. (2017). https://twitter.com/HanneEskjaer/status/936546896654594049 (accessed 24 April 2018).

Finland (2017). http://formin.finland.fi/public/default.aspx?contentid=356546 (accessed 27 May 2018).

Frederiksen, M. Q. (2017). *The Greenland conference '17. The ambitious Arctic: Cooperation, mining and infrastructure. Arctic Cluster of Raw Materials.* Copenhagen, Denmark: ACRM.

Gad, U. P. (2016). *National identity politics and postcolonial sovereignty games: Greenland in the margins of Europe.* Monographs on Greenland 353 (Man & Society 43) series. Copenhagen: Museum Tusculanum Publishers.

Gad, U. P. (2018a). Grønlandsk identitet og udvikling – danske trusler og muligheder. Sprogdebatten under hjemme- og selvstyre, in Tróndheim, G., Marquardt, O., & Høiris, O. (eds) *Grønlændernes syn på Danmark, danskere og dansk sprog og kultur* (pp. 257–277). Aarhus: Aarhus Universitetsforlag.

Gad, U. P. (2018b). Race and racism in Greenlandic identity politics: The Empire racializes back. And forth. Paper presented to the conference on *Race and Racism in Contemporary Denmark*, Aalborg University.

Gad, U. P., Jacobsen, M., & Strandsbjerg, J. (2018). Introduction: Sustainability as a political concept in the Arctic, in Gad, U. P., & Strandsbjerg, J. (eds) *Politics of sustainability: Reconfiguring identity, space, and time in the Arctic* (pp. 1–18). Routledge Studies in Sustainability. London: Routledge.

Hammeken-Holm, J. T. (2017). Greenland Minerals and Energy has the controlling interest in the Kuannersuit project. https://naalakkersuisut.gl/en/

Naalakkersuisut/News/2017/06/130617-Stadig-bestemmende-indflydelse-i-Kua nnersuit-projektet (accessed 27 May 2018).

Hankinson, G. (2007). The management of destination brands: Five guiding principles based on recent developments in corporate branding theory. *Journal of Brand Management*, *14*(3), 240–254.

Kongehuset (2017). http://kongehuset.dk/taler/hkh-kronprinsens-tale-ved-arctic-conference-sustainable- development-goals-in-the-arctic-local-and (accessed 24 April 2018).

MFA (2017). http://um.dk/en/foreign-policy/the-arctic/the-sdgs-in-the-arctic/ (accessed 24 April 2018).

Michelsen, P. (2017). Danmark ætlar at steðga føroyskum virksemi í altjóða samfelagnum. 1 December 2017. http://www.uvmr.fo/fo/kunning/tidindi/danmark-aetlar-at-stedga-foroyskum-virksemi-i-altjoda-samfelagnum/ (accessed 24 April 2018).

Nuttall, M. (2017). *Environment, resources and politics in Greenland: Under the great ice*. London: Routledge.

Olins, W. (2002). Branding the nation – the historical context. *Journal of Brand Management*, *9*(4), 241–248.

Ren, C. B. (2012). Envisioning Greenland: Contested naturecultures in the making. *Conditions*, (11/12), 154–155.

Ren, C. B., & Blichfeldt, B. S. (2011). One clear image? Challenging simplicity in place branding. *Scandinavian Journal of Hospitality and Tourism*, *11*(4), 416–434.

Ren, C. B., & Rasmussen, R. K. (2017). "Future Games": Enacting innovation in Greenland. *Arctic Yearbook*, *6*, 247–258.

Ren, C., & Thomsen, R. C. (2016). The 2016 Arctic Winter Games: "Now we do what we do best". *Arctic Institute*, March 2016. https://www.thearcticinstitute.org/2016-arctic-winter-games/ (accessed 24 April 2018).

Rosing, M. (ed.). (2014). *To the benefit of Greenland*. Ilisimatusarfik: University of Greenland.

Samuelsen, A. (2017). http://um.dk/en/foreign-policy/the-arctic/the-sdgs-in-the-arctic/speeches/anders-samuelsen/ (accessed 24 April 2018).

Thisted, K. (2014). Imperial ghosts in the North Atlantic: Old and new narratives about the colonial relations between Greenland and Denmark, in Göttsche, D. & Dunker, A. (eds) *Colonialism across Europe: Transcultural history and national memory* (pp. 107–134). Bielefeld: Aisthesis.

Thisted, K. (2015). Pioneering nation: New narratives about Greenland and Greenlanders launched through arts and branding, in Evengård, B., Nymand Larsen, J., & Paasche, Ø. (eds) *The new Arctic* (pp. 23–38). Cham: Springer.

VisitGreenland (2017). Greenland. A pioneering nation. https://www.govmin.gl/images/stories/faelles/mineral_resources_act_unofficial_translation.pdf (accessed 24 April 2018).

14. Gastro Scandinavism: the branding of New Nordic Cuisine as a discursive space for forging new identities

Kim Simonsen

We tend to think that products and genres such as Scandinavian design, brands like LEGO and Nordic crime fiction have put Scandinavia on the map, but new Nordic food and Noma have created the same kind of branding. New Nordic gastronomy is used in different roles such as place marketing, destination branding and place making (Berg et al., 2000). Within the last 10 to 15 years, new Nordic food has become a brand on the international stage of cuisine. This chapter analyses how the branding of place and the French notion of *terroir* in New Nordic Cuisine has worked as a form of pan-Scandinavist branding for peripheral areas in the north; here, I have coined the term *Gastro Scandinavism* through the contraction of gastronationalism and Scandinavism. The chapter asks questions such as: Are these branding strategies and the relation to place or terroir a throwback to earlier forms of nationalism, e.g. romantic nationalism? The chapter will determine the role played by food in national identity constructions, both in the past and the present. The material analysed will be New Nordic cookbooks, manifestos, images from promotional books of the New Nordic Food Movement, and debates over the status of new Nordic food with a focus on the restaurants Noma and the Faroese KOKS.

This chapter is divided into three sections. The first is a general introduction to the study of nationalism and food as well as the branding of food. Then follows a discussion of the consequences of the "nordification" and creation of a new Gastro Scandinavist terroir. This leads to the last section on the Nordic sense of terroir and Gastro Scandinavism found in Nordic cookbooks.

BRANDING NORDIC FOOD: IN THE BEGINNING WAS NOMA

Until recently, the French Michelin Guide did not cover Scandinavia – the area was not considered to have a single restaurant worth visiting (Skyum-Nielsen, 2010, p. 12). Instead, French and Italian cuisine dominated in the international language of gastronomy. As a result, the north was locked in a fight over status and power in a centralised system, favouring the South. There were no unified national dishes of the north – in fact, a unified Scandinavian food or kitchen did not exist, nor was there a unified culinary tradition of gourmet food. Gastronomy in the north is dependent on its construction by the New Nordic Food Movement.

To use the term "regional" about many countries at once, from Greenland to Sweden and Iceland, in relation to food or culture would

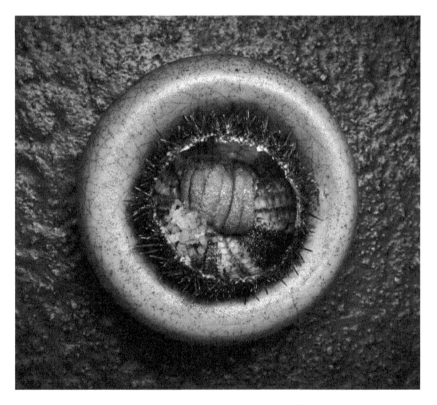

Source: http://gistogvist.fo/Lysingar/koks/KOKS_2016_web.pdf.

Figure 14.1   From KOKS, Faroe Islands: sea urchin eggs

be controversial (Cook and Crang, 1996). The notion of Scandinavia is a modern construction; Scandinavia is not a country in the same way that Europe is not a country but a geographical area in the world. However, the notion of Scandinavia is related to images and a brand. In this chapter I work with an expanded notion of Scandinavia, and I am also referring to the region as the north.

The everyday foods of places such as Iceland, Denmark, Norway and Sweden were turned into national traditions in the nineteenth century. The national commemoration of Icelandic food was a part of a wave of nineteenth-century romantic nationalism, which can be witnessed in the festival of *Þhorrablóti*, where they eat "hákarl", fermented Greenland shark. This is a festival comparable to Burns Night in Scotland. Denmark, Sweden, Finland and Norway have older forms of traditional food, but not in the same commemorative form as in Iceland. The nationalism scholar Joep Leerssen (2006) states that the cultivation of culture in Romantic nationalism can be outlined in three types of endeavour: salvage, fresh productivity and propagandist proclamation. In the case of Scandinavism, we find folklore, national costumes, national anthems, national landscapes and national commemorations such as the Norwegian festival that occurs annually on 17 May. Food is also a consistent part of the national identity (Ichijo and Ranta, 2016).

In Denmark, the traditional Christmas lunch is highly ritualised and nationalised, with food like "flæskesteg" (pork-roast), cured herring and kale cabbage. Norwegians have "pinnekjøt" (fermented lamb) and "rakfisk" (fermented cod). The Swedes have "surströmming" (highly fermented Baltic herring). However, most of these traditional forms of food are not a part of New Nordic Food, although they promote produce from these areas.

One of the key components of the New Nordic Food Movement was the drawing up of a manifesto. This occurred in November 2004 when the duo behind Noma invited the movers and shakers of the region's food world to a symposium on New Nordic Cuisine. The New Nordic Food Manifesto was drawn up by some of the region's top chefs and food professionals. Its ten points expressed the values of a New Nordic Cuisine.[1] The idea of the manifesto had been inspired by the success of Danish film and the DOGMA 95 filmmaking manifesto. Through the New Nordic Food Manifesto, the stakeholders wanted to create a new brand of regional and local food, but also to rediscover and change the status of already known food resources in a process to recognise the region's food culture. It was

---

[1]   See http://www.norden.org/en/theme/ny-nordisk-mad/the-new-nordic-food-manifesto (accessed 1 May 2018).

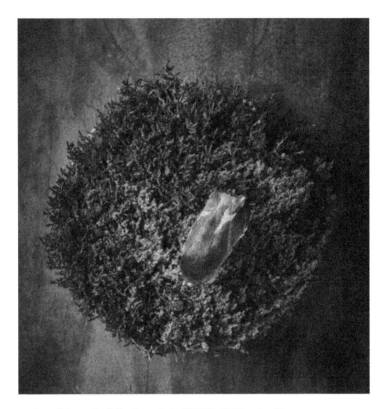

Source: http://gistogvist.fo/Lysingar/koks/KOKS_2016_web.pdf.

Figure 14.2   From KOKS, Faroe Islands: fermented lamb

a daring proposal, since the chefs in Denmark tended not to have a kind word to say about their own culinary heritage. Despite the favouring of French cuisine, the Nordic food "revolution" did not want to copy French food, nor that of any other kitchen (Redzepi, 2010).

The founders of the New Nordic Food Manifesto had a vision in which the North needed to reinvent their own food and cuisine, not purely from traditional roots, but through an avant-garde way of thinking, to make the modern meet the traditional. Thus, the founders wanted to combine leading skills in gastronomy with the best of local ingredients, which are often found in the most unlikely places, such as the Arctic and sub-Arctic region.

With New Nordic Food, we encounter not only a national branding, but a pan-national branding or what I refer to as a pan-Scandinavian national branding. National branding is defined as a deliberate action to convey and promote ideas, images and values regarding national identity

(Aronczyk, 2013, p. 105; Volcic and Andrejevic, 2011, p. 3). These notions can also be linked to the term *gastronationalism*, which is associated with the idea of national branding and identity expression occurring through the medium of food (DeSoucey, 2010). Gastronationalism is:

> a form of claims making and a project of collective identity, [it] is responsive to and reflective of the political ramifications of connecting nationalist projects with food culture at local levels. (DeSoucey, 2010, p. 433)

The pan-national ideology of Scandinavism is mostly remembered as an unsuccessful nineteenth-century political movement promoting Scandinavian unity. Ultimately, the ideology is considered to have foundered when Denmark stood alone in the war with Prussia in 1864. However, cultural Scandinavism has longer roots and a more persistent presence and afterlife in cultural exchange, Scandinavian corporation and the modern-day Nordic Council is a result of this (Simonsen, 2017). As a pan-national movement Scandinavism is still the leading idea behind modern-day political and cultural promotions of the north. The nationalism scholar Louis Snyder defines pan-nationalisms as:

> politico-cultural movements seeking to enhance and promote the solidarity of peoples bound together by common or kindred language, cultural similarities, the same historical traditions, and/or geographical proximity. (Snyder, 1984, p. 49)

Pan-nationalism can therefore be viewed as a form of nationalism distinguished by being associated with a claimed national territory, or which does not correspond to existing political boundaries. This general definition is painting nationalism on a broader canvas to include all who by reason of geography, race, religion, or language, or a combination of any of them, are included in the same category – this is the backdrop to the notion of Gastro Scandinavism used in this chapter.

FROM TERROIR TO GASTRO SCANDINAVISM – WHAT ARE THE CONSEQUENCES OF THE "NORDIFICATION" OF TERROIR?

The French word *terroir* is defined as the combined conditions offered by nature – soil and sun, wind and rain – that endow food with its unique identity. When we study how the Nordic culinary wave presents itself in books and how it is imaged in relation to the promotion of certain restaurants like Noma, KOKS and Fäviken in Sweden, we find that the

Figure 14.3   From KOKS, Faroe Islands: fermented cod

cookbooks and folders are filled with intense representations of Nordic landscapes to promote a relation with the origin of the food. The chefs are seen in media representations, films, TV shows and cookbooks wandering through nature as lonely sorcerers or druids in front of a background of nature, such as the Atlantic Ocean, which tells a story about their hidden force, that they are in a pact with nature, the local environment, and that the food comes from an approach to living a simple authentic and mini-malist life in rural or peripheral areas. The chef can make seaweed, herbs or previously unknown berries into an international luxury commodity, and tomorrow appear on the cover of the *New York Times* or the *New Yorker*.[2] In addition, the more peripheral the food is, the more authentic food critics believe it to be.

---

[2]   See, for example, Graham (2016).

The New Nordic Food Manifesto is not only firmly terroir-bound but also a throwback to the discourse of Scandinavism promoting the whole Nordic region. This can be construed as a mercantile form of nationalism or pan-nationalism, but all forms of nationalism are cultural. Nationalism is a political instrumentalisation of a national self-image. And an important point often forgotten is that identities are determined by exchange and recognition from the outside and are not created from within.

In the New Nordic Food Manifesto, three of the declared aims are related to the local environment. The New Nordic Food Movement intends to "express the purity, freshness, simplicity and ethics associated with the region", to reflect the changes in seasons, and to use ingredients and produce "whose characteristics are particularly excellent in Nordic Climate".

For one of the founders of Noma, René Redzepi, success was not so easily achieved. Eventually the ongoing teasing and jokes from his peers affected Redzepi's mental health and, during a trip to Greenland with Claus Meyer, he had a mild mental breakdown (Simonsen 2004). However, he and Meyer went on to open Noma at the warehouse in Copenhagen known as *Nordatlantens Brygge* (North Atlantic Wharf), a cultural centre for Iceland, Greenland and the Faroe Islands. They had to wait two years before Noma was awarded its first Michelin Star. In 2010 they were selected as the best restaurant in the world, and have been given this honour another four times since. Subsequently, the story of their difficult start up and eventual success was employed in an efficient branding campaign for the restaurant (Skyum-Nielsen, 2010, p. 11).

Redzepi learned to use the French concept of terroir to advance the prestige of the New Nordic Food. Terroir is the point of connection made between cuisine, taste, history, memory and landscape. Its meaning is ascribed by culture, transforming it into a significant category, as soil, landscape and surroundings. The scholar Szilvia Gyimóthy sees the recent emergence of a unique food culture in the Nordic region as a demand driven by chefs in Copenhagen (Gyimóthy, 2017).

The notion of terroir has shifting interpretations depending on the culture and the moment in history (Trubek 2008). Despite the focus on the local, it must be acknowledged that when New Nordic cookbooks use the concept of terroir, they are at one and the same time emulating the French and stepping out of the shadow of French gastronomy. For New Nordic Food is inspired by French nouvelle cuisine, or the new French kitchen of the 1960s and 1970s, where simplicity was in focus related to seasons and the pursuit of extremely fresh produce. Of course, the simplicity of new Nordic cooking is also inspired by the minimalism and freshness of Japanese cuisine, though this influence is often overlooked.

Trubek (2008) shows how terroir is an important cultural category regarding national identity. She highlights the role of the taste of food – rock, grass, hillside, valley and plateau, which are all part of the construction of e.g. vernacular and national landscapes (Trubek, 2008). Here we face an important aspect of the branding of the New Nordic Food Movement, since national identities are determined by exchange and recognition, where other nations recognise the distinctness of the identity (Harbsmeier, 1986, p. 50). The creation of a national identity is therefore constituted in the difference between "us" and "the others"; to have established a certain terroir is not enough, it must be perceived from the outside.

THE BIRTH OF THE GASTRO SCANDINAVIAN COOKBOOK

Cookbooks in Scandinavia have not, until recently, covered Scandinavian cuisine, primarily because, as mentioned before, Scandinavian food did not exist. There was no united culinary tradition that could be referred to. In 2013 Claus Meyer[3] published *Ny nordisk hverdagsmad* (New Nordic Everyday Food) along with several other leading food experts. It was distributed by the famous supermarket association FDB,[4] which helped in promoting and selling the book to a greater public than if it had been available in bookshops alone. A more globally oriented book is Simon Bajada's (2015) *The New Nordic: Recipes from a Scandinavian Kitchen*, which was written in English so that it was accessible to an international audience. The cookbook highlights everyday recipes common in Scandinavian homes, and focuses less on fine dining and more on traditional techniques such as pickling and smoking.

International publishers Phaidon have published several coffee-table cookbooks about Noma and Redzepi. In one of these, the publishers describe Redzepi as part of the:

> cutting edge of gourmet cuisine, combining an unrelenting creativity and a remarkable level of craftsmanship with an inimitable and innate knowledge of the produce of his Nordic terroir. (Redzepi, 2010, p. 13)

---

[3] A large part of the success of new Nordic food can be contributed to Meyer. He was a prior co-owner of Noma and has a successful history of entrepreneurship in the world of food. Meyer recently sold his businesses to an investment fund for US$115 million and moved to New York, where he has established several New Nordic restaurants e.g. Agern in Grand Central Station.

[4] In 2018 1.6 million Danes were members of FDB.

Source: http://gistogvist.fo/Lysingar/koks/KOKS_2016_web.pdf.

Figure 14.4   From the main chef at KOKS, Faroe Islands (1)

Mention is also made of the strong connection Redzepi has to the region, as can be seen in dishes of his such as Newly-Ploughed Potato Field or The Snowman from Jukkasjärvi. These have been painstakingly constructed to express the array of Nordic ingredients used. Another example can be found in Redzepi's use of pebbles, which he picks up in the local regions, in the presentation of his dishes. In this way, Redzepi is directly identifying the food with the land from which it has sprung.

Through the influence of Noma and the New Nordic Food Manifesto, several international cookbooks have been published which focus not only on the food itself, but the accompanying beautiful images. Together, the dishes and images reinforce the relationship between nature, place and cultural roots. For though Noma's or KOKS' dishes are avant-garde in their expressions, they always entail a search for new, old or forgotten ingredients, a search which involves foraging among local fields for wild produce. In Noma's case, they source horse-mussels from peripheral areas like the Faroe Islands, the purest possible water from Greenland, and sheep or game from Lapland. Here we see the pan-national or Scandinavist scope of the New Nordic Food Movement, which invites a new theory for understanding nationalism. Of course, it must be recognised that initially such specific ingredients were only available in a few elite restaurants. Chef Trina Hahnemann tried to change this with her international bestseller, *The Scandinavian Cookbook*. Hahnemann has been a crucial factor in the mass dissemination of the newfound passion for Nordic food and has played an important role in getting people to cook Nordic style in their own homes:

> Nordic food is an everyday cuisine that can inspire people in the northern hemisphere to eat both locally and seasonally. It's about tradition and eating from your "back yard" in a new and modern context. But it's also about great food, cooked in the kitchen and eaten together at the table. (Hahnemann, 2008, p. 24)

Food scholar Bi Skaarup does not appear to have the same appreciation for the sense of tradition that inspired Hahnemann. Instead he claims that New Nordic Food was not a nostalgic turning back of the clock to times gone by, but rather the culinary leaders and innovators had started to cultivate produce from the Nordic area. A few years later the Scandinavian food activists gained international fame and the whole region went from a gastronomic backwater to a fine dining destination (Skaarup, 2013).

THE GASTRO SCANDINAVIST SUPER TERROIR

The book about KOKS takes us on a 290-page long journey (Redzepi, 2012b). There is very little text in the image-dominated work, which takes us on a tour de force through landscapes and produce, where the geographical relationship between produce, land and people is emphasised. From the first establishing shot of the landscape, to ultra-close-up images of moss and rocks, we only slowly begin to understand that this is in fact a cookbook. This massive luxury edition aims to make the reader grasp the intrinsic relationship between *taste* and *place*. Relating specifically to the Faroe Islands, KOKS makes it clear that the islands offer a super terroir. This idea is echoed in Redzepi's words: "Langoustines were so intense and so briny that they were simply mesmerising. Still this day . . . Faroese examples are my benchmarks" (Redzepi, 2012a, 15). Here we see how Redzepi is elevating terroir and goût de terroir – the "taste of the earth"

Source: http://gistogvist.fo/Lysingar/koks/KOKS_2016_web.pdf.

Figure 14.5   From the main chef at KOKS, Faroe Islands (2)

– as material version of local identity. This idea gives us a strong dynamic between people and place, as is made clear, visually, in the case of the New Nordic cookbooks. Through these images, we are reminded of a connection between Gastro Scandinavism, at the same time both promoting and creating a relation between the Nordic people, the landscapes and food. However, it is important to recognise that the idea of a Nordic terroir relates strongly to marketing and storytelling, since there are no "typical" Nordic landscapes (they are varied), and the Nordic people are culturally different, with various language barriers, such as Greenlandic, Finnish, Icelandic, Sami, and so on.

Bearing in mind, then, the search for an authentic Nordic sense of terroir, it becomes necessary to look at romantic nationalists and the thoughts of the philosopher Johann Gottfried von Herder. He believed that treasures were to be found among the ordinary people, in their proverbs, ballads and customs (Herder and Rohfleisch, 1946). We can find an echo of that romantic notion in the promotion of New Nordic Food:

> you'll find a treasure trove of other delights. What comes to mind? Sea urchins, razor shells, scallop, whelk. And before I forget it, a plethora of different kinds of seaweed. . . . Faroese lobster, the delicacy that is drawn out of the fjords around Tórshavn is without a doubt of exceptional quality. (KOKS, n.d., 2016)

Not surprisingly, elements of rural landscapes are a popular motif in the cookbooks. When investigating the different terroirs, landscapes, sea-scapes and urbanscapes in books about Noma and KOKS, we find that quaint images of life in small Scandinavian villages, forests, fields and coastal regions are as popular as the more unforgiving yet still pictur-esque and sublime panoramas. These quaint images are highly charged with an almost existential and characterological meaning for the Nordic state of mind. We could easily refer to this as the "official Scandinavian iconography" seen from the perspective of non-Nordic people. There is an emphasis on rural areas, extreme forms of nature, small forgotten towns and even smaller villages. These are idealised and glorified. Most representations of the different national Nordic landscapes are rendered via certain genres and traditions of landscape representations, like the sublime or the picturesque. The landscapes are represented as mild and embracing, while the seascapes are wild, unforgiving and merciless. There are hardly any images of socioscapes or modern urbanscapes, which, again, is a throwback to iconography associated with Scandinavism and nineteenth-century romantic nationalism. Nevertheless, it cannot be denied that the New Nordic Food Movement has been important in con-necting the Nordic countries. Moreover, it has served in re-actualising and refurbishing the Nordic peripheries from a Gastro Scandinavist sentiment. Yet, the idealistic original vision of the movement, which included not using truffles, olive oil and Burgundy wines, has recently been contested and ultimately abandoned in the new Noma 2.0, which opened in the spring of 2018. Former Noma chef Christian Puglisi is one of the critics of the original New Nordic Food Manifesto. In his cookbook *Relæ: A Book of Ideas* (2014), he suggests that the regional focus is not in tune with the globalised world in which he lives. Therefore, the idea of an authentic or even "lost" Nordic order or terroir, which should be rediscovered, is an obsolete way of thinking.

As mentioned above, I coined the term Gastro Scandinavism through the contraction of gastronationalism and Scandinavism. In the long nine-teenth century – usually defined as the period from 1790 to 1914 – an emergence of cultural nationalism occurred in most nations of Europe. At the same time, a new national self-image appeared in most nations, and in this construction culture and cultural heritage played a new role and was instrumentalised to serve ideological aims. National and pan-national self-images do not emerge from nowhere, but from the "mangrove swamp" of different ethnic self-images. Scandinavism has a much similar genesis, where nodal actors worked out of a notion of common Scandinavian heritage (Simonsen, 2017). Seeing Scandinavia and, moreover, the entire north as a unity meant strengthening its image in the world. From the start, Noma and the New Nordic Food Movement were not interested in acting on a Danish national scale; they had ambitions for the North and global ambitions, even though the idea of making a Nordic gastronomy sounded insane to food critics and chefs. The founders of Noma, René Redzepi and Claus Meyer, revealed in an interview that other chefs had mocked them, asking, "Are you going to make whale blubber pizza?" (Redzepi and Meyer, 2006, p. 9). Redzepi had initially been inspired by the chefs of the avant-garde[5] Catalan restaurant elBulli, then the best restaurant in the world, where he had served an internship. elBulli was run by Ferran Adrià, who has been described as the most imaginative generator of haute cuisine on the planet. He reinvented, re-branded, vernacularised and made previously unfashionable Catalan food a global brand.

A year after the signing of the Manifesto, Nordic politicians responded with the Århus Declaration, in which the Nordic ministers of fisheries, agriculture, forestry and food announced their support for the New Nordic Food Program.[6] In 2006 the Nordic Council of Ministers funded a program called New Nordic Food Enhancing Innovation in the Food, Tourism, and Experience Industry (2007–2009) with US$5 million. Soon afterwards, the Nordic Council of Ministers initiated the New Nordic Food Manifesto as a way of boosting the production and consumption of traditional food products.[7]

A part of this ongoing politicising of the New Nordic Food Movement can be seen in the Embla Food Award, which is awarded to the best in Nordic food, or in the idea of Nordic food diplomacy, which is a means of telling a story through Nordic cuisine. A recent example of this

---

[5]   The artistic idea of the avant-garde is often used in relation to cutting edge restaurants, but this notion is also becoming an empty signifier, a superlative used to praise innovation in a certain context.

[6]   See Nordic Council of Ministers (2015).

[7]   In 2009, the bank Nordea and the Nordea Foundation gave US$20 million to the OPUS project. The project was based at the University of Copenhagen and done in cooperation with Claus Meyer and others. OPUS stands for 'Optimal well-being, development and Health for Danish children through a healthy New Nordic Diet'.

comes from a speech given by Danish President Lars Løkke Rasmussen in Washington, DC, where he advised Barack Obama to get inspired by New Nordic Cuisine, which involves such things as moss, bark and ants.

Furthermore, in 2008, the Nordic Council of Ministers and the Nordic Innovation Centre launched the New Nordic Food Programme, with 14 food ambassadors, for an international audience at the Bocuse d'or Europe chef competition in Lyon. National support, such as those listed here, suggest the extent to which banal nationalism can be elevated in "Nordic", "French" or "British" recipes and ingredients, and that those recipes carry stories about national borders and national history. In this regard, the New Nordic Food Movement has evidently been driven by the desire for a common culinary identity and heritage in the north.

CONCLUSION: GASTRO SCANDINAVISM

Despite wavering from the initial aims of the movement, New Nordic Food is an homage to place and to the concept of terroir, as well as to a well-known and successful image of the north and to the growing strength of the brand of Scandinavia. Noma and New Nordic Food have united the different regions of the north in celebrating Nordic food, through creating a culinary culture which did not previously exist. The New Nordic Food Movement has been a part of redefining the idea of the Nordic by means of an ideological reorientation, which can be conceptualised, analysed and emulated in an international context.

In this chapter, we have used Nordic cuisine to engage with and analyse the international interest in everything "Nordic", and how that cuisine is connected to a geographical idea about place, as well as a desired moral orientation. This changed Nordic perspective enables us to think about the interconnectedness of nations, regions and their pursuits to gain recognition from the world outside. Furthermore, the relative strength of the New Nordic Food Movement can be explained out of a deep-felt longing for a better and stronger sense of identity, and a more prestigious self-image of Scandinavians, which can be understood as Gastro Scandinavism.

Through Gastro Scandinavism, Nordic cuisine has contributed to the self-image of the people of the whole region. It has cultivated a subtle and often unacknowledged sense of national pride. Restaurants like Noma have tapped into the idea of identity and its relationship with food and place. The restaurant is presented as a cool Nordic minimalist space that is slightly primitive, with skins of animals and rugged tables set in old and historic buildings. Through the forward-thinking of institutions such as Noma, the way has been paved for peripheral areas like the North of

Norway, Iceland, Greenland and the Faroe Islands to escape their former marginalisation. It becomes apparent that food is a crucial aspect of the cultural heritage of nations. Food is a part of our collective memory and material culture. It is used to simultaneously produce and reproduce national identity in a time of globalisation.

REFERENCES

Aronczyk, Melissa (2013) *Branding the Nation: The Global Business of National Identity*, New York, Oxford Univerity Press.

Bajada, Simon (2015) *The New Nordic: Recipes from a Scandinavian Kitchen*, Richmond: Hardie Grant.

Berg, Per Olof, Anders Linde-Laursen and Orvar Löfgren (2000) *Invoking a Transnational Metropolis: The Making of the Öresund Region*, Lund: Studentlitteratur.

Cook, Ian and Philip Crang (1996) "The world on a plate: Culinary culture, displacement and geographical knowledges", *Journal of Material Culture*, 1 (2), 131–153.

DeSoucey, Michaela (2010) "Gastronationalism: Food traditions and authenticity politics in the European Union", *American Sociological Review*, 75 (3), 432–455.

Graham, Adam H. (2016) "Faroe Islands, fermentation drives the menu bites", *New York Times*, 12 August. https://www.nytimes.com/2016/08/14/travel/raest-restaurant-torshavn-faroe-islands-denmark.html (accessed 4 April 2018).

Gyimóthy, Szilvia (2017) "The reinvention of terroir in Danish food place promotion", *European Planning Studies*, 25 (7), 1200–1216.

Hahnemann, Trina (2008) *The Scandinavian Cookbook*, Kansas City: Andrews McMeel Publishing.

Harbsmeier, Michael (1986) "Danmark. Nation, kultur og køn", *Stofskifte. Tidsskrift for antropologi*, 13, 47–73.

Herder, Johann Gottfried von and Josef Rohfleisch (1946) *Auszug aus einem Briefwechsel über Ossian und die Lieder alter Völker*, Schöninghs Textausgaben 246, Bremen: Schöningh.

Ichijo, Atsuko and Ronald Ranta (2016) *Food, National Identity and Nationalism: From the Everyday to the Global*, Basingstoke: Palgrave Macmillan.

KOKS (n.d.) Website. http://www.koks.fo (accessed 4 July 2019).

Leerssen, Joep (2006) "Nationalism and the cultivation of culture", *Nations and Nationalism*, 12 (4), 559–578.

Meyer, Claus (2013) *Ny nordisk hverdagsmad*, Copenhagen: Strandberg Publishing.

New Nordic Food (n.d.) Website. http://www.newnordicfood.org/ (accessed 4 July 2019).

Nordic Council of Ministers (2015) *The Emergence of a New Nordic Food Culture: Final Report from the Program New Nordic Food II, 2010–2014*. https://www.norden.org/en/publication/emergence-new-nordic-food-culture (accessed 4 July 2019).

Puglisi, Christian (2014) *Relæ: A Book of Ideas*, London: Ten Speed Press.

Redzepi, René (2010) *Noma: Time and Place in Nordic Cuisine*, London: Phaidon.

Redzepi, René (2012a) "Foreword", in *KOKS*, London: Books for Cooks – Bent C. Forlag APS, pp. 3–5.

Redzepi, René (2012b) *KOKS*, London: Books for Cooks – Bent C. Forlag APS.

Redzepi, René and Claus Meyer (2006) *Noma nordisk mad*, Copenhagen: Politikens Forlag.

Simonsen, Kim (2004) "Noma", *Sosialurin*, 15 (12), pp. 12–19.

Simonsen, Kim (2017) "The cultivation of Scandinavism – The Royal Northern Society of Antiquaries' international network, seen through the letters of Carl Christian Rafn", in Jes Fabricious Møller et al. (eds) *Skandinavisme*, Odense: Syddansk Universitetsforlag, pp. 1–10.

Skaarup, Bi (2013) "The New Nordic diet and Danish food culture", in Patricia Lysaght (ed.) *The Return of Traditional Food*, Lund: Lund University Studies, pp. 33–42.

Skyum-Nielsen, Rune (2010) "The Perfect Storm", in René Redzepi (ed.) *Noma: Time and Place in Nordic Cuisine*, London: Phaidon, pp. 11–17.

Snyder, Louis L. (1984) *Macro-Nationalisms: A History of the Pan-Movements*, Westport, CT: Greenwood Press.

Trubek, Amy (2008) *The Taste of Place: A Cultural Journey into Terroir*, London: University of California Press.

Volcic, Zala and Mark Andrejevic (2011), Nation branding in the era of commercial nationalism, *International Journal of Communication*, 5, 1–21.

15. Appropriation of the Nordic brand in the Estonian political discourse 1997–2017: consistencies and contestations

Piia Tammpuu, Külliki Seppel and Kadri Simm

INTRODUCTION

This chapter studies the appropriation of the Nordic brand and its dynamics in the Estonian political discourse over two decades, from 1997 to 2017. Our study departs from the assumption that the peculiarity of the Nordic branding is not confined to the strategies of place branding applied for representing the Nordics, but includes long-standing efforts to export the 'Nordic' also as a societal model (Browning 2007) and a set of certain values and norms (Ingebritsen 2006) to be copied and followed by others. We aim to explore the impact of these efforts by analysing the ways in which Estonian politicians have incorporated Nordicity in their political rhetoric to legitimate their programmes in domestic political struggle and assert Estonia's belonging to the Nordics.

The twenty-year period under observation is characterised by complex processes of state-building and consolidation in Estonia, which followed the restoration of independent statehood in 1991 after the half-century long Soviet regime and subsequent transitional reforms implemented in the first half of the 1990s. The particular political setting thus implies a certain receptiveness for importing concrete policies as well as values, norms and practices in more general terms. Furthermore, state-building also encompassed crafting a new identity and image, which would support the political goals of the governments of the restored state and help to dissociate itself from the burdensome past of Soviet occupation. The latter has also involved launching special nation-branding campaigns aimed at re-building Estonia's international reputation and image as a 'normal European state' (see e.g. Bolin and Ståhlberg 2010; Jansen 2008; Jordan 2014; Pawłusz and Polese 2017). While Estonia's attempts at defining and positioning itself as a Nordic country in the post-Soviet context have mainly been associated with foreign policy needs (see e.g. Lagerspetz 1999) and external audiences (Bolin and Ståhlberg 2010), our analysis seeks to demonstrate that the appropriation of Nordicness implies not only the branding of the country in the eyes of foreign audiences but equally among the domestic publics.

Several factors explain the attractiveness of the Nordics as certain role models and an identity reference in the Estonian context. Given Estonia's geopolitical position as the northernmost Baltic state, Nordic countries have had a significant influence on Estonia's national identity due to their geographical and cultural proximity (Lagerspetz 1999). Being histori- cally part of the same geopolitical space as the Nordic countries (Clerc and Glover 2015), the positioning of Estonia as essentially a European country and its post-Soviet 'return to the West' has also been occurring through the 'Nordic gate' (Lauristin and Vihalemm 1997; cf. Feldman 2000; Jurkynas 2004). Besides cultural and geopolitical commonalities, the contemporary political significance of the Nordic model as a success- ful socio-economic constellation on the global scale and the prominent role of the Nordics in world politics further explicate the authority and significance of the Nordic countries in the Estonian context. Recognised as successful norm-setters in the international political arena, the Nordic countries also took a leading role in cooperating with their Baltic neigh- bours to support the transitional reforms and their preparation for European integration (Bergman 2006; Browning 2007; Jurkynas 2004; Musial 2015).

On the other hand, there are also aspects which problematise and ques- tion the view of Estonia and the other Baltic states as 'eager followers' of the Nordics (cf. Musial 2015). The first governments of the restored Estonian state, inspired by the Thatcherist and Reaganist ideology that was at its peak in the early 1990s, introduced neoliberal economic and social policies that were quite at odds with the Nordic model. Also, the Soviet occupation as a cultural and political interruption of the former democratic capitalist regime has complicated the smooth transmission of the values and norms common to the Nordic democracies into the Estonian context. Apart from these factors, the sustainability and viability of the Nordic model in the changing political realities within Europe and outside has been a much discussed topic in the literature throughout the period covered in this chapter (see e.g. Browning 2007; Ingebritsen 2006; Lawler 1997; Mouritzen 1995). Therefore, we expect the utilisation of the Nordics as a particular reference point and the positioning of Estonia as a 'Nordic country' to be not necessarily consistent but rather a varying and contested discursive practice over the years.

Based on a study of political discourses of the leaders and major spokespersons of Estonian parliamentary parties across the political spectrum, this chapter has two major foci. First, how and in which contexts has the Nordic model been included in the Estonian political discourse? And, second, how has Nordicity been appropriated for positioning Estonia in the domestic political context? Our analysis is based on a systematic collection of media texts published in the Estonian-language news media in the years of 1997–2017, which include explicit references to the Nordic countries or Nordicity by the selected group of politicians. The temporal starting point of the analysis marks the rise of the Nordic dimension as an alternative to the Baltic connection in the Estonian political discourses, still dominant in the beginning of the 1990s (Jurkynas 2004, p. 21). The empirical material thus allows us to trace the consistencies and variations within the aforementioned aspects both in terms of the political-ideological spectrum as well as in temporal perspective.

EXPORTING AND APPROPRIATING THE NORDIC AS A BRAND

Regardless of their relatively small size and remote geographic location on the northern rim of Europe, the Nordics have become recognised as states capable of exercising 'collective authority beyond their borders that exceeds their military or economic weight' (Ingebritsen 2006, p. 1). Such symbolic authority draws on the deliberate and persistent strategies of the Nordic countries in communicating and promoting their model of democracy as a signifier of certain values, norms and practices, which Ingebritsen has pointedly defined as 'norm entrepreneurism' (Ingebritsen 2006). An alternative way of conceptualising these activities is through the rather straightforward marketing or 'branding' prism (Browning 2007), which, either conceptualised as place branding or nation branding more specifically,[1] can be seen as a method of soft power that lies in the ability to shape the preferences of others due to the attractiveness of a country's culture, political values, ideals and policies (Nye 2004).

The values, norms and practices at the core of the Nordic model as an internationally 'marketable brand' include both outward-oriented principles, such as a peace-building approach in international relations, internationalist solidarity and multilateral security, which have been guiding

---

[1]   Generally, nation branding can be seen as a specific type of place branding besides city branding and regional branding, focused on the strategic shaping of a country's image and reputation (see e.g. Campelo 2017).

the foreign policy agendas of the Nordic countries, as well as values and norms that have their historical roots in domestic policies of the Nordics, such as egalitarian social democracy and environmental norms (see e.g. Browning 2007; Ingebritsen 2006). Altogether, these have come to define the Nordic 'exceptionalism' as a difference from or superiority compared to the 'overall standard' (Browning 2007; Ingebritsen 2006; Mouritzen 1995).

The extensive and multifaceted role of the Nordic countries in assisting the complex social, political and economic transformations in the Baltics since the early 1990s has accordingly been interpreted as a deliberate strategy to strengthen their authority both in the Baltic region as well as in Europe at large by exporting Nordic principles, standards and practices to their southern neighbours (Browning 2007; Ingebritsen 2006; Jurkynas 2004; Musial 2015). Their efforts in the Baltics have been considered to be rather successful. For example, as Musial (2015) argues, the Nordics 'quickly became role models and sources of inspiration in several domains as they epitomised Western European governance and welfare, and were close neighbours across the Baltic Sea' (p. 262). Furthermore, the Nordic countries had proved that, despite being similarly relatively small and geopolitically peripheral in Europe, they can still achieve an outstanding and influential international reputation and standing (Ingebritsen 2006). The Nordics, especially Finland and Sweden, had also strong economic interests in Estonia (as well in other Baltic states) by quickly becoming the main foreign direct investors and export markets for the country (Feldman 2000; Jurkynas 2004). Thus, according to Musial (2015), the strategies of the Nordic countries in the post-1991 Baltics involved efficient use of the Nordic power of attraction supported by targeted investment strategies, which eventually resulted in the acceptance and implementing of the new norms and standards on the part of the Baltic states. These aspects also help to understand why the Nordics have had a clear 'competitive advantage' compared to the Baltics as a significant identity reference for Estonia. Being anchored in the burdensome Soviet past (as well as in its post-Soviet realities) that Estonia has deliberately wished to disassociate itself from, the Baltics have simply failed to offer an attractive alternative to the Nordics in advancing the political ambitions and agendas of the country (cf. Jurkynas 2004; Lagerspetz 1999).

However, the view of the Baltics as 'eager norm-followers' of the Nordics (see e.g. Musial 2015) is problematic, as it downplays possible conflicts and controversies included in such attempts to transmit and recontextualise norms and values. Hence, we propose to consider the reception and adoption of such initiatives through the concept of appropriation, which generally refers to the adoption and adaptation of foreign concepts, practices or symbols by taking them out of one context and putting them into another. Essential to these processes is the aspect of resignification – that is, investing cultural objects or forms with an adapted content that is often far-removed from the 'original'. In other words, instead of mere copying or imitation, appropriation involves the alteration of the initial meaning and content through its re-contextualisation, according to the intentions and interests of the adopter (Gorman 2016; cf. Schneider 2003, p. 224). In this respect, appropriation can be seen as a discursive mechanism through which meaning is constituted and negotiated (Lorentzen 2017). Unlike theoretical approaches of cultural and norm diffusion, which tend to focus on structural factors of adoption, appropriation as a theoretical instrument thus highlights the role of adopters, including their purposes and motives as crucial factors explaining the modes and outcomes of adoption processes (Gorman 2016). Accordingly, the concept of appropriation offers an alternative theoretical approach to scholarship on norm diffusion and institutional transfer of norms by making visible processes of re-interpretation, modification and normative change as well as by emphasising the capacities of the local actors to shape meanings and manipulate institutional transfers in practice (Draude 2017).

In analysing norm adaptation, what has to be taken into account is that the norms themselves may change over time. According to Browning (2007), some of the elements that have been recognised as part of the Nordic model have been 'Europeanised' over time and melded with European practices and processes, decreasing Nordic exceptionalism. Also the Nordics themselves seem increasingly to have difficulties to adhere to previous 'Nordic norms', for example, by being pushed from the welfare model and related norms towards a more neoliberal agenda by the elites. Besides, as Ingebritsen (2006) argues, in some areas like immigration and cultural diversity the Nordics have been unable to sustain the role of 'norm entrepreneurs' due to internal conflicts over values such as cultural preservation versus multiculturalism.

THE NORDICS AS A REFERENCE POINT IN THE ESTONIAN POLITICAL DISCOURSE

Our analysis shows that references to 'Nordicity' as a specific development model have had two peaks in the Estonian political rhetoric – in the late 1990s/early 2000s and early 2010s – both of which can be associated with a certain 'crisis of development' in Estonia following economic crises and a related search for a new way forward (Lauristin and Vihalemm 2017, p. 61).

While the Nordics have been present in the political rhetoric of the leaders and major spokespersons of different parliamentary parties, clear contrasts appear in terms of the thematic foci between the politicians from different poles of the political spectrum. Predictably, the social democrats representing the left-wing position in the Estonian political system have tended to highlight the traditional features of the Nordics as success-ful 'welfare societies', such as strong commitment to social security and equality. However, in the rhetoric of the right-wing parties, which have set the political course for the major part of the re-independence period (until 2016), the Nordic model is used more selectively: the key associa-tions related to the Nordic countries are limited to economic prosperity and high levels of socio-economic development and living standard. The other side of the Nordic socio-economic progress, such as high taxes and redistributive policies, are generally either overlooked or criticised.

Besides references to the 'Nordic model' in general, more specific political, social or economic features have also been highlighted in politi-cal debates. Some elements have appealed across political divides, for example, in the early 2000s, the Nordic countries served as examples of successful 'knowledge economies'. In others, politically motivated differ-ences in how the Nordic values and practices are interpreted and presented are clearly visible. For example, in the debates on labour market reforms and redesigning of labour regulations in 2005, the key focus was on the concept of 'flexicurity' as a synthesis of both flexible and secure labour relations. While the left-wing politicians mainly highlighted the security aspect achieved through collective agreements and strong labour unions in the Nordic countries, right-wing politicians on the contrary emphasised the Nordic experiences of 'easy firing and hiring' as a way to make labour relations more flexible and adaptable to economic needs. On a more abstract level, the debates also include references to more general values and norms attributed to Nordic democratic traditions, political culture and society. The examples include democratic governance and a high level of trust towards political institutions.

The comprehensiveness of the topics testifies to the importance of the Nordic countries as the most 'significant others', either as close neighbours or the role models against whom to benchmark Estonia's development. Yet, significantly, there are several societal values and norms generally associated with the Nordic model that appear either only episodically in Estonian political discourse or are rather contested or rejected. The rare mentioning of the Nordics in relation to gender equality, listed as one of the key elements of Nordic identity (see e.g. Landgrén 1998, cited in Lagerspetz 1999, p. 19), can be seen here as a reflection of the marginal status of gender issues in Estonian society. Likewise, references to the

Nordics are missing in relation to environmental norms and values, which can be explained by the weakness of the green political parties in Estonia. The references to the Nordics in connection with values and norms related to socio-cultural diversity and multiculturalism have occurred in the right-wing (populist) discourse in the negative context (as a warning), indicating the sensitivity and ambivalence of these issues in the Estonian political setting.

Although the Nordics have been frequently employed as a general reference point by Estonian politicians, more specific country-based references can also be distinguished. From all the Nordic countries, Finland and Sweden have received the lion's share of references. Finland is culturally, economically and socially the closest country to Estonia due to linguistic similarities, shared historical experiences and long-term cultural connections, and a high level of interaction between the two populations, both in terms of tourism and labour migration.

While Finland's dominance in the political rhetoric is partly related to factors not specifically related to its 'Nordicity', Sweden, on the contrary, represents the embodiment of the Nordic model as a specific type of socio-economic organisation of society and is also the main target of the critique of the welfare society. Sweden is also hailed for its 'advanced' political culture and norms, and stable democratic political system. Other Nordic countries have entered the discussions within specific political topics. For example, Denmark came into focus during the major redesigning of the Estonian labour policy when its branded concept of 'flexicurity' was the buzz-word across the political spectrum. Norway was highlighted as an example during the EU accession negotiations by the opponents of accession as a viable form of relations with the EU. Iceland has been missing to a large extent from the political discussions altogether.

Though the Nordics are mostly depicted as carriers of certain common norms and values, differences between particular Nordic countries are also recognised and contrasted. For example, in the context of Estonia's accession to the EU, the differences between Finland and Sweden in their engagement to EU politics have been highlighted. Recently, in the context of the refugee crisis the different political positions between Norway and Denmark as more 'conservative' and 'selective' in their immigration policies on the one hand, and Sweden and Finland as more 'liberal' and 'open' on the other hand have been marked.

POSITIONING ESTONIA – A 'NORDIC' COUNTRY?

The other facets of using the Nordic countries as a continual political and ideological reference concern the representation of Estonia as a 'Nordic country' and the attempts to construct its own versions of 'Nordicity'. Unlike the slogans crafted for the branding campaigns that have aimed at building the image of Estonia as 'Nordic' (see e.g. Jansen 2008; Jordan 2014; Pawłusz and Polese 2017), the ways in which the Nordics have been rhetorically employed by national politicians for positioning Estonia and presenting its political aims in domestic political discourse have been far from unanimous or uniform.

Estonia as Becoming a 'Nordic' Country

The most consistent motive occurring in the national political discourse over the years, and equally employed by politicians from different ideological strands of the political spectrum, is that of Estonia as striving *to become a 'Nordic' country*. Here the Nordics primarily represent the *telos*, the ultimate goal for Estonia, particularly for their high living standards and wealth. Underlying the particular motive is the idea of 'catching up' with the Nordics, that is, reaching the high level of socio-economic development and prosperity generally associated with them:

> over the last 20 years, we have been mobilised by another dream – to catch up, to get closer to, to live as well as they live in Finland and elsewhere in the free world. (Siim Kallas, rightist-liberal Reform Party, 9 December 2006)

This motive also frames another type of rhetoric suggesting Estonia as *not being a 'Nordic' country – yet*. Here the Nordics serve mainly as a benchmark against which to compare the country's overall progress and advancements in different policy areas, particularly in the late 1990s and early 2000s.

'Lagging behind' the Nordics is often explained by the Soviet occupation as a political and economic interruption in the developmental trajectory of the country. Here comparisons with Finland are repeatedly made to justify Estonia's handicap:

> Finland did not have to survive 50 years of occupation and therefore the Finnish living standard is now remarkably better than it is in Estonia. . . . 20 years have not been enough in order to recoup the lost time and achieve the living standard which is possible for Finns. (Andrus Ansip, rightist-liberal Reform Party, 10 May 2012)

The Soviet past is also blamed for Estonia's 'socio-cultural disadvantage' compared to the Nordics. For example, deficits in political culture are explained via the experience of living under the Soviet regime:

> if somewhere in Sweden, Finland or Germany a minister of interior would be caught listening in on his political rivals, his own party would sack him forever. Of course the same would be done to the party by the electorate. We can ask why it did not happen here. The people grown up in the Soviet system do not see a problem in that. Then everyone was listened in on daily basis. (Eiki Nestor, leftist Social Democratic Party, 31 October 2002)

On the other hand, the claim of Estonia *as moving further away from the Nordics*, instead of becoming a Nordic, has been used by leftist and centrist politicians to criticise the neoliberal policies of the right-wing governments of the country:

> our prime minister Andrus Ansip believes in the flexible labour market. His predecessor, current European commissioner Siim Kallas has proposed Denmark as a good role-model for Estonia. . . . if Estonia's labour market was based on the same principles as in Denmark, I would cry with happiness. Unfortunately, it is not so and government's plans are not taking us closer to Denmark, but to Bangladesh . . . (Eiki Nestor, leftist Social Democratic Party, 8 November 2005)

However, regarding the Nordics as the *telos*, the motive of Estonia as *already a 'Nordic' country* occurs from the late 2000s as a measure and judgement of the advancements that the country has made so far, especially under the governance of the right-wing coalitions. As the following extract illustrates, being 'Nordic' is actually conflated with 'being European' in Estonian political discourse, which indicates the largely overlapping significance of the 'Nordic' and the 'European':

> We have built a proper Nordic country during a short time: Estonia has become one of the most European of countries. (Andrus Ansip, rightist-liberal Reform Party, 3 January 2011)

Furthermore, Estonia is also claimed to perform 'even better' than the Nordics by implementing more 'efficient' (social) policies or by providing more 'generous' public benefits to its citizens.

However, the exclaimed lack of Nordic values and norms in Estonian society is an aspect that continuously appears in the political discourse of the Estonian social democrats throughout the two decades analysed here. For example, as Jevgeni Ossinovski, the leader of the Social Democratic Party since 2015, argues:

> Let us compare the values of the inhabitants of Estonia and Sweden. [. . .] How can we explain that only 58 per cent of Estonian people disagreed with the statement 'if there is job scarcity, men should have greater right to work than women?' While 93 per cent of Swedish respondents do not consider this acceptable. [. . .] Only when such value-based foundation is laid, can we speak of Sweden as a realistic development goal for Estonia. (Jevgeni Ossinovski, leftist Social Democratic Party, 26 January 2016)

In general, the attempts to (re-)define and (re-)position Estonia as 'Nordic' in domestic political discourse seem to be driven more by the perceived present-day socio-economic and political realities of Estonia and the Nordic countries rather than any historical and cultural similarities and connections.

Questioning the Nordic Model as an 'Estonian Way'

While the economic prosperity associated with the Nordics has served as a worthy target for the country and has equally been yearned for by Estonian politicians across the spectrum, the proposed ways for reaching this goal have been much more contested and divergent.

The political discourse of right-wing parties that have dominated the government coalitions tends to reject the long-term policies underlying the Nordic model as the potential 'Estonian way'. Mainly the high tax rates required for the welfare expenditures and the redistributive policies as well as the progressive tax policies characteristic of the Nordic countries have been contested throughout the years.

An even more explicit rejection occurs in relation to the alleged 'crisis of the welfare state' as an outcome of 'overindulging' and 'generous distributive policies', associated not only with the Nordics (and in this context particularly with Sweden) but also with Germany as another prototype 'welfare society':

> I call for not redistributing. Let's look at the situation in which Germany and Sweden are today. I think that we still do not have the right to be lazy and start a street-conversation with a friend on the topic: how many days you have been on sick leave this year already? (Juhan Parts, rightist-conservative Res Publica, 19 December 2003)

A rhetorical move included in the extract below is to present 'social' as synonymous with 'socialist', thus attributing a negative past-related connotation to the former. In general, this kind of rhetoric is particularly evident in the discourse of the rightist-conservative politicians, which – at least implicitly – is meant to contest the political positions of local social democrats standing for 'social values':

> The Nordic as a target is a bit vague and originates from a socialist dream. We have already seen in close history what this may bring along. (Margus Tsahkna, rightist-conservative Union of Pro Patria and Res Publica, 16 January 2016)

However, a more 'moderate revision' of the Nordic model and its 'financial pillars' is also characteristic to Estonian social democrats, who, nevertheless, suggest the 'Scandinavian way' to be also the only 'Estonian way':

> Estonian tax burden is approximately 37–39 per cent of the GDP [gross domestic product]. In the Nordics, it is approximately 50 per cent. Which would be the optimal level for Estonia? Definitely lower than it is in the Nordics. [. . .] But it is still possible to reach Scandinavia only via [the] Scandinavian way. (Sven Mikser, leftist Social Democratic Party, 29 March 2012)

Similarly, Nordic immigration policies and related norms and values have been rejected as 'too liberal' not only by the conservative and the right-wing populist parties (the latter being represented in the Estonian Parliament since 2015) but also by rightist-liberal politicians:

> We can see what problems have arisen from too liberal immigration policies in many Western European countries. We do not have to go very far. We can see these problems at our Northern neighbours. It is completely foolish to repeat the same mistakes that others have made. (Andrus Ansip, rightist-liberal Reform Party, 9 September 2010)

Proposing Its Own Model – Estonia as 'The Nordic Tiger' and 'The New Nordic'

Instead of adopting the 'Nordic way' to become 'Nordic', in search for a new way forward after the economic crisis in 2008–2009, alternative versions of the Nordic model have been proposed, particularly by the rightist-liberal Reform Party that acted as the leading partner in government coalitions between 2005 and 2016. In 2010, Prime Minister Ansip introduced his vision of Estonia as 'The Nordic Tiger' (*Põhjamaade Tiiger*) – a country primarily characterised by rapid economic growth and high competitiveness, high-quality education and energy security:

> Estonia has to become the Nordic Tiger – a country with the fastest growing economy in the region and a country providing the best education like the Nordics. [. . .] 'The Nordic Tiger is a modern, flexible and efficient state, which can offer the best in these fields.' (Andrus Ansip, rightist-liberal Reform Party, 13 June 2010)

As revealed from the label and the foci of this vision, certain elements, such as the rapid economic growth, high competitiveness and technological innovativeness, taken from the nation or country brand(s) of the fast developing Asian economies known as 'Asian Tigers' have been combined within the Nordic frame.

This political vision was further elaborated and presented by the Reform Party as its election platform in the parliamentary elections of 2015, entitled now as 'The New Nordic' (*Uus Põhjamaa*). By emphasising the quality of being 'New', Estonia as opposed to the 'Old Nordics' was suggested to be 'more dynamic and flexible'. According to Taavi Rõivas, the successor of Ansip as the leader of the Reform Party and the Prime Minister of Estonia (2014–2017), the vision of Estonia as the 'New Nordic' entails the following:

> the New Nordic – is a well-protected and economically successful country, which secures equal opportunities, values the family and bears European values. The New Nordic is Estonia's great narrative – a better secured, wealthier and [of demographically] increasing population. [. . .] We have rather good premises for reaching this goal – Estonia is already in several fields on the top of the world. Our premises for economic growth are good because of the educated Estonian people, [a] favourable environment for entrepreneurship as well as for the low level of state loan. We are still distinguished [from the Nordics] by a gap in the living standard, the closing of which requires efforts but is possible. We are not satisfied until Estonian living standard is at least equal to Finland. (Taavi Rõivas, rightist-liberal Reform Party, 16 January 2015)

Thus, compared to the previous idea of Estonia as the 'Nordic Tiger', the vision of Estonia as the New Nordic was somewhat broader, including also aspects usually associated with the Nordic model such as equality, security, and family welfare. However, these values were still presented through the prism of neoliberalism, for example by stressing equal opportunities rather than equal outcomes and placing family welfare in the service of demographic growth as a driver of economic development.

Estonian social democrats, while positioning themselves as standing for a 'socially more protective' approach, are still premised on the high competitiveness [of the state] as the political end when referring to their own Nordic model:

> The aim of the Social Democratic Party is a Nordic model which is targeted at achieving high competitiveness [of the state] but which also offers people solutions in case innovative and risk-prone initiatives do not succeed. (Sven Mikser, leftist Social Democratic Party, 4 February 2012)

However, the Social Democratic Party has failed to communicate its version of 'Estonian Nordicity' as persistently and steadily as the rightist-liberal Reform Party.

Nevertheless, the vision of Estonia as The New Nordic has largely lost its prominence since 2016 when the rightist-liberal Reform Party had to give up its long-term position in the Estonian government. Besides, the significance of the Nordics as a target for Estonia has explicitly been contested by the populist Estonian Conservative People's Party, most notably in relation to liberal immigration policies attributed to the Nordics and to the unfolding 'migration crises' in Europe:

> The Reform Party's dream about the New Nordics has scattered not only due to the stagnant politics of the reformers themselves but at least equally as a result of the migrant crisis that has buried the Nordics. (Mart Helme, right-wing populist Estonian Conservative People's Party, 19 January 2016)

This leaves us with the question whether these shifts will be an indication of the longer 'decline of the Nordic brand' in the Estonian political discourse or rather the fluctuant and selective nature of its appropriation.

CONCLUSIONS

The Nordics as a development model to be achieved or, on the contrary, to be avoided, has been a consistent but also contested reference point in Estonian politics. In general, it is not the cultural and historical traits perceived as commonly shared with Nordic countries but rather their present-day social, political and economic characteristics that have constituted the Nordics as a significant reference point for Estonian politicians. The long-term adherence to the Nordics as a symbolic *telos* for Estonian society, however, has implied only selective appropriation of the elements associated with the Nordic identity and model.

The meaning and significance of the Nordics has shifted according to the ideological stance of the political actor as well as the particular political situation and theme, thus making it a 'floating signifier' in Estonian political discourse. While the Estonian social democrats have been more consistent in appraising the Nordic model as a comprehensive development plan and critiqued Estonia's distance from it, the right-wing parties that have dominated the government coalitions have employed the Nordic model rather selectively and instrumentally through the neoliberal filter. Estonia's goal of becoming 'as wealthy and developed as the Nordics' has not been accompanied by efforts to adopt either the economic or social policy based on the more egalitarian type of distributive justice, reminiscent of the Nordic model (cf. Browning 2007; Lagerspetz 1999). Our study also reveals the difficulties associated with self-identifying as

'Nordic': societal values and norms, such as gender equality and respect for cultural diversity as part of the overall norm of social equality, as well as stringent norms of political conduct, generally associated with the Nordic democratic politics and society, are not equally rooted in the post-Soviet Estonian context.

In this regard, the selective appropriation of Nordicity in the Estonian political discourse also echoes some of the contested aspects of the Nordic model within the Nordic societies, such as the political pressures to move from a welfare model towards a more neoliberal agenda (Browning 2007; Stråth 2004) as well as domestic conflicts over migration policies (Ingebritsen 2006). However, as the Estonian case demonstrates, becoming a 'European country' in terms of membership of the EU, has not decreased the relevance of the Nordic identity and model as a political reference point. On the contrary, the visions of Estonia as a Nordic Tiger and the New Nordics, proposed by the rightist-liberal Reform Party in parliamentary elections in 2010 and 2015 respectively, occurred after Estonia's EU accession in 2004.

However, as Browning emphasises, discussions about the declining 'market value' and relevance of the Nordic model and norms as a brand do not necessarily entail the decline or loss of Nordic identity(ies) as such (Browning 2007, p. 28). In this respect, the idea of Estonia as historically and culturally belonging to the Nordics will presumably also maintain its relevance as part of the (geo)political identity of the country.

ACKNOWLEDGEMENT

This research has been supported by the European Union and European Regional Development Fund through the Centre of Excellence in Estonian Studies and is related to the research projects IUT20-5 and IUT20-38 (funded by the Estonian Ministry of Education and Research).

REFERENCES

Bergman, A. (2006), 'Adjacent internationalism: The concept of solidarity and post-Cold War Nordic–Baltic relations', *Cooperation and Conflict*, **41** (1), 73–97.
Bolin, G. and P. Ståhlberg (2010), 'Between community and commodity: Nationalism and nation branding', in A. Roosvall and I. Salovaara-Moring (eds), *Communicating the Nation*, Göteborg: Nordicom, pp. 79–101.
Browning, C. S. (2007), 'Branding Nordicity: Models, identity and the decline of exceptionalism', *Cooperation and Conflict*, **42** (1), 27–51.

Campelo, A. (2017), 'The state of the art: From country-of-origin to strategies for economic development', in A. Campelo (ed.), *Handbook on Place Branding and Marketing*, Cheltenham, UK and Northampton, MA, USA: Edward Elgar Publishing, pp. 3–21.

Clerc, L. and N. Glover (2015), 'Representing the small states of Northern Europe: Between imagined and imaged communities', in L. Clerc, N. Glover and P. Jordan (eds), *Histories of Public Diplomacy and Nation Branding in the Nordic and Baltic Countries: Representing the Periphery,* Leiden and Boston: Brill Nijhoff, pp. 3–20.

Draude, A. (2017), 'The agency of the governed in transfer and diffusion studies', *Third World Thematics*, **2** (5), 577–587.

Feldman, G. (2000), 'Shifting the perspective on identity discourse in Estonia', *Journal of Baltic Studies*, **31** (4), 406–428.

Gorman, B. (2016), 'Appropriating democratic discourse in North Africa', *International Journal of Comparative Sociology*, **57** (5), 288–309.

Ingebritsen, C. (2006), *Scandinavia in World Politics*, Lanham, MD: Rowman & Littlefield.

Jansen, S. C. (2008), 'Designer nations, neo-liberal nation branding – Brand Estonia', *Social Identities,* **14** (1), 121–142.

Jordan, P. (2014), 'Nation branding: A tool for nationalism?' *Journal of Baltic Studies*, **45** (3), 283–303.

Jurkynas, M. (2004), 'Brotherhood reconsidered: Region-building in the Baltics', *Journal of Baltic Studies*, **35** (1), 1–31.

Lagerspetz, M. (1999), 'The Cross of Virgin Mary's Land: A study in the construction of Estonia's "Return to Europe"', *Finnish Review of East European Studies*, **6** (3–4), 18–28.

Landgrén, L.-F. (1998), Lecture delivered at Finns Folkhögskola, Esbo, Finland.

Lauristin, M. and P. Vihalemm (eds) (1997), *Return to the Western World*, Tartu: Tartu University Press.

Lauristin, M. and P. Vihalemm (2017), 'Eesti tee stagnaajast tänapäeva: sotsiaal-teaduslik vaade kolme aastakümne arengutele', in P. Vihalemm, M. Lauristin, V. Kalmus and T. Vihalemm (eds), *Eesti ühiskond kiirenevas ajas: elaviku muutumine Eestis 2002–2014 Mina. Maailm. Meedia tulemuste põhjal.* Tartu: Tartu University Press, pp. 60–95.

Lawler, P. (1997), 'Scandinavian exceptionalism and European Union', *Journal of Common Market Studies,* **35** (4), 565–594.

Lorentzen, J. (2017), 'Norm appropriation through policy production: Rwanda's gender policies', *Third World Thematics*, **2** (5), 658–674.

Mouritzen, H. (1995), 'The Nordic model as a foreign policy instrument: Its rise and fall', *Journal of Peace Research*, **32** (1), 9–21.

Musial, K. (2015), 'Benevolent assistance and cognitive colonization: Nordic involvement with the Baltic states since the 1990s', in L. Clerc, N. Glover and P. Jordan (eds), *Histories of Public Diplomacy and Nation Branding in the Nordic and Baltic Countries: Representing the Periphery.* Leiden and Boston: Brill Nijhoff, pp. 257–279.

Nye, J. S. (2004), 'Public diplomacy and soft power', *The Annals of the American Academy of Political and Social Science*, **616**, 94–109.

Pawłusz, E. and A. Polese (2017), '"Scandinavia's best-kept secret": Tourism promotion, nation-branding, and identity construction in Estonia (with a free guided tour of Tallinn Airport)', *Nationalities Papers*, **45** (5), 873–892.

Schneider, A. (2003), 'On "appropriation": A critical reappraisal of the concept and its application in global art practices', *Social Anthropology*, **11** (2), 215–229.
Stråth, B. (2004), 'Nordic modernity: Origins, trajectories and prospects', *Thesis Eleven*, **77** (5), 5–23.

16. Phantasmal brand Sweden and make-believe in political speech

Mikael Andéhn

POST TRUTH VERSUS THE COHESIVE FANTASY OF REALITY

> Look at what happened last night in Sweden . . .
> (Donald J. Trump. 45th President of the USA, 18 February 2017)

We might never know what really happened "last night in Sweden". This statement by the 45th President of the United States, a man much maligned for his recurrent tendency of acting as a mythomoteur of contemporary social discourse through his ultracrepidarian excesses, drew massive media attention. It seemed that nobody knew what events were referenced in this statement, after the fact, it seems most likely these events originated in the imagination of an American journalist who extrapolated more widely than what has been typical for people in this profession historically. Nevertheless, the statement is indicative of something more profound in the workings of media in contemporary society, and which holds particular pertinence in the context of geographical knowledge.

Examining how Sweden is represented in international media reveals a particular phantasmal quality of places (see Gao et al., 2012). As the global media ecology increasingly encompasses, and is greatly shaped by messages that often reference events that never take place and situations, and descriptions of situations, that are not reflected in the lived experience by the people involved. In other words, it increasingly involves falsehoods and absurdities that are presented as if they were worthy to be considered to be truths in their own right. This tendency has earned them the moniker "post truths". In the present work post truth is treated as a tendency of moving beyond the dichotomy of true and false, which leaves (un)qualified statements as meaningful simply by virtue of their reception, and "where appeals to emotion are dominant and factual rebuttals or fact checks are ignored on the basis that they are mere assertions" (Suiter, 2016: 25). The determining factor for valuing speech so becomes the scope of its conveyance, which comes to displace the necessity for any claims to veracity, where the title of a "post truth" is granted to statements only when they are understood as deviating from what we generally construe as "true" a property, which itself, as we shall see, has a naturally tenuous nature. The process of becoming literate in the form of communication post truths represent can readily be likened to a socialization into an alternative reality, constituted by a nonalethic form of speech (see Stokke and Fallis, 2017), i.e. one that is not concerned with the truth-value of its content, a reality which is constituted by a new form of media literacy with its own conceptual technology, which we will explore shortly. First, we need to establish some fundamental traits of the object of focus of the post-truth myth-making process, place. The idea of place identity, i.e. inherent properties of a place, as something distinct from place image, i.e. the perceptions of a place, is inherently problematic. This is not the least true in the context of address in which place generally finds itself defined, that is, through the assignment of meaning rendered through experience (Relph, 1976; Tuan, 1977), which invariably seems to fail to ever reach the potential of discerning some nature of places that could be construed as constituting *essential* identities. Rather, grasping for the identity of places seems to always require some privileging of accounts, such as a legal spatial delimitation, as representing a particular form of the place among many other competing versions. Indeed particularly Tuan's (1977) account of place appears greatly contingent on a very direct form of encounter thought to generate experiences, meaning that place is rendered phenomenologically. But this focus on experience as capable of generating some unified account, as Debord tells us, cannot hold in the context of modern media, as mediated experience "should be understood as the systematic organization of a breakdown in the faculty of encounter, and the replacement of that faculty by a social hallucination" (1967/1994: 63). Granted, if any mediated account is a social hallucination, this new mythological use of places in post-truth discourse is hard to make justice as something truly separated from the already tenuous link to a claim to reality held by other accounts of places. Yet such a separation seems almost necessary from any perspective geared towards dispelling the confusion post-truth statements produce. Indeed, if one examines accounts of place, particularly comparing places such as Sweden, Berlin or the USA to those places that have little claim to reality in the strict sense, such as Valhalla, Heaven or El Dorado, it becomes evident that places are *always* mythological if mediation can generate place-defining experience. As a toponym is always a discreet signifier for an, at best, approximate spatiality that requires a secondary regime to frame it (see Deacon, 1997; Casey, 1993). Some other means of separating post truth from the ordinary understanding of place is thus needed to proceed in dissecting the nature of post truths in the context of place. But before endeavouring to account for such a separation we shall engage in exploring the phantasm of the example at hand, the mythologies of the nation of Sweden.

THE MEANS OF PHANTASM

About a thousand years removed from the era of Vikings and with the Swedish empire long since collapsed, Sweden is often described as having enjoyed more than 200 years of peace. Having remained quasi-neutral during both the Great War and the Second World War, Sweden became a rich nation in the post-war era, due in part to its intact infrastructure and social stability, which allowed it an advantage over the war-torn countries recovering from these great conflicts (see Nordstrom, 2000). The country joined neither NATO (North Atlantic Treaty Organization) nor the Warsaw pact during the Cold War, officially following a non-alignment policy in its dealings with the superpowers, although it retained close connections to western countries, and finally joined the European Union (EU) in 1995. The non-alignment policy was also coupled with a long dominance of a moderate leftist political party, in which consensus between labour unions and corporate interest was emphasized. This political orientation was popularly referred to as "the third way", between socialism and capitalism. Both the principles of the third way and non-alignment were perhaps embodied most palpably by the politics of Olof Palme (the prime minister of Sweden 1969–1976 and 1982 up until his assassination in 1986). Palme, even though he was the leader of the moderate leftist Social Democrats, was a staunch and outspoken critic of not only the American aggression in the Vietnam War, but also of the suppression of the Prague spring by the Soviet Union. His anti-colonial rhetoric, taken together with the fact that Sweden had a history of comparatively very modest involvement in overseas colonies of its own, as well as a very marginal role in the slave trade and colonial oppression that serves as an onus on the historical reputation of many European nations (see Harrison, 2007), served to render a mythology of moral superiority that arguably bubbles just under the surface of the media discourse in the country to this day. This peculiar tendency was further compounded by the mythologies surrounding, for instance, Dag Hammarsköld (UN Secretary-General and posthumous Nobel peace prize recipient) and Raoul Wallenberg (credited with saving in excess of 10,000 Jewish Hungarians from German occupation during the Second World War). Indeed, this reputation, which was also mirrored in discourse outside Sweden (Hinshaw, 1949), and the non-alignment policy, rendering a veneer of neutrality, allowed Sweden to exert considerable so called soft power (Nye, 2008). This state of affairs was thought to enable Sweden to act as a "bridge" between the superpowers (Myrdal, 1960). This account of historical reality relayed here is generally understood as true, i.e. it constitutes the "ordinary mythology" of the nation of Sweden, and has served to greatly increase the visibility and importance of the country. Indeed, by all accounts Sweden would otherwise most likely have exerted a very modest geopolitical influence in the absence of these mythological resources. Further, Sweden in many ways epitomizes the Nordic model of a political history of a strong influence from the moderate left resulting in relatively minor income discrepancies across social classes. The country has also pursued a strong orientation towards a dual earner model, which has been argued to have resulted in the country having the smallest gender inequalities of any of the European welfare states (Korpi, 2000). Sweden also has a history of relatively liberal immigration policies (Sainsbury, 2006). Having been a net immigration country since the Second World War, the nation has owed much of its increase in population to immigration in the last 80 years (Statistiska Centralbyrån, 2018). In recent decades immigration has also accelerated significantly having brought a significant cultural influence and changes in the political landscape in tow. One particularity of this tendency is that immigration to Sweden has historically been dominated to a large extent by asylum seekers, as opposed to, for instance, New Zealand in which the immigration policy has historically prioritized meeting the need for certain professional competences (Bauer et al., 2000). Sweden also performs very well in various factors comparative to other countries, as the country is frequently featured at the very top of various estimates of development and quality of life writ large[1] and is the one of the leading, if not the first, nations in terms of gender equality across several metrics.[2]

Here, we arrive at a point where the logic behind the use of Sweden as a reference point in political speech is beginning to crystallize. The ordinary mythology of Sweden's idealized history, as presented here, in conjunction with its political present renders a certain set of "reputation assets" (Anholt, 2005: 119), or – one may note – liabilities, which in summation can be said to constitute "brand Sweden", both of which are, naturally, derived from a selective accounting of history that is riddled with silenced and emphasized components. The example here lends further support to the, perhaps self-evident, but nevertheless pertinent idea that "place

---

[1] See http://www.oecdbetterlifeindex.org (retrieved 18 January 2018).
[2] See http://eige.europa.eu/rdc/eige-publications/gender-equality-index-2017-measuring-gender-equality-european-union-2005-2015-report (retrieved 16 January 2018).

brands exist even without place brand*ing*" (Giovanardi et al., 2013: 379 emphasis in original; see also Olins, 2002). For Sweden, particularly, the history of non-alignment and "third way" political orientation allows for a unique non-recognition into certain dominant supranational geographical orders, the EU notwithstanding. Following Andéhn and Zenker's (2015) proposition that a place's relation to other places in a "system of geographical abstractions constitutes a piece of information more vital than any other" (p. 25) in defining it, Sweden's mythology is meaningfully separable from the aforementioned dominant orders. Specifically, Sweden's mythology allows it some degree of avoiding an "iconicity of similarity" (Deacon, 1997: 75; see also L'Espoir Decosta and Andéhn, 2018) with entire swathes of other nations that may be more readily ordered into having belonged to either the free-market west or the socialist east. At the same time, meanwhile, it has been noted that Sweden has appeared to have been given the role of the exemplar nation of various mythologies that could just as readily be attributed to one of the other Nordic countries, and to a lesser extent even the Netherlands (see Marklund, 2013). Sweden, it seems, has emerged as a synecdoche of the entire Nordics. Further, it seems that many of these ordinary mythologies simply enjoy a stronger connection, specifically to brand Sweden, than they do to any other Nordic country, or the Nordics in general, which may have interesting implications for the understanding of both the mythologies and the place, as the stronger association would render Sweden more readily referable as a representation of political mythologies related to feminism and multiculturalism (see Andéhn and L'Espoir Decosta, 2016).

These factors, taken together, render an easily discernible basis of Sweden's function as a rhetorical device in contemporary politics, as a situation emerges in which the potential of various failures of Sweden becomes a reference for promoting various shades of neoliberal, social conservative and reactionary politics, while the idea of its success is equally central to proponents of feminism, multiculturalism and social democracy. This is hardly something new, as it was noted as early as the 1960s that the interest in Sweden and Swedish politics "caused some alarm among American conservatives who feared that socialism could be introduced by stealth into the free-market United States by using Swedish precedents" (Marklund, 2013: 275). What this state of affairs yields in practice is that the success of Sweden, or lack thereof, has long been a point of interest for political actors with sometimes very little direct stake in the country. This has, in turn, led to a situation in which the ordinary mythologies associated with Sweden, ranging from its association to sexual liberation in the 1950s and 1960s to its current challenges pertaining to the integration of the large numbers of refugees, are prone to be the subject of the simplification and value-laden foregone conclusions inherent in political discourse. It appears that the ordinary mythologies, once leveraged in political speech, hold much of the same potential of rendering a place into a monoculture as branding the place would (Pasquinelli, 2010). Political speech, in the context of how ordinary mythologies are construed, arguably shares the commonality of marketing that in its form as communication is boiled down to its most readily digestible form, which invariably entails the trimming away of many cumbersome uncertainties and complexities (see Horkheimer and Adorno, 1979). On the basis of this outline of the ordinary mythology of Sweden, we now turn to exploring how this account can coexist in a context in which it is leveraged as a component of post-truth statements, in which accounts that run counter to the ordinary mythology are becoming commonplace.

POST TRUTH AS MEDIA

Following Barthes (1972) we learn that a "myth cannot possibly be an object, a concept, or an idea; it is a mode of signification, a form" (107), which presents us with a useful alternative understanding that can be leveraged to address post truths. If we take this statement pointing to "form" one step further we might venture an understanding of these post truths as even representing their own form of conceptual technology, i.e. media (as per the definition proposed by McLuhan, 1994). McLuhan (1994) famously construed things as separate as clothing to the telegraph as technological means of providing affordances to human beings beyond what would otherwise have been available to them. In understanding post truth as media we are afforded a new vehicle for approaching the effects of these statements, as on the one hand performing an extension of human power, reach or speed (McLuhan, 1994) or as replacing, or even disabling faculties once possessed (Carr, 2011). In the present work, we shall find that post truths are indeed imbued with the ability to extend human potential, as McLuhan (1994) proposes, rendering post truth to something which can be approached as a form of media-technology.

In order to go further with the examination of post-truth speech acts, as well as the reference they make to mythologies, we must first draw a line in the sand, as we encounter a fundamental problem of mythologies which automatically extends to bar any means of ordering them into a typology based on their veracity, particularly in painting some myths as more "authentic" or more "real" than others. To return to Barthes "myth is not defined by the object of its message, but by the way in which it utters this message: there are formal limits to myth, there are no 'substantial' ones" (1972: 107). Yet if the understanding of post truths is formulated around the erasure of the distinction between facts and fiction, how can any account that seeks to elaborate on its use be sustained in the light of the observations that *no* myths are substantial? Here, we are aided by the seminal work of Slavoj Žižek (2009), who captures that truth is always formed in reference to a fantasy which serves to form a cohesive account of itself and thus comes to act as if it was true, and which also makes evident that an alternative "true reality", or a pre-ideological state, is an impossibility. By extrapolation we come to understand two things, first, that post-truth statements are not more false, by any strict objective means, than any other accounts, as a "truth" being deemed as "objective" is not a meaningful basis of distinction of the relative veracity of myths. Second, we also note that it is possible to sustain mythological accounts even in the face of evidence of their falsehood, as Žižek (2009) notes that ideology, taking the form of a symbolic act, has a curious power to resist dismissal through everyday experience. We seem to be capable of sustaining competing accounts of reality and act upon them as-if true even if they are mutually incompatible (see also Jameson, 1981). So far the idea of post-truth myth-making and the "ordinary myths" we take to constitute reality, which we have encountered even in times that predated mass-media, seem altogether compatible. So what does the post truth achieve for all its attempts at reframing reality? Entertaining the idea of post-truth speech being a form of media-technology, we can see how it comes to constitute an affordance that McLuhan (1994) framed as the extension of human power, speed and reach. While framing this form of myth-making as media we already challenge its prima facie conventions of understanding, but where does this alternative accounting lead us?

To state it directly, we encounter a situation in which it is indeed possible to assign a status of "more real" to one mythology over the other. Place becomes possible as simultaneously imbued with an hegemonic "ordinary mythology", while serving as a mythological referent in a post-truth statement. For the purposes of understanding a place via this typology, a distinction between these two can be rendered in that one represents a myth which is understandable as *discretely* distanced, while the other is *acutely* distanced, from the "truth" the fabric of the fantasy of collective reality presumes. This distinction, while seemingly gradient, produces two completely separate sets of speech technology that are engaged in mutual referencing. In other words, post truth is a form of anti-myth, a media that since it is understood as falsehood either if you agree or disagree with its political implication, prompts a recurring examination of what is understood as a functional political phantasm versus what operates on the traditional basis of establishing "truth", i.e. that which effectively references the ideologies that are traditionally employed to arrive at a "cohesive fantasy of reality".

Post truths are thus not meant to align to the hegemonic cohesive account of reality, rather they serve a different function, in that they demonstrably energize discourse and prompt action, without ever having to qualify as "true" or even necessarily *dispositionally* true in relation to one another (Matreavers, 2014). This function of post-truth mediation lies exactly in the identification of statements as not compatible with "ordinary mythologies", that is, exactly the process in which they are identified as what we would construe as falsehoods if we made reference to an ordinary mythology. Post-truth statements, in this mode, do not make for a convincing competitor for a "cohesive fabric of a fantasy of reality", although it should be noted that they can indeed form a so called dispositional belief, i.e. coherence within the make-believe world, in the framework they create in aggregation (Matreavers, 2014; also Leslie, 1994). The perhaps more interesting function of post truths is how they signal political orientation and reinforce tribal membership, by referencing a political unconscious in which these myths, still known to not be true, perform the function of a call to action. To exemplify, the "ordinary mythology" of Sweden might be one of a society struggling to realize its promise of a welfare state and a paragon of social equality, in the face of social changes, while a post truth may characterize the place as overrun by radical Islamists, gang crime and various perils associated with that "great other" that serves as the threat there is a need to mobilize against politically even as far away as in the USA. Neither of these competing accounts can be shown to be true in any absolute sense, but their concurrent utterance allow for a paradoxical situation in which the latter is leveraged to dispel the former. What is certain, in all of these free-flowing accounts of Sweden, is that the current use of the place as a rhetorical signal is always preceded by an ordinary mythology which serves as the point of origin of its counterpart post truths. The question remains, how do post truths perform their function?

MAKE-BELIEVE, TRUTH AND PLACE

If we return to the idea of post truth as a form of media, considering the phantasmal nature of ordinary mythologies (Debord, 1967/1994; Žižek, 2009), it behoves us to further account for how post truth differs from ordinary mythologies as they both relate to place. If we follow Casey (1993: 330) in his asserting that "stripping away cultural and linguistic accretions, we shall never find a pure place underneath", how can we maintain that post-truth statements are simply not an act of further engaging with the rendering of ordinary mythologies of place? In considering how post-truth statements are herein defined as not being considered for the status of "truth" we approach a tentative answer to this problem. Since these statements are not understood as representation of the fantasy of a coherent fabric of reality, one may argue that they never truly attain the status of what Harvey (2001) called "sites for the production of geographical knowledges". Instead these statements enable a different function.

In the use of Sweden as a rhetorical device, i.e. the statement "look at what happened last night in Sweden", we do not require further explanation of what actually happened. Instead, we here understand through the previous establishment of Sweden as a shorthand example of, for instance, failed immigration, or the dangers of Islamism, to the American right – all while simultaneously serving as a welfare state paragon to the American left. Here the use of place emerges as a political shibboleth. Specifically as the implied meaning of what happens in Sweden, it can be understood to refer to a failure of multiculturalism, feminism or some other opposed political ideology. This reveals something inherent about post-truth speech acts, as it captures how these can be understood, prima facie, as not representing their own apparent verbatim representation, or as a reference to the ordinary myths, but instead operating within a system of speech in which the statement becomes a reference to a specifically contextualized shared political understanding that enacts resistance to the ideology represented by ordinary mythology. For instance, stating that immigrants are overrepresented in violent crime statistics is not only an attack against what is understood as a multicultural hegemony, but also something that follows a set, tropified narrative path that sparks recognition among those that experience themselves as subjugated by the hegemony of multiculturalism. Here, we arrive at the core function of post truths, in that one may understand them as a means of refusal to genuflect to the dominant ideologies that the ordinary mythologies are often leveraged, if not even sometimes created, to support. In doing so, post truths also allow for an negotiation of *interpellation* (Pfaller, 2014) in that they allow for an imagination in which a particular dominant ideology is suspended (Althusser, 1969/1977 in Pfaller, 2014). Post truths thus take on the role of what Pfaller (2014) calls "ownerless illusions" in that they constitute a reference to beliefs held by no one, but that can, nonetheless, be engaged with as if true. This even enables people who in no way take the post truths to represent what is typically construed as truth, i.e. the ordinary mythologies, to engage with these statements and even derive jouissance from the relief from interpellation they render without ever having to engage with them as "truth" (Walz et al., 2014). Thus, post truths not only serve to relieve those engaging with them of the strain of the complexity of the ordinary mythologies for an often far simpler world view, but they also provide a means by which the dominant ideologies can be challenged by proxy, all without having to endure the dissonance that considering these statements as having to qualify as competing ordinary mythologies would invariably render. Herein lies a crucial potential of post truths: the means to resist dominant ideologies without the investment of having to formulate, or even believe in, an account counter to them.

Practically, in engaging with a post truth one understands that what is being said is "false", but also that this falsehood reveals the phantasm at the roots of what is considered "true" – the same "truth" that is indeed leveraged in the formulation of, and in support of, the dominant ideology. This reveals that there is no absolute basis for the ordinary mythologies, and – by extrapolation – the ideologies they support, just as for the post truth used to dispel them. Post-truth media thus emerge as a mode of make-believe that can be leveraged to dispel ordinary mythologies. This is not to say that statements that are received by most as post truths are not taken as reflecting realities by others. Indeed, the idea of post truth as media, presented here, is contingent on the receiver implicitly identifying it as separate from the "truth" of an ordinary mythology. But in this context it is important to note that discourse on, for instance, social media allows events to draw visibility to places in a previously unprecedented manner, and these events have major influence on the reputation of the places as well (Andéhn et al., 2014; Sevin, 2013). It should also be noted that this influence is in no way necessitated by the events actually taking place. For the reputation of the specific place Sweden, its ordinary mythologies are nevertheless affected by the use of it as a component of political speech, even if this speech falls into the category of post truth. The signifier "Sweden" endures, but it does so with the idea of the chimera of "Sweden", as holding some lasting monolithic meaning, being further chipped away. Here is where place branding is most directly affected, as the ordinary mythologies – the material of evoking place meaning – now shaking at the fundament, can no longer be evoked without risking a simultaneous evocation of an opposing post truth.

CONCLUDING REMARKS

This chapter has constituted an attempt at unpacking one of the riddles of the so called post-truth politics, which is becoming increasingly pertinent in wake of the rise of hybrid media (Suiter, 2016). Having established some linkage between the uses of places and the working of their mythologies, the chapter has attempted to discern whether a line can be drawn between certain mythologies and others based on their claim to truth – an impossible task. We instead find that once a falsehood, presented as a post truth, is identified as such, it acts as a form of conceptual technology, i.e. as *media* (McLuhan, 1994). As such, post-truth statements become a means to an alternative understanding which enables an array of previously impossible thoughts and actions. In an attempt to approach this media in the spirit of thinking "critically of the entire agencement of cultural production" (Hietanen and Andéhn, 2017: 542), we find that post truths indeed have the potential to dispel ordinary mythologies. Post truths, once examined, reveal that they and ordinary mythologies share the curse of an inherent tenuousness in their claims to represent any absolute reality.

The implications for places, here exemplified by Sweden, is that the mythologies of places come to be revealed as, if not inherently fragile, at least subject to a complex interplay of various forms of political use. Indeed, what one sometimes encounters as "place identity" in place branding literature is revealed to be exactly as nonsensical as one first suspects. As Barthes (1972) and Debord (1967/1994) assert, there is no objective means by which one myth can be held up over another; there is no place left if cultural connotations are evacuated (Casey, 1993). Further, the very means of place identity, the ordinary mythology, emerges as a *target* by virtue of the political ideology that through the same mythology becomes attributed to the place. Post truths also represent an exceptionally versatile tool in terms of their rhetorical use, as they do not need to compete for the status of a permissible part in a cohesive fabric of reality held by ordinary mythologies to enact their potential. But perhaps even more interesting is that post truths, in their dispelling of ordinary mythologies, have a more profound allure in their capacity to serve as a means of resisting dominant ideologies and undermine meaning attributed to places in the process of branding them, a potential derived from their ability to enable an imagined lapse of the tyranny of the reality of dominant ideologies, rendering an alternative phantasm in an act of emancipatory political make-believe. To grasp post truths in a more general sense, one may conclude that the experienced subjugation is the cause, and the suspension of the dominant ideologies enacting this subjugation, the goal. But here it should be offered that the effect of post truth widely overshoots this goal. It has been noted that, for instance, "[t]he belief among voters that politicians lie is near ubiquitous in contemporary political systems" (Rose, 2017: 555), a simple statement that indicates the scope of the context in which post truth strives. Here, we encounter a consequence of the greater tendency that post truth emerges as the perhaps most visible component of. We are witnessing something akin to a Deleuzo-Guattarian disappearance of falsehood in political discourse, in that lies and blatant misrepresentations are now so commonplace that they have become expected! This issue is likely to be aggravated by the mechanisms outlined in this text, that post truths serve a function beyond the alethic, one that operates by a logic of whether they are effective attacks on dominant ideologies rather than whether they are true or false. Further, post truths are impervious to attack by the means of political discourse that operate as if contingent on a negotiation of ordinary mythologies. As Lockie (2017) states: "When factual claims are judged according to their emotional and ideological consistency, we cannot expect that lobbing more factual claims into the public domain will necessarily challenge anyone's beliefs" (1). Herein lies the fundamental take away of the present work: post truth does not operate in discourse by conventional means, it does not engage in a contest towards claims of veracity; instead it provides emotional gratification derived from the resistance towards what is understood as the dominant ideology. Given these circumstances it is not unfeasible that we shall see an expansion and elaboration of the impact and use of post truth as media in the future and it would bode well to further examine the nature of this media in preparation for the destabilization they herald.

REFERENCES

Althusser, L. (1969/1977). Ideologie und ideologische Staatsapparate (Anmerkungen für eine Untersuchung). In L. Althusser (Ed.), *Ideologie und ideologische Staatsapparate* (pp. 37–71). Hamburg/Berlin: VSA.

Andéhn, M. & L'Espoir Decosta, J-N. P. (2016). The variable nature of country-to-brand association and its impact on the strength of the country-of-origin effect. *International Marketing Review, 33*(6), 851–866.

Andéhn, M. & Zenker, S. (2015). Place branding in systems of place – on the interrelation of nations and supranational places. In S. Zenker & B. P. Jacobsen (Eds.), *Interregional place branding* (pp. 25–37). Heidelberg: Springer.

Andéhn, M., Kazeminia, A., Lucarelli, A., & Sevin, E. (2014). User-generated place brand equity on Twitter: The dynamics of brand associations in social media. *Place Branding and Public Diplomacy, 10*(2), 132–144.

Anholt, S. (2005). Some important distinctions in place branding, *Place Branding and Public Diplomacy, 1*(2), 116–121.

Barthes, B. (1972). *Mythologies*. New York: Noonday Press.

Bauer, T. K., Löfström, M., & Zimmermann, K. F. (2000). Immigration policy, assimilation of immigrants and natives' sentiments towards immigrants: Evidence from 12 OECD countries. *IZA Discussion Paper, 187.*

Carr, N. (2011). *The shallows: What the Internet is doing to our brains.* New York: W. W. Norton & Company.

Casey, E. S. (1993). *Getting back into place: Toward a renewed understanding of the place-world.* Bloomington: Indiana University Press.

Deacon, T. (1997). *The symbolic species – the co-evolution of language and the brain.* New York: W. W. Norton and Company.

Debord, G. (1967/1994). *The society of the spectacle.* New York: Zone Books.

Gao, B. W., Zhang, H., & L'Espoir Decosta, J-N. P. (2012). Phantasmal destination: A post-modernist perspective. *Annals of Tourism Research, 39*(1), 197–220.

Giovanardi, M., Lucarelli, A., & Pasquinelli, C. (2013). Towards brand ecology: An analytical semiotic framework for interpreting the emergence of place brands. *Marketing Theory, 13*(3), 365–383.

Harrison, D. (2007). *Slaveri – en världshistoria om ofrihet: 1500–1800.* Lund: Historiska Media.

Harvey, D. (2001). *Spaces of capital – towards a critical geography.* Edinburgh: Edinburgh University Press.

Hietanen, J. & Andéhn, M. (2017). More than meets the eye: Videography and production of desire in semiocapitalism. *Journal of Marketing Management, 34*(5–6), 539–556.

Hinshaw, D. (1949). *Sweden: Champion of peace.* New York; Putnam.

Horkheimer, M. & Adorno, T. W. (1979). *Dialectic of enlightenment.* London: Verso.

Jameson, F. (1981). *The political unconscious: Narrative as a socially symbolic act.* London: Methuen.

Korpi, W. (2000). Faces of inequality: Gender, class, and patterns of inequalities in different types of welfare states. *Social Politics: International Studies in Gender, State & Society, 7*(2), 127–191.

L'Espoir Decosta, J.-N. P. & Andéhn, M. (2018). Looking for authenticity in commercial geographies. In J. M. Rickly & E. S. Vidon (Eds.), *Authenticity & tourism: Materialities, perceptions, experiences* (pp. 15–31). Bingley: Emerald Publishing.

Leslie, A. M. (1994). Pretending and believing: Issues in the theory of ToMM. *Cognition, 50*(1–3), 211–238.

Lockie, S. (2017). Post-truth politics and the social sciences. *Environmental Sociology, 3*(1), 1–5.

Marklund, C. (2013). A Swedish Norden or a Nordic Sweden? Image politics in the West during the Cold War. In J. Harvard & P. Stadius (Eds.), *Communicating the North: Media structures and images in the making of the Nordic region* (pp. 263–287). Farnham: Ashgate Publishing.

Matreavers, D. (2014). *Fiction and narrative.* Oxford: Oxford University Press.

McLuhan, M. (1994). *Understanding media: The extensions of man.* Cambridge: MIT Press.

Myrdal, G. (1960). *Beyond the welfare state: Economic planning and its international implications.* New Haven, CT: Yale University Press.

Nordstrom, B. J. (2000). *Scandinavia since 1500.* Minneapolis: University of Minnesota Press.

Nye, J. S., Jr (2008). Public diplomacy and soft power. *The Annals of the American Academy of Political and Social Science, 616*(1), 94–109.

Olins, W. (2002). Branding the nation – the historical context. *Journal of Brand Management, 9*(4–5), 241–248.

Pasquinelli, C. (2010). The limits of place branding for local development: The case of Tuscany and the Arno valley brand', *Local Economy, 25*(7), 558–572.

Pfaller, R. (2014). *On the pleasure principle in culture: Illusions without owners.* London: Verso.

Relph, E. (1976). *Place and placelessness.* London: Pion.

Rose, J. (2017). Brexit, Trump and post-truth politics. *Public Integrity*, *19*(6), 555–558.

Sainsbury, D. (2006). Immigrants' social rights in comparative perspective: Welfare regimes, forms in immigration and immigration policy regimes. *Journal of European Social Policy*, *16*(3), 229–244.

Sevin, E. (2013). Places going viral: Twitter usage patterns in destination marketing and place branding. *Journal of Place Management and Development*, *6*(3), 227–239.

Statistiska Centralbyrån (2018). *Befolkningsutveckling; födda, döda, in-och utvandring, gifta, skilda 1749–2016.* Retrieved 23 January 2018 from http://www.scb.se .

Stokke, A. & Fallis, D. (2017). Bullshitting, lying, and indifference toward truth. *Ergo*, *4*(10), 277–309.

Suiter, J. (2016). Post-truth politics. *Political Insight*, *7*(3), 25–27.

Tuan, Y. F. (1977). *Space and place: The perspective of experience.* Minneapolis: University of Minnesota Press.

Walz, M., Hingston, S., & Andéhn, M. (2014). The magic of ethical brands: Interpassivity and the thievish joy of delegated consumption. *Ephemera*, *14*(1), 57–80.

Žižek, S. (2009). *First as tragedy, then as farce.* London: Verso.

17. Nordic place branding from an indigenous perspective

Anne Heith

There is a history of othering the Sámi people and describing their traditional territory as a periphery. However, "the peripheral north" may be enacted, marketed, and branded in various ways (Bærenholdt & Granås 2008). A topic discussed in Umeå in connection with the city being a European Capital of Culture in 2014 was the program's focus on Sámi culture. Critical Sámi voices claimed that the Sámi were exploited and commodified. There were also representatives of the Sámi who argued that highlighting Sámi culture was all right as long as Sámi entrepreneurs benefitted from the exposure in marketing and media (Heith 2015a, 2015b). The debate reflects the fact that today the Sámi are concerned with the ways they and their culture are used as well as with issues related to Sáminess as a brand. One potential problem that tends to come to the fore in discussions like the one in Umeå is the exotification of people in branding and marketing. Paulgaard claims that reinforcing core contrasts between the majority population and groups seen as exotic and different is characteristic of the tourism industry (Paulgaard 2008, 55). While Sámi entrepreneurs who benefit from this kind of use of Sáminess may find it acceptable to use exotification, there is a sensitivity to differentiation of groups related to a colonial history. The issue of using Sáminess in marketing is furthermore complicated by attempts at toning down differences between the Sámi and the majority population. This is the theme of a brochure with the title *Fördomar och förklaringar* ('Prejudices and explanations') distributed by the Sámi Parliament's Information Centre in Sweden (Skielto and Enoksson n.d.). The purpose of the brochure is to inform people about stereotypical notions of the Sámi people – to a high degree the same kind of stereotypes used in the marketing of tourist attractions. These contradictions testify to the fact that uses of Sáminess and stereotypes are contextual and performed by diverse agents with different agendas and cultural affiliations.

To understand the aversion to the use of Sámi culture in present day branding and marketing of the North one has to go back to history, a history that many Sámi today find painful. In the nineteenth century scientists went north to document the people, land, fauna and flora in a region conceived of as a wilderness at a remote distance from the civilized world. The indigenous people of this region, the Sámi, were photographed and measured. Their artifacts and holy objects were collected and taken to museum collections in European metropolises. Under the influence of Darwinistic ideas of the survival of the fittest there was a belief that the Sámi would not survive in the modern world. As a remnant from ancient times they and items connected with their culture were exhibited and stored in museums.

Sámi people with reindeer were displayed at the Egyptian Hall in London in 1822–1823 and at Hagenbeck's Zoo in Hamburg in 1875 (Lehtola 2013). From the vantage point of the organizers and spectators the Sámi were seen as "a wild, exotic people" from a distant part of Europe that had not been reached by civilization. As Europe's only indigenous people the Sámi were marketed as an attraction. The view on the Sámi has shifted according to ideological embedding and due to the temporal strata when narratives were produced. They were seen as an inferior race in accordance with the science of race biology, but they could also be viewed as a positive contrast to modern man living in close contact with nature. Like other so called primitive people the Sámi were seen as living a more "authentic" life than modern man in narratives connected with romanticized ideas of nature, authenticity, and a simple way of life.

Whether the Sámi were seen in a positive light as noble savages, or as representatives of an inferior race, they were constructed as the Others. In the 1920s and 1930s there was a public debate on the threat of degeneration in Sweden. In 1921, the State Institute for Race Biology was founded in Uppsala. Its first director, Herman Lundborg, saw it as a mission to teach the Swedish people about the danger of blending "races". In his opinion the so called "Nordic racial character" should be kept as pure as possible. Scientists like Linnaeus, Retzius and Lundborg contributed models of racial hierarchies and ideas of racial differentiation which continued to exclude groups of people from the idea of the people for centuries. This history is a suppressed theme of later narratives of the modern, democratic Swedish people's home, which has had an immense impact on the Swedish self-image as a progressive, modern nation, exceptional in its dissemination of welfare and equal opportunities. It is only during the last decades that this image has been shattered through a focus on the exclusion of certain groups from the idea of the people, and the suggestion that the people's home was founded on a selective idea of the people. It has been proposed that the social democratic people's home launched by the politician Albin Hansson in a speech in 1928 was an ethnic system: "The

Swedish people's home in Per Albin's classical version was without doubt meant for ethnic Swedes [. . .]" (Hettne et al. 1998, 400, my translation).

Through the centuries there have been multiple narratives about the land of the Sámi, which today is called Sápmi. In the seventeenth century when Sweden was a great power with colonial ambitions, chancellor Axel Oxenstierna expressed the opinion that the north was an India with riches to be harvested. In this period of time, when colonization and the establishment of mines began the process, which deprived the Sámi of the lands they had traditionally used. The contemporary poet David Vikgren (2013) draws attention to this history in the poem *Skogen, malmen, vattenkraften*, "The forest, the ore, the water power" which repeats the words "skogen", "malmen", and "vattenkraften" in various combinations, drawing attention to the most important natural resources that have been extracted from the north, and contributed to Swedish wealth creation (Vikgren 2013). Today "extractive violence" is a prominent theme among Sámi activists, politicians, ordinary people, and cultural workers protesting against the establishment of mines (Sehlin MacNeil 2017). One example from recent years is when British Beowulf Mining planned to start a mine in Gállok (Kallak). This engendered massive protests, which made it clear that the mining company's plans to transform the land to an industrial area was not going to be accepted silently by Sámi. They wanted to preserve the lands as pastures for reindeer and a cultural heritage to be passed on to future generations.

The conflict at Gállok points both to a history of colonialism whereby the land of the Sámi has been exploited, and to contemporary protests against colonization. After the Second World War a wave of decolonization took off in which former colonies started to demand rights and sovereignty. People from former colonies, indigenous peoples and minorities became more visible in political debates in a period shaped by the spatial turn in the humanities and social studies (Westphal 2011). At the outset of the mobilization of indigenous peoples globally the Sámi already were actively involved. When the World Council of Indigenous Peoples (WCIP) was founded in Port Albern, Canada in 1975, Sámi from Sweden, Finland and Norway were among the founders. One of the council's conferences took place in the city of Kiruna in Sápmi. The current cooperation among indigenous peoples is built on the 20 years of work done by the WCIP.

Today, there is an international movement of indigenous peoples providing a forum for actions promoting the rights of indigenous peoples. There are also Sámi Parliaments in Norway, Sweden and Finland working for Sámi rights on various fields. An international orientation is found in the pioneer Nils-Aslak Valkeapää's poetry books *Trekways of the Wind* (1994) and *The Earth, My Mother* (2017), which both use the idea of a global indigenous collective sharing experiences of loss. This notion is also used in the works of later generations, for example in the official video of the Sámi singer Sofia Jannok's album *ORDA – This is my land* (Jannok 2016a). The video, which contains film sequences from international demonstrations by representatives of indigenous peoples protesting against climate change, evokes an indigenous collective protesting against a western view of nature as a resource which it is legitimate to exploit. The album, which is explicitly critical of Swedish colonialism, contains a track with recordings from the proceedings of a court case when Girjas Sámi village prosecuted the Swedish State concerning the right to administer the use of the mountain areas of the village. The voice of the representative of the State is heard denying that the Sámi have the right to the land, while Jannok's song stands for protest against a repressive state. Clearly this Sámi protest does not fit into the image of the equal nation without social conflicts; rather it points to the theme of colonial complicity highlighted in critical narratives of colonialism in the Nordic nation-states (Keskinen et al. 2009).

In connection with the development of tourist attractions in northern Scandinavia, new aspects of exploitation have been foregrounded by Sámi who do not accept cultural appropriation of elements from Sámi culture used for marketing northern Scandinavia as an attractive destination for visitors. Tourism utilizing Sáminess has been targeted as neocolonial. This type of tourism is initiated by stakeholders who come from outside the culture, with no connection to the Sámi community but who still use elements connected to Sámi culture. In Finland this has given rise to a vigorous debate and protest against exploitative tourism. The debate has been particularly lively concerning the branding of the city of Rovaniemi, marketed as the "Official Hometown of Santa Claus". Examples of cultural appropriation include the sale of items marketed as genuine Sámi handicraft, but which are copies made by non-Sámi. Another is an event called an "Arctic Circle-crossing ceremony" said to be an ancient "Lappish" tradition, but which in reality is a fiction produced by people from the Finnish tourist industry. As a response to Sámi protest, a project has been initiated aiming at the development of ethical guidelines from the Sámi point of view for responsible and sustainable Sámi tourism product development and presentation in Finland. The project is presented on the website of the Sámi Parliament in Inari, Finland (Sámi Council of Finland n.d.).

Decolonization related to the spatial turn in the humanities has provided tools for the analysis of neocolonialism and phenomena such as cultural appropriation in the tourist industry and its branding of places as attractive destinations. Today there is an awareness among indigenous peoples globally of exploitation and, with the establishment of fora such as the Sámi parliament and international organizations working for the rights of indigenous peoples, the protests of indigenous peoples are being heard. Indigenous cultural workers contribute to this by actively engaging in cultural production disseminated worldwide through electronic media. Sofia Jannok's contribution to the construction of a Sáminess which challenges a colonizing discourse in the music video to the album *ORDA – This is my land* (Jannok 2016b), was awarded for "best music video" at ImagineNative Canada, the world's largest indigenous film festival. The film shows beautiful Arctic scenery with mountains and snowy landscapes, reindeer herds and Sámi people in colorful traditional costumes. If it had not been for the detail that some of the Sámi carry machine guns and Sofia Jannok's lyrics emphasizing that "this is my land" the film might have seemed inviting and exotic in a pleasing manner for presumptive visitors. In this particular film the Sámi are not portrayed as peaceful people living in harmony with nature, but as a resilient people fighting for their rights to the land and culture that has been colonized. It is obvious that in the wake of decolonization, a new fora have emerged from where indigenous perspectives challenging colonialism in all its forms may be expressed and that this has proved to be a corrective for producers of exploitative and false narratives of the Sámi people and its culture. However, the current situation is complex. While there are Sámi entrepreneurs involved in branding and the development of touristic experiences, there are also Sámi artists and activists focused on struggle and resistance in a manner alien to the commercially oriented tourist industry. Both groups have in common that they share a resistance to top-down initiatives that have excluded Sámi from planning and management of activities related to Sámi territory and culture.

To conclude, today the Sámi parliaments of the Scandinavian countries take an active interest in issues related to the branding and marketing of Sámi culture (Skielto & Enoksson n.d.). This implies that Sámi agency and entrepreneurship are highlighted as essential elements of sustainable and ethically responsible tourism. As the ethical guidelines developed by the Sámi parliament in Inari show, there is no tolerance of exploitation of elements from Sámi culture or dissemination of top-down, ridiculing images and narratives of the Sámi. This new narrative of Sámi entrepreneurship in the tourist industry co-exists with Sámi anticolonial protest against plans to use the lands of the Sámi, be it for the establishment of mines, wind power parks in the mountains, or the marketing of hunting trips to areas used by reindeer herders. As an indigenous people the Sámi have a claim on the land. Land use, as well as immaterial and material culture, are potentially attractive assets which may stimulate branding and marketing of tourism in Sápmi by the Sámi themselves.

REFERENCES

Bærenholdt, J. O. and B. Granås (eds) (2008) *Mobility and Place: Enacting Northern European Peripheries*. Aldershot: Ashgate Publishing.

Heith, A. (2015a) "Indigeneity, Cultural Transformations and Rethinking the Nation: Performative Aspects of Sámi Elements in Umeå 2014", in B. Lundgren and O. Matiu (eds), *Culture and Growth: Magical Companions or Mutually Exclusive Counterparts?*, UNEECC Form Volume 7. Sibiu: Lucian Blaga University if Sibiu Press, 110–126.

Heith, A. (2015b) "Enacting Colonised Space: Katarina Pirak Sikku and Anders Sunna", *Nordisk museologi/The Journal of Nordic Museology*, special issue: *Rethinking Sámi Cultures in Museums*, 2015 (2), 69–83.

Hettne, B., S. Sörlin and U. Østergård (1998) *Den globala nationalismen*. Stockholm: SNS Förlag.

Jannok, S. (2016a) *ORDA – This is my land*, CD. Göteborg: Gamlestans Grammofonbolag.

Jannok, S. (2016b) *This is my land*, official video: https://www.youtube.com/watch?v=riXVuhlMNQA (accessed 13 June 2018).

Keskinen, S., S. Tuori, S. Irni and D. Mulinari (eds) (2009) *Complying with Colonialism: Gender, Race and Ethnicity in the Nordic Region*. Farnham: Ashgate Publishing.

Lehtola, V.-P. (2013) "Sami on the Stages and in the Zoos of Europe", in K. Andersson (ed.), *L'Image du Sápmi II*. Örebro: Humanistic Studies at Örebro University, 324–352.

Paulgaard, G. (2008) "Re-Centering Periphery: Negotiating Identities in Time and Place", in J. O. Bœrenholdt and B. Granås (eds), *Mobility and Place: Enacting Northern European Peripheries*. Aldershot: Ashgate Publishing, 49–59.

Sámi Council of Finland (n.d.) "Culturally Responsible Sámi Tourism", website of the Sámi Council, Inari, Finland: https://www.samediggi.fi/ongoing-projects/culturally-responsible-sami-tourism/?lang=en (accessed 13 June 2018).

Sehlin MacNeil, K. (2017) *Extractive Violence on Indigenous Country: Sami and Aboriginal Views on Conflicts and Power Relations with Extractive Industries*. Umeå: Department of Culture and Media Studies and Vaartoe – Centre for Sámi Research.

Skielto, A. and Enoksson, M. (n.d.) *Fördomar och förklaringar* [Prejudices and explanations], brochure written by A. Skielto and M. Enoksson, with illustrations by A. Suneson. Sweden: Samiskt informationscentrum.

Valkeapää, N.-A. (1994) *Trekways of the Wind*, 2nd edition. Kautokeino: DAT.

Valkeapää, N.-A. (2017) *The Earth, My Mother*. Kautokeino: DAT.

Vikgren, D. (2013) *Skogen, Malmen, Vattenkraften*. Luleå: Black Island Books.

Westphal, B. (2011) *Geocriticism: Real and Fictional Spaces*. New York and Houndmills, Basingstoke: Palgrave Macmillan.

18. Market-mediated feminism and the Nordic: a commentary on the political dimension of place branding

Cecilia Cassinger

The chapters in Part III of this volume, entitled Politics of Disruptive Nordic Place Branding, concern the use of the Nordic brand as a form of narrative resource to achieve political ends. The contributions deal with how imaginaries of the Nordic are rhetorically employed in domestic politics (Tammpuu et al; Andhén) and to renegotiate boundaries of the geopolitical landscape (Ren et al; Simonsen). Due to the focus on the mobilisation of the Nordic brand by nation-states, the contributors consult concepts within the research field of nation branding, which – in part – follows a critical tradition of place branding informed by media and communication studies. Nation branding used to be closely connected to political propaganda and diplomatic rhetoric to build and maintain geopolitical relationships. In recent decades, however, the theory and practice of nation branding have become more oriented towards the promotion of domestic trade and economic politics. Regardless of a political or economic orientation, nation branding practices are intended to give nations a competitive edge within the greater narrative of globalisation (Aronczyk, 2008). Place branding and nation branding converge conceptually insofar as they refer to a set of selected narratives and meanings intended to endow a geographical place with a positive image. However, nation branding differs from place branding in that it is often considered as a political tool to foster national identities, and strengthen economic development and international relations (Kaneva, 2011). Volcic and Andrejevic (2011) argue that nation branding is a form of soft power and "the continuation of warfare by other means in an era of capitalist globalization" (2011: 599).

In this closing comment, I would like to briefly reflect on feminism and gender equality as core political components of the Nordic brand. The aim is not to examine Nordic gender equality and feminism as systems of ideas or activist practices, but rather to examine market-mediated feminism and gender equality in the construction of the Nordic brand. What interests me here is to examine how political ideas are culturally brokered (Cohen, 1985) when made marketable to foreign (and domestic) audiences and mobilised in the place branding discourse. Nordic feminism is a particularly interesting example of the branding of politics, since it is used in both progressive and reactionary discourses to either support or challenge the essence of the Nordic brand. The political landscape in the Nordic countries is increasingly polarised around reactionary and progressive values. Progressive values are often associated with social equality and tolerance, while reactionary values are connected with provincialism and moral superiority of national traditions.

Moreover, feminist perspectives are missing in place branding research. Although argued to constitute fruitful research trajectories to advance critical theory and enrich the study of national identity and nationhood, feminist-informed approaches and gender analyses are largely absent in the field. A few exceptions are Rankin's (2012) gender analysis of the Canadian federal government's nation branding strategy and Jezierska and Towns' (2018) study of Sweden's feminist foreign policy in relation to the Progressive Sweden brand. Jezierska and Towns (2018) demonstrate that Sweden's nation branding strategy differs from more conservative forms of "nation branding practices that draw on a familiar repertoire of androcentric representations of women as passive objects of male discovery, desire and/or protection" (p. 57). Because of their radical ambition to rewrite history and challenge persistent patriarchal structures, feminist-informed approaches are well-suited to offer alternative brand narratives of nationhood.

THE NORDIC GENDER EQUALITY MODEL

The Nordic region is a particularly interesting site at which to think through feminist issues and develop distinct feminist-informed approaches in place branding research and practice. The Nordic welfare model is often argued to represent "a dominant analytical paradigm in feminist scholarship" (Lister, 2009, p. 253). The Nordic Council of Ministers stresses the liberal political values in the Nordic gender equality model in the promotion of the Nordic brand; however, feminism's radical potential is generally avoided. The focus of the Council's attention is on reports and exhibitions on shared and paid parental leave, subsidised day-care, and gender and climate policy (see e.g. The Nordic gender effect at work, 2018). During the 1970s and 1980s, the Nordic region institutionalised gender equality policies and adopted many so-called woman-friendly policies (Borchorst and Siim, 2008). The Norwegian political scientist Helga Hernes (1987) was influential in conceptualising the gendered dimension of the Nordic welfare model. She argued that the emphasis of the Nordic welfare states on social equality could potentially make them woman-friendly and state feminist (Borchorst and Siim, 2008). The traditional social democratic favouring of redistribution policies to diminish class differences paved the way for social equality, including gender equality. Women were integrated into the labour force and gained access to the public sphere; public care policies, such as state financed day-care, were developed (Hernes, 1987). These actions were important to break the barrier between the private and the public sphere and particularly the division between the family and the state, which historically cemented the patriarchal order of the welfare state and prevented women from gaining full citizenship. The traditional social democratic citizen, for instance, refers to the breadwinner citizen worker, the cultural trope of the male working-class hero (Anttonen, 2002). Yet, Hernes (1987) suggested that the women-friendly policies of the Nordic welfare states made it possible for women to gain full citizenship as care-givers (mothers), political actors, and workers.

BRANDED FEMINISM – COOL BUT HARMLESS

Even though the Nordic Council of Ministers nowadays stress gender equality as "integral to Scandinavian citizenship" (Lister, 2009: 248), there are important differences related to "the extent of institutionalization of gender equality" in the Nordic countries (Borchorst and Siim, 2002: 92). For example, Denmark is often mentioned as an exception to the Nordic gender model due to its relatively weak institutionalisation of gender equality compared with other Nordic countries (Lister, 2009). In Denmark, as a result of feminism being positioned as an extra parliamentary movement, feminism was never made part of political agenda setting and gender issues are regarded as less important in Danish politics (Borchorst and Siim, 2008). By contrast, Sweden has had a stronger tradition of feminist movements and state feminism. Borchorst and Siim (2002) argue that the reason for the progression of feminism in Sweden is that the state has served as a vehicle for developing feminist thinking and provided an arena for women's activism. This implies that Sweden could claim to be a feminist space as opposed to other place brands. In 2015, Sweden got a self-defined feminist government and a feminist-informed approach to foreign and security policies (Aggestam, Bergman-Rosamond and Kronsell, 2019).

The feminist foreign policy may be understood as embedded in a global discourse of gender equality to ensure sustainable development, peace and international security, as well as in a domestic political discourse to signal a move towards a progressive and less consensus-driven foreign policy. The feminist foreign policy may also be seen as part of an effort to strengthen the progressive brand of Sweden (Jezierska and Towns, 2018). In the action plan for Sweden's feminist foreign policy, the Minister of Enterprise and Innovation states that:

> A feminist foreign policy strengthens competitiveness and the Sweden brand. Gender equality offers men and women the same conditions to flourish, and generates jobs. (Government Offices of Sweden, 2015)

What happens to feminism when it becomes part of the nation branding discourse? Jezierska and Towns' (2018: 57) answer is that "feminism disappears from view in the 'Progressive Sweden' brand". They mean that focus is shifted from feminism's radical political claims of structural change to a focus on gender equality issues. Explanations for the disappearance of feminism may be found in the nature of brand and market mediation. The ultimate goal of branding is to create coherence, simplicity and attention. Messages and ideas are thus reduced in complexity and repackaged in order to fit the commodity logic of the market. Nation brands are commodity signs whose meanings and values are decided within a global cultural system of brands (Kaneva, 2018). When mediated through brand Sweden, the feminist foreign policy converges with a popular feminism, which is highly visible in a global brand and consumer culture (Banet-Weiser, 2018). Popular feminism is characterised by liberal values and drained of its radical potential to contest the status quo. Expressions of popular feminism can be observed in celebrity led campaigns promoting feminist issues for the United Nations (UN), the artist Beyoncé performing in front of a gigantic neon sign displaying the word "Feminist", or advice in a women's magazine on feminism as the new fashion. Referring to the work of Scharff (2013), Gill (2016) observes how feminism has "moved from being a derided and repudiated identity among young women [. . .] to becoming a desirable, stylish, and decidedly fashionable one" (p. 611). She contends that the market mediates a positive version of feminism, which is "encumbered by its desire *not* to be angry, *not* to be 'difficult,' *not* to be 'humourless' . . ." (2016: 618). In the liberal market version, feminism is cool, but emptied of radical political content, thus harmless.

PROGRESSIVE VERSUS REACTIONARY PLACE BRANDS

The high visibility and wide circulation of feminism in recent years have activated intense forms of misogyny (Gill, 2016). The new mutual relation between popular feminism and popular misogyny (Banet-Weiser, 2018) is visible in the polarisation of the Nordic political landscape. Far-right populist parties that openly express xenophobic and misogynous views nowadays co-exist with growing feminist parties (Mawe, 2017). In the 2014 election, the Swedish political party, Feminist Initiative, gained seats in several municipal councils in the urban regions as well as in the EU parliament. Central to the positioning of the Nordic feminist parties is the opposition to reactionary nationalism and far-right populism (Mawe, 2017). Following Feminist Initiative, feminist parties in Norway, Denmark and Finland have used the catchphrase "In with the feminists. Out with the racists!" to recruit voters (Hustad, 2017).

The progressive values traditionally associated with the Nordic are challenged by the growth of a reactionary nationalism represented by far-right populist parties. In the reactionary nationalist ideology, family policy is central. Almost like a mirror of the main character Offred's fate in Margaret Atwood's (1985) dystopian novel *The Handmaid's Tale*, a woman's role is primarily defined by her ability to reproduce and support men as the nation's defenders. The heterosexual nuclear family is viewed as the foundation on which the nation is built and an assurance of healthy and normal values (Vickers, 2006). In reactionary nationalism, nation branding may thus be posited as a form of biopolitics intended to control women's reproductive abilities (cf. Ek, 2011). In the nationalist rhetoric of right-wing populism, feminism and gender studies lead to de-masculinisation and destruction of society as we currently know it (Vickers, 2006; Yuval-Davis, 1997). Gender research is frequently discredited as pseudo-science. Hungary's far-right government recently decided to discontinue financial support to gender studies degrees at state universities. The discontinuation of support is chiefly motivated politically (i.e. gender studies is ideology and not science), but is also rationalised by means of a market logic (i.e. there are no jobs for gender scholars). The Hungarian government's policies are lauded by the Nordic far-right, such as the Sweden Democrats, which currently constitutes Sweden's third largest political party.

Feminist lenses are important to identify and name systems of inclusion and exclusion in the making of nationhood and nation brands to help us understand how gendered orders can be altered. Could then nation branding be used as a vehicle for reactionary nationalists or progressive feminists? Aronczyk (2008) argues that nation branding does not embrace "the chauvinistic and antagonistic elements of reactionary nationalism" and is a rather "benign way to communicate national interests" in its "ability to assemble diverse motifs of heritage and modernization, domestic and foreign concerns, and economic and moral ideologies in the projection of national identity" (p. 43). The nation brand should not only mediate the nation as a moral orientation, but also as a market to invest in (Aronczyk, 2009). Given the economic, rather than political, nature of branding, it is unlikely that place brands would represent either reactionary or progressive interests. Branding neutralises political messages in order to appeal to a diverse international public. Kaneva (2018) refers to *simulation nations* in order to illuminate how nation brands are made up as commodity signs in order to seduce international media audiences. Simulation nations are informed by the logic of the media and market, rather than political ideology. Stahlberg and Bolin (2016) similarly state that nation branding empties nationhood of ideas of belonging and community, representing a cosmopolitan view on the nation as appearance. In articulating cosmopolitan viewpoints, however, nation branding may (unintentionally) offer counter-narratives to reactionary nationalism and its focus on provincial xenophobic and misogynous values. Feminist-informed approaches to place branding advance the knowledge of such counter-narratives and their effects. In her book *The Promise of Happiness*, Ahmed (2010) provides us with a plausible way of conceptualising a feminist approach to place branding. She writes:

> Feminist consciousness can thus be thought of as consciousness of the violence and power that are concealed under the language of civility and love, rather than simply consciousness of gender as a site of restriction of possibility.

Ahmed's brief explication proposes that a feminist approach to Nordic place branding would entail the continuous unmasking of the taken for granted moral "Nordic" values in the promotion of the region. The chapters in this part of the book intriguingly demonstrate how such unmasking can open up spaces of new ways of knowing and thinking about the region. Hopefully, they will pave the way for further re-narration of the Nordic and its imaginaries.

REFERENCES

Aggestam, K., Bergman-Rosamond, A. & Kronsell, A. (2019). Theorising feminist foreign policy, *International Relations*, 33 (1), 23–39.
Ahmed, S. (2010). *The promise of happiness*. London: Duke University Press.

Anttonen, A. (2002). Universalism and social policy: A Nordic feminist revaluation. *Nora: Nordic Journal of Women's Studies*, 10 (2), 71–80.

Aronczyk, M. (2008). "Living the brand": Nationality, globality and the identity strategies of nation branding consultants. *International Journal of Communication*, 2, 41–65.

Aronczyk, M. (2009). How to do things with brands: Uses of national identity. *Canadian Journal of Communication*, 34, 291–296.

Atwood, M. (1985). *The Handmaid's Tale*. London: Vintage Classics.

Banet-Weiser, S. (2018). *Empowered: Popular feminism and popular misogyny*. Durham, NC: Duke University Press.

Borchorst, A. & Siim, B. (2002). The women-friendly welfare states revisited, *Nora: Nordic Journal of Women's Studies*, 10 (2), 90–98.

Borchorst, A. & Siim, B. (2008). Woman-friendly policies and state feminism: Theorizing Scandinavian gender equality. *Feminist Theory*, 9 (2), 207–224.

Cohen, E. (1985). The tourist guide: The origins, structure and dynamics of a role. *Annals of Tourism Research*, 12 (1), 5–29.

Ek, R. (2011). Creating the creative post-political citizen? The showroom as an arena for creativity. *Culture Unbound*, 3, 167–186. Retrieved from http://www.cultureunbound.ep.liu.se.

Gill, R. (2016). Post-postfeminism? New feminist visibilities in postfeminist times. *Feminist Media Studies*, 16 (4), 610–630.

Government Offices of Sweden (2015). Ministry of Foreign Affairs. Accessed 15 December 2018. https://www.government.se/government-policy/feminist-foreign-policy/ministry-for-foreign-affairs-presents-action-plan-for-feminist-foreign-policy/.

Hernes, H. M. (1987). *Welfare state and woman power: Essays in state feminism*. Oslo: Norwegian University Press.

Hustad, K. (2017). Denmark's new feminist party declares, "Out with the racists! In with the feminists!" *Public Radio International*, 4 December. Accessed 17 December 2018. https://www.pri.org/stories/2017-12-04/denmarks-new-feminist-party-declares-out-racists-feminists.

Jezierska, K. & Towns, A. (2018). Taming feminism? The place of gender equality in the "Progressive Sweden" brand. *Place Branding and Public Diplomacy*, 14 (1), 55–63.

Kaneva, N. (2011). Nation branding: Toward an agenda for critical research. *International Journal of Communication*, 5, 117–141.

Kaneva, N. (2018). Simulation nations: Nation brands and Baudrillard's theory of media. *European Journal of Cultural Studies*, 21 (5), 631–648.

Lister, R. (2009). A Nordic nirvana? Gender, citizenship, and social justice in the Nordic welfare states. *Social Politics: International Studies in Gender, State & Society*, 16 (2), 242–278.

Mawe, I. (2017, 4 April). Feminist parties moving forward in the Nordic countries. Nordic Information on Gender (NIKK). Accessed 17 December 2018. https://www.nikk.no/en/news/feministiska-partier-pa-frammarsch-i-norden/.

Nordic Co-operation (n.d.) Website. Accessed 3 September 2018. https://www.norden.org/.

Rankin, P. (2012). Gender and nation branding in "The True North Strong and Free". *Journal of Place Branding and Public Diplomacy*, 8, 257–267.

Scharff, C. (2013). *Repudiating feminism: Young women in a neoliberal world*. Farnham: Ashgate Publishing.

Stahlberg, P. & Bolin, G. (2016). Having a soul or choosing a face? Nation branding, identity and cosmopolitan imagination. *Social Identities*, 22 (3), 274–290.

Vickers, J. (2006). Bringing nations in: Some methodological and conceptual issues in connecting feminisms with nationhood and nationalisms. *International Feminist Journal of Politics*, 8 (1), 84–108.

Volcic, Z. & Andrejevic, M. (2011). Nation branding in the era of commercial nationalism. *International Journal of Communication*, 5, 598–618.

Yuval-Davis, N. (1997). *Gender and nation*. London: Sage.

PART IV

Conclusion

19. The Nordic wave of place branding: a manifesto

Cecilia Cassinger, Andrea Lucarelli and Szilvia Gyimóthy

This book has sought to bring together instances of the emerging Nordic wave in place branding. By means of displaying different empirical cases, conceptual analysis, and methodologies, we have attempted to provide a foundation for further endeavours to unpack and project the underlying contours of Nordic place branding. In the work in the book we have extended the perspective on Nordic place branding from being an object of study to a specific approach to branding practice and policy, a sensitivity to research, and as a type of hybrid scholarship. These features of Nordic place branding allow the concept to travel in different geopolitical and scholarly directions and, by way of cross-pollination, expand place branding research and practices on an international scale.

The aim of this final chapter is to assemble the key insights of the contributions in the book into a comprehensible Nordic approach towards place branding that can be distinguished from other approaches in the field. Nordic place branding is situated conceptually, empirically and epistemologically in the field by offering a manifesto for research in which the peculiarity of the Nordic, as we know it here, is outlined. Thereafter, the tenets of the manifesto are discussed in terms of their significance and value for the international field of place branding, their transferability to other contexts, and their orientation and affect in international practices. Finally, we propose a future agenda of research and practice, which includes a critical reflection on the possible impact and expansion of the view presented in the book.

SURFING THE NORDIC WAVE

In the book, we use the ocean wave as a figure of thought to represent the Nordic as a particular movement to place branding that others may emulate or flow with. Waves appear as unique disturbances in the ocean that are reiterated during certain periods of time. Eventually, however, all waves reach the shore and return to the ocean. Unlike schools and paradigms, waves have no boundaries, they move in different directions. Waves are counter-expressions of essentialism, since they evolve, disappear, and are replaced by new waves. Hence, this book describes the Nordic as a liquid movement situated in a particular time and space. The 18 contributions in the book all catch the Nordic wave, albeit at different vantage points. They offer insights that are germane to opening the way for a more specific formulation of a Nordic place branding manifesto. Such a manifesto should be seen as a way to summarise, position and brand the type of scholarships, academic engagement, and practices that we see examples of in this book. The transdisciplinary and international research expressed in many of the chapters allows us to capture a first feature of the wave, namely the global importance of the implications and consequences of Nordic place branding.

The figure of the wave is in line with Nordic scholarship that traditionally has emphasised the use of metaphors and narratives in management (e.g. Berg, 2001; Czarniawska-Joerges and Sevón, 2005). The wave enables us to recognise that the concepts, empirical cases and methodologies presented in the different chapters are not the only ones and not even the first ones, since waves are created by their relations to other waves. In this regard, the manifesto, presented here, is not only based on the contributions in this book, but refers to previous waves in terms of previous studies (e.g. Browning, 2007; Pamment, 2016) and pioneering research in place branding (e.g. Kavaratzis et al., 2017) on the shoulders of which this book stands. Moreover, the figure of the wave enables us to recognise that the concepts, empirical cases, and methodologies presented in the contributions need to be read in dialogue with international place branding discourses (e.g. Asian, Arabic or Anglo-Saxon regional features). The manifesto is composed by different floating elements that, despite being part of the same ocean of place branding, are brought in from different directions, by different meteorological conditions, via different waves (i.e. different concepts, empirical cases and methodologies in the chapters). These waves, while being located and centred around a specific area, due to their liquid properties spread into different areas of the ocean and may thus encounter or merge with other waves that are directed towards different shores (i.e. continental or European approaches). In Table 19.1, we attempt to position the Nordic approach as situated in between the management and critical perspectives in place branding research.

Table 19.1   The Nordic wave in place branding research

	Management approach	Critical approach	Nordic wave
Conceptualisation	Multi-disciplinary	Interdisciplinary	Transdisciplinary
	Instrumentalist	Deconstructionist	Constructionist
	Essentialist ontology	Determinist	Relational
	Concept-driven	ontology	ontology
		Issue-driven	Problem-driven
Methodological	Critical realist	Critical	Interventionist
approach	Post-positivist	Postmodernist	(engaged
			scholarship,
			participatory)
Scale and scope	Mono-dimensional	Two-dimensional	Multi-
of research	Compartmentalised	Relativist	dimensional
	Colonialist	Post-colonialist	Process-based
			De-colonialist
Knowledge	Technical	Emancipatory	Therapeutic
objective	Functionalist	Agnostic	Diagnostic
Ideological	Market-driven	Anti-capitalist	Sustainability
orientation	capitalism	Inclusive	Social welfare
	Growth		
Place branding	Heterotopia	Dystopia	Utopia
metaphor			

PECULIARITY OF THE NORDIC WAVE

The Nordic approach outlined in Table 19.1 represents a distinct *forma mentis (mindset)* of place branding, positioned not only related to academics and practitioners, but also among other stakeholders (e.g. visitors, politicians, media, citizens, as well as Nordic and non-Nordic audiences) that are involved in place branding processes in the Nordic region and beyond. The Nordic wave represents a particular regime (Bertilsson and Rennstam, 2018), which is superimposed by different situated values cutting across each other, thus having different implications and significances for stakeholders. This relational ontology is addressed in Chapter 9 on trans-local communities, diagnosing contested implications of trans-local activities for residents and tourists, as well as entrepreneurial and governmental activities. While acknowledging asymmetric power constellations, Nordic branding scholars are not settled with providing a critical description of these, but, rather, engaged in processes of negotiation, compromises as solutions. We chronicle the overlap, and navigation between situated values is illuminated in the branding of Greenland (Chapter 13), as well as in the construction of Nordicness in the symbolic and material enactment of the New Nordic Cuisine (Chapter 2), bringing together local, trans-local and international stakeholders at various political, entrepreneurial and socio-cultural levels. We reflect upon the conditions, opportunities and consequences of an open place branding ecology including the diverse resources and relational capital of restaurant owners, employees, cultural diplomats, and businessmen. We have demonstrated that the cross-cutting practices of heterogeneous branding agency was the key to reaching inter-national significance of political value (see Chapters 14 and 15), and eco-nomic value (Chapters 2 and 3). The peculiarity of the Nordic approach could furthermore be observed at an epistemic-methodological level in the emergence of a research network able to address different values and produce different implications for researchers, practitioners, local popula-tions, tourists, as well as research funds, as demonstrated in the chapter on slow brand formation (Chapter 7), Sámi involvement (Chapter 11), tourist landscape engineering (Chapter 8), and even practitioner engage-ment (Chapter 10).

Overall, this type of scholarship, research design, stakeholder interac-tion, and collaboration, emerging from the different chapters and com-mentaries, allows us to distil the unique features which characterise the Nordic place branding approach. Here we will address three peculiarities: (1) global reflexivity and responsibility; (2) legitimisation of place branding practices and research funding; and (3) shifting geopolitical boundaries.

Global Reflexivity and Responsibility

The Nordic wave has implications for different stakeholders working and dealing with place branding practices and theories. It highlights both a sense of global reflexivity and trans-local responsibility. Global respon-sibility refers not only to how different concepts and theories are treated within Nordic scholarship (i.e. research that attempts to appropriate and transform foreign concepts, theories and models for furthering research), but also to how the scientific process of creating and transforming place branding concepts and creating best-practices could have an impact – both positive and negative – on place branding theories and practices. In other words, this means that the Nordic approach has an international outlook, even though we have to be cautious of not falling back on the narrative of the Nordic "role model" to be replicated in other parts of the worlds, both near (Chapter 14), but also far away (Chapters 13 and 15). Trans-local responsibility refers instead to how researchers, being aware of their role in the Nordic-societies, in different ways seek to engage with the so-called third mission of research (i.e. consulting, advising, debating, participating), locally and trans-locally, thus bringing different practices together and creating continuing collaborative networks (Chapters 2, 3, 6, and 8). This type of engagement functions as a pool for other researchers, practitioners and public authorities, which in turn adopt similar constellations in creating opportunities for collaborative activities and funding platforms for common research.

Legitimisation of Place Branding Practices and Research Funding

A second peculiarity of the Nordic wave is the legitimisation of place branding scholarship and practice in the Nordic socio-cultural and political context. The type of research, advice, reports, and practitioner–academic collaborations (Chapters 7 and 9) which are characteristic of the Nordic approach legitimise place branding practices and function as drivers in political and policy decisions, building planning schemes, and creating place-making activities. Legitimising place branding practices to a broad set of audiences is important given that place branding is financed by means of tax-funded public (or semi-public) resources. This makes legitimisation and justification processes regarding the long-term vision and objective of the place brand important. Reaching consensus around the values of the place brand across political parties, in councils, parliaments and communities at large is a peculiar feature of Nordic place branding. Nordic ideas of fairness and justice also have implications for Nordic research funding policies. Driven by the principle of reducing inequities and providing equal chances to marginalised communities, regional development and research funding positively discriminates subaltern perspectives. At first sight, the channelling of disproportionally large amounts to engage with peripheral regions and indigenous communities may seem a noble, but ineffective approach to directing research focus to "places that don't matter". However, by giving academic consideration to subaltern voices and issues and participating in branding solutions, researchers are intersecting path-dependent negative trajectories and contributing to building alternative futures – very much in line with the performative, action-research based imperative envisaged by Gibson-Graham (2008).

Shifting Geopolitical Boundaries

Place branding has had relatively little interaction with geopolitics, despite the centrality of branding for understanding competitions between nation-states and regions in the contemporary world order (Browning and Ferraz de Oliveira, 2017). In the landscape of post-Cold War globalisation, geopolitics merges with geo-economics, which turns place branding into the exertion of non-coercive soft power (Volcic and Andrejevic, 2011). The symbolic and cultural significance of place branding converge with a general interest within geopolitical studies on "the renewed relevance of reputation and prestige politics in the context of emergent powers" (Browning and Ferraz de Oliveira, 2017: 646). The contributions in the book consider different scales of place branding from supra-national (Chapter 4) to subnational spaces (e.g. Chapters 10 and 11). Borders, actual and imaginary, divide geographical territories. Boundary making and place naming are privileged practices of definition and categorisation. Borders are to be defended and protected, sometimes through arms and hostile rhetoric, which are underscored in the chapters on branding the indigenous Sámpi region (Chapter 11), branding Greenland (Chapter 13), and the reactionary politics of the Trump administration (Chapter 16). These contributions remind us that place branding is not an innocent managerial practice, but involved in continuous boundary-making practices and struggles over Nordicity. Borders confine our movement and imagination of where we can and cannot go, and what it is possible to think. However, we also learn that borders are not fixed, but can be diminished, expanded and abolished and it is always possible to break free from disadvantageous frames. This is especially relevant to place branding, since the space of what we may call the geobrand is performed through narratives of the region. As emergent Nordic place-making practices demonstrate, compelling imaginaries are re(b)ordering the imaginary wasteland of remote and insignificant territories (Chapter 12). Following the figure of the wave and the utopian orientation of the Nordic approach, the borders of the Nordic geobrand are fluid and flexible, moving back and forth depending on winds (or external agendas). This is how indigenous territorial borders have been upheld under the occupation of nation-states. Such borders are brought into being by performing spaces in songs and stories about the land (Verran, 1998). Viewing the Nordic approach to place branding as a performance of space also means that the borders of the geobrand are not fixed for once and for all, but may be reconstructed through narration and negotiation.

FUTURE OF THE NORDIC WAVE

In one way or the other, the contributions in this book deal both with boundary making, community and belonging, and exclusion, struggle and contestation. The Nordic brand wishes to serve as a humanitarian example for others to follow, promoting social equality and welfare models. Such claims come with an implicit assumption of moral superiority, which raises questions of intolerance and exclusion. In view of the rise of a new type of nationalism, the relationship between politics and place branding becomes a pressing issue. Many of the efforts in place branding – as this book shows – are state governed projects at the municipal level. These projects are dependent on a political apparatus and consensus across political parties regarding the values and vision of the brand. Place branding practices are part of creating and forging local, national and regional identities. Today, perhaps as a counter-reaction to increased global mobility, we are experiencing a political moment where provincialism is set against cosmopolitanism. Many struggles and disputes over borders in the Nordic region remain, particularly in relation to new nationalism, populism, and the discontent with globalisation. The Nordic region has its own problems to deal with despite wanting to be a moral example for others.

The history and geography of any place shapes patterns of thoughts, practices, identities, and opportunities. There is always a risk of stereotyping the Nordic and its mythical place qualities, characterised by welfare, social equality and peace. This book dismantles this utopian idyll, and reveals how the Nordic countries deal with their own share of problems related to colonial history, and involvement in international armed conflicts as well as social, ethnic and territorial marginalisation. We have shown that behind the streamlined homogeneous surface, there is grave tension between the few cosmopolitan, branded highlights and the insignificant majority. The polarisation between places that don't matter vs. those that do may create new territorial conflicts and give rise to populism (Rodríguez-Pose, 2018). This is also becoming more apparent in the Nordic countries, which face an unprecedented polarisation of the political landscape, as reactionary and progressive movements are growing in size. We contend that there is a need for alternative narratives of the Nordic that can challenge centres of power and create spaces in which voices of displaced groups can be heard.

REFERENCES

Berg, P. O. (2001). The summoning of the Øresund region. In B. Czarniawska-Joerges & R. Solli (Eds.), *Organizing metropolitan space and discourse*. Solna: Liber, 175–191.

Bertilsson, J., & Rennstam, J. (2018). The destructive side of branding: A heuristic model for analyzing the value of branding practice. *Organization*, *25*(2), 260–281.

Browning, C. S. (2007). Branding Nordicity: Models, identity and the decline of exceptionalism. *Cooperation and Conflict*, *42*(1), 27–51.

Browning, C. S., & Ferraz de Oliveira, A. (2017). Reading brand Africa geopolitically: Nation branding, subaltern geopolitics and the persistence of politics. *Geopolitics*, *22*(3), 640–664.

Czarniawska-Joerges, B., & Sevón, G. (Eds.). (2005). *Global ideas: How ideas, objects and practices travel in a global economy* (Vol. 13). Copenhagen: Copenhagen Business School Press.

Gibson-Graham, J. K. (2008). Diverse economies: Performative practices for "other worlds". *Progress in Human Geography*, *32*(5), 613–632.

Kavaratzis, M., Giovanardi, M., & Lichrou, M. (Eds.). (2017). *Inclusive place branding: Critical perspectives on theory and practice.* London: Routledge.

Pamment, J. (2016). Introduction: Why the Nordic region? *Journal of Place Branding and Public Diplomacy*, *12*(2–3), 91–98.

Rodríguez-Pose, A. (2018). The revenge of the places that don't matter (and what to do about it). *Cambridge Journal of Regions, Economy and Society*, *11*(1), 189–209.

Verran, H. (1998). Re-imagining land ownership in Australia. *Postcolonial Studies: Culture, Politics, Economy*, *1*(2), 237–254.

Volcic, Z., & Andrejevic, M. (2011). Nation branding in the era of commercial nationalism. *International Journal of Communication*, *5*, 598–618.

Afterword: riding the Nordic wave in place branding – or does the Nordic exist and will it travel?

Mihalis Kavaratzis

WHAT MIGHT THE 'NORDIC' BE?

The first lines of this brief afterword to the book *The Nordic Wave in Place Branding* are written on an aeroplane, which has just taken off and is flying at full speed towards its destination. Although the plane appears placeless, flying above the earth, I try to hold on to a 'sense of place' by thinking of the place we took off from a few minutes ago and the place we will arrive at in a few hours. Although we are not flying over the Nordic region and I have not yet read the manuscript of the book, I also have a sense of the 'Nordic'. Trying to think of what the 'Nordic' might mean, I am forced to rely on my own scant resources, that is, my very limited experience of visiting Nordic countries and my boundless exposure to stereotypes over the 'Nordic'. In the placeless aeroplane, I have absolutely no doubt in my mind: the 'Nordic' is a set of countries that somehow have managed to live what, for the rest of us, is a dream of equality, inclusivity, participatory democracy and the welfare state (perhaps stained – but only a little – with the recent rise of the politically extreme right). Surely, the rest of the world should be trying hard to copy all that. Yet, it's not. Why not, I wonder? Is there something typically 'Nordic' about the 'Nordic' and its values? Are the 'Nordic' propositions too 'Nordic' to be of relevance to other places? Is this mixture of dreams what *The Nordic Wave in Place Branding* will be about?

DOES THE 'NORDIC' EXIST AND IN WHAT FORM?

We can take it further and ask: Does the 'Nordic' really exist? Yes, the book convincingly argues, the Nordic does exist. It is here around us, not necessarily as a spatial entity but rather as a series of propositions, some of which I could predict and some of which I couldn't: egalitarianism, participation, transparency, equality, dialogue, openness, feminism, sustainability and more are explored and evidenced in the chapters of the book. Starting to read the book from a non-Nordic vantage point, at the intersection of slight hesitation (and suspiciousness) and wild enthusiasm (and hope), one word comes to mind: utopia. Surely in any other part of the world, where transparency is still imaginary, egalitarianism is still an unfamiliar term, inclusivity is still an illusion, gender relations are still troubling and social justice is still a cause for revolutions, the 'Nordic' can only be utopia. But if it can, to any extent, form an active ideal, a live myth or even – dare I say? – a reality within the Nordic region, then maybe it's not as utopian as it first sounds.

The editors start with the desire for the book to go beyond the 'Nordic' as geographical space, moral orientation and normative discourse – and the book certainly does that. While the 'Nordic' has an obvious spatial dimension (which, in the case of this book, provides a very suitable and interesting empirical research setting), this is probably really minor amongst its features. More than spatial, the 'Nordic' is conceptual; in other words, the subject of the book is not so much the 'Nordic' as a set of countries and their practices but 'Nordicity' as a set of ideas and propositions. In the chapters of the book, the 'Nordic' does not only become a context for empirical research on place branding but a specific way of practising place branding. The 'Nordic' does not only become a socio-cultural context but also a political context and a very specific one at that. The 'Nordic' also becomes a theoretical point of view and an almost ideological proposition with specific contents. The 'Nordic' is indeed quite specific and, therefore, rather special. All the book's chapters demonstrate that in one way or another.

Of course, it is not interesting in itself to see what the 'Nordic' is, what Nordic place branding looks like and why it is special. What is more interesting is to think whether the ideals, values and practices that form what is cleverly called in this book the 'Nordic wave in place branding', can be useful in any form or shape for places outside the Nordic region. As I read more and more of the book's contributions, I discover more and more about the 'Nordic': I disentangle the 'Nordic' from the 'Scandinavian' (that I have always confused), I come close to Nordic pop music (that I have never heard – except ABBA, that is), I sense the New Nordic Cuisine (that I have only fleetingly tasted), I remember the prison in Horsens (that I have actually visited), I discover about branding the Nordic Cool in Washington, DC, I add 'Slow Adventure' to my list 'Slow Food' and 'Slow City', I learn about the myth of brand Sweden in the post-truth era and so much more. In all this, I get deeply engaged in a consideration of what the Nordic finally is, but I also find myself immersing in a contemplation of what the Nordic is not. And it suddenly strikes me that the value of the 'Nordic' might not lie in what *it is* but in what *it is not*. Let me explain . . .

WHAT IS (NOT) THE NORDIC?

The final paragraphs of this brief Afterword are written in the Eurostar as it travels under the English Channel leaving Britain behind and approaching France in a few minutes. This brings to mind the notion of 'travelling ideas' (Czarniawska-Joerges and Sevón, 2005), an idea mentioned repeatedly in the book. When ideas travel, they affect the fields to which they travel. As our train heads towards Brussels, the 'capital of Europe', I cannot help wondering whether Nordic place branding might ever be accepted and adopted in Europe (or the Anglo-Saxon world or – why not? – beyond). Other Nordic approaches have not necessarily travelled very well, why would this one? First, we don't all want to be 'Nordic', neither as ideal nor as practice, and rightly so, even if we agree with the Nordic values . . . Second, half of the world's political systems and current conditions make a Nordic approach seem very distant and utopian (in fact, frustratingly so). Third, there is something about the specificity of place identity that makes us think of the need for specificity in place branding and that might work as a warning against any attempt to help the 'Nordic' travel.

There is also the other side of the coin to consider: when ideas travel, they themselves are affected by the fields in which they travel (Czarniawska-Joerges and Sevón, 2005). They borrow elements of the new context they have entered, and they can never leave these new elements behind; they are transformed. What would that mean for Nordic place branding? The answer is given in the book and in something that I find particularly agreeable and rather refreshing: the flexibility – and even elasticity – with which the editors and contributors treat the notion of the 'Nordic'. I attempt here an – inevitably inept – re-interpretation of what they say and, to do that, I wish not to state what the 'Nordic' is, what values it stands for and what it proposes. These are explained very well in the whole book and are encapsulated brilliantly in the editors' manifesto at the end. The apt reader will surely find ideas that I do not have the competence to capture. Instead, I wish to interpret what the book says for me, by stating three propositions that the 'Nordic' is NOT. So, the 'Nordic' is not an '*All-or-Nothing*' proposition. Rather, it is distributed, it is shared unequally between people who use (some of) it and participate in it in different ways. In this sense, Nordic place branding can be picked up, attempted, left unused or unfinished and it can still make its contribution to global place branding (of course, I inaccurately use 'global' here as the opposite of 'Nordic'). That also means that the 'Nordic' is not a '*Take-It-or-Leave-It*' proposition. On the contrary, the 'Nordic' has whatever meaning people negotiate over it. So, Nordic place branding can indeed be understood or misunderstood, formed and reformed anywhere into a new shape of Nordic place branding (which, of course, ironically means that it will not be Nordic but something else). In turn, that means that the 'Nordic' is not a '*Once-and-for-All*' proposition. On the contrary, it keeps changing, it is always becoming. So, Nordic place branding is not what it is now, but it always becomes something when people encounter it and work with it, whether within the Nordic region or outside.

To a great extent, these three characteristics are attributes of all ideas and, therefore, of all place brands. In my view, this constitutes a valuable lesson from the 'Nordic' – and from this book – in the sense that this flexibility and elasticity feel to an outsider part of the 'Nordic' approach, or, at least, a result of a 'Nordic' conceptualisation. If, outside the Nordic region, people understand their place brands in these three ways, then the 'Nordic' has travelled; it has affected, and it has been affected. Nordic place branding, then, will be very much like the Danish Hot Dogs that have apparently conquered New York as described in Chapter 2 of the book: not *made in* the 'Nordic' but *made with the values of* the 'Nordic'. And who doesn't like a good hot dog?

REFERENCE

Czarniawska-Joerges, B., & Sevón, G. (Eds.). (2005). *Global ideas: How ideas, objects and practices travel in a global economy* (Vol. 13). Copenhagen: Copenhagen Business School Press.

Index

1980s 43, 81, 229
2000s 43, 143, 196

Aaland Islands 4
Aarhus School of Architecture (AAA) 96
ABBA 69
aesthetic strategies 154
Africa 36
Agenda 2030 168
alternative tourism 86
Älvdalen 144
Älvstaden 56
ambassadors 113
Anglo-Saxon 4
Anholt-GfK Nation Brand Index 42
antecedents 26–8
anthropomorphic 155
appropriation 11, 87, 191, 194–5, 224
archetypal 96
Arctic 15, 160–64, 168–70, 178, 224
Arcus 47
Ark of Prosperity 82
Arlanda airport 48
atmosphere 95
attractiveness 55
Austin 40, 45–8
authenticity 114
Aviccii 39

Baltic region 194
Bergen 15
Berlin 45
Billboard list 39
Bodø 14–16
borealism 79
Bornholm 112
brand
    cool 230
    development 76
    entrepreneurial 163

identity 171, 175, 179, 191, 208
loyalty 129
manual 70, 72
proto- 73
slow adventure 76
Sweden 207–17, 228
unmanageable 160
brandscapes 155
BRØD 15, 16, 18, 20, 22
Business Finland 44
Business Sweden 43

capitalism 2.0 118
Carlsberg 47
Chinese language 31
Claus Meyer 13, 21, 181–2, 187
co-branding 50, 166
co-creation 65, 94
co-design 155
co-destruction 56, 65
cohesion policy 86
Cold War 28
collaborative practices 106
collective
    decision making 54
    productive supra-national capital 26
colonial 139
colonialism 223–6, 242
commodification 80
common branding agenda 49
communal space 18
communitarian model 156
communities, engagement of 112
community involvement 93
consensual governance 132
consensus 4, 68, 107
constructions 14
contested heritage 125
cooperative 118
Copenhagen 13
cosmopolitanism 231, 242

Council for Promotion of Sweden
    Abroad 43
creatification 119
creative
    hub 39
    industry 101
critical approach to place branding
    238
cross-appropriate 155
cross-border place branding 76
cross-national collaboration 28
cross-sectoral collaboration 92, 103
culinary tradition 17
cultural
    markers 146
    values 20

Danish Hot Dogs 21
de-colonizing 140
de-differentiation 110
degree, autonomy of 59
democracy 4
democratic process 59
Denmark 4, 11, 15, 44, 47, 71
design interventions 92
destination management organisations
    (DMO) 12, 155
destructive branding 56
determinism 96
diffusion 13
digital market 50
digitalisation 39–40
diplomacy 170–71
discourse 4
Disneyfication 132
distrust 63

Economist, The 30
Egholm Elsebeth 100
entanglement 92
environmental ethics 87
equality
    gender 204, 210, 228–30
    social 204, 214, 241
essentialist 95
Estonia 191–8
ethnic districts 139
ethnocentric 154
EU regionalization policy 85
Europe 30–36

European 2
    Capital of Culture 101
    Union 76
exceptionalism 28
exoticism 143
exotization 86
experience design 148
experiencescapes 155
Export Music Sweden 43

Fanø 112
Faroe Islands 4, 169, 181
Fäviken 179
feminism
    approach 228
    foreign policy 211
    market mediated 230
    nordic 228, 227, 230
    state 229
Finland 4, 43
Finland Promotion Board 43–4
Finnvera 44
fishing industry 15
foraging 83
friluftsliv 77
frontier 143
Fund for the Promotion for Denmark
    43
fuzzy concepts 85
Fyn 15

game-changer scenarios 153
gender equality 2, 101
gentrification 119
geographical determinism 96
geopolitics 210, 227, 240
Gini coefficients 81
global music scene 39
Gothenburg 55–65
Gotland 112
Greater Stockholm 73
Greenland 4, 160, 162
gross domestic product (GDP) 81

Hans Christian Andersen 15
heavy service responsibilities 54
hedonics, consuming of 13
hegemonic 158
heritage governance 125
Himkok 47

homogenous masse 29
Horsens 124
Horsens State Prison 124
House of Scandinavia 47–9
Huffington Post 30
Hvide Sande 91, 98
hybrid cultural manifest 154
hygge 12, 18, 20, 23, 32, 100

Ibsen Henrik 77
Iceland 4, 43
Iceland Music Export 43
iconic political brand 70
ideology 179
    identity politics 171
    market 154
    national 175–6, 182, 189, 228
    place 208, 217
    nordic 196, 203–4
Idre Sápmi Lodge 144
IKEA 43, 69
image change 129
imaginaries 161, 227, 241
imagined community 11
imagineering 125
inclusive place branding 94
indigenous tourism 139
Innovation Norway 44
institutional logic 155
internal collaboration 65
INTERREG 82
inter-regional harmonization 28
interventional place making 105
Inuit 4, 164
invisible population 118

Jannok Sofia 224–5
John F. Kennedy Center for the
    Performing Arts 25
Jutland 15

KOKS 179, 184
Kos 18–19
Kygo 39

labelling system 147
Läckberg Camilla 101
lagom 30
Langeland 15–16
Lapland 144

Latin America 26, 36
lavvu 143
law of Jante, 20–22
Lego 43
lifestyle entrepreneur 115
lipophobia 17
Live at Heart 48
local
    governance 110
    patriotism 157
Local Action Group (LAG) 112
London 45
Lonely Planet 71

Maaemo 20
made in Denmark 21
management of values 56
manipulative rhetoric 155
marginalization 111
matchmaking event 103
media-technology 212
Mediterranean 13
Metallica 133
metaphor 1
Michelin star 20
midnight sun 15
migration 110
Millennium 30, 100
mining
    arctic 166–7
    Gállok conflict 223
mobility 111
moodboards 104
mooring 111
moral orientation 4
multi-local lives 110
multi-scalar 59, 117
music
    industry 39, 40, 45
    innovator 40
Music Export Denmark 43
Music Finland 43, 45
Music Norway 43
myth 1, 12,15 20, 77
mythologies 18, 209–12

nation
    simulation 232
national
    differences 33

identity 78
interests 60
nationalism
    gastro 175, 179
    pan- 178–9, 181
    reactionary 231
    romantic 175, 177, 185–6
nature-based tourism 83
Nazis 12
new Danish cinema 11
new Nordic 21
    cookbook 185
    cooking 164
    cuisine (NNC) 11, 13
    food 22, 30, 175–8, 181, 186
    manifesto 20, 175–8, 181, 187–8
    movement 176, 181, 186
    vision 201–3
New Public Management (NPM) 55
New York 21
Noma 13, 19, 21, 47, 175, 183
non-governmental organizations
    (NGOs) 12
nonstandard regionalization 86
Nordens Venedig 73
Nordic
    approach 236, 241, 246–7
    architecture 97
    collaboration 28
    cool festival 25, 28, 35
    cooperation 45
    cuisine 2, 6, 11, 13, 30,175, 188, 239,
        245
    egalitarian workplace 19
    egalitarianism 22, 245
    exceptionalism 21, 194–5
    feminism 228
    foreign policy 28
    history 2, 29
    ideals 55, 65
    Innovation House 46
    institutionalised values 54
    landscapes 12, 20, 91, 94–5, 180,
        185–6
    lifestyle 30
    margins 160
    model 5, 25, 28, 30, 192–6, 200–204,
        210, 131, 134
    Noir 14, 30, 92, 99, 105
    pan- 7, 45, 153

place branding 1, 8, 54, 92, 103, 189,
    221, 227, 232, 236
place-making 153, 241
playlist 45
region 1, 4, 11, 25, 31–3, 39, 42–5,
    49, , 55, 68, 74, 94, 99–112, 140,
    181, 228, 238, 242, 244–7
societal model 21
supranational branding strategy 36
supranational place brand 36
terroir 6, 155, 182, 185
values 22, 196, 232, 241, 246
wave 1, 100, 236–41, 244–5
welfare 2, 4, 12, 21, 167, 169, 228–9
welfare state 2, 4, 100, 167–8, 200,
    214–15, 229
Nordic Council of Ministers 26, 34, ,
    45, 187–8, 228–9
Nordic Music Export Programme
    (NOMEX) 45, 49, 50
Nordicity 1, 2, 5, 7 , 69, 82, 85, 191,
    193–7, 202, 204, 241, 245
Nordicness 11, 12–25, 32 192, 239
Nordland 15, 17
Norse symbols 12
Northern lights 15, 149
Norway 4, 11, 15–18, 25, 42–7, 71, 74,
    83, 95, 139, 145, 149, 177, 189
Norwegian
    Arts Abroad 44
    Energy Partners 44
    fjords 15
    nose-to-tail 148
    nostalgia 17–18, 117
    Public Diplomacy Forum 43
NYT 14–21

Odense 15
off-peak 100, 104
Örebro 48
orientalism 79
Oslo 20, 39, 44, 46
Osos 47
othering 139, 141, 150, 221
outdoor recreation 77–9, 85, 89

Palme Olof 209
Palo Alto 46
participatory place branding 106
patrimonialisation 154

performances 11, 13–14, 79, 153
peripheries 76, 82 86–7, 153, 155–6, 186
phenomenological tradition 95
place-making 77, 91, 105, 117, 119–20, 139, 149–50, 153-8, 240–41
    practices 77, 92, 124, 150, 153
political
    collaborations 32
    discourse 8, 191, 193–6, 198–9, 203–4, 212, 218, 230
    speech act 212, 215
polarisation 93, 231, 242
popular music 6, 39–41
population density 92
postcolonial 7, 141
    anti-colonial rhetoric 209
    decolonialization 172, 224–5
    sensitivity 169, 197, 221, 236
post-truth 208, 212–17
power asymmetries 120
product-country imagery 13
pro-growth strategies 54
Promote Iceland 43, 45
    provenance-label 155
    provotyping 92–3, 96, 98–9, 105

quality of life 30, 76, 81–2, 105, 113, 141, 210

recreational landscapes 118
regional vision 72
reindeer
    herding 60, 139, 143, 145–6
    industry 60
relational aesthetics 96
Rene Redzépi 13, 181–4, 187
reputation management 127
resident–visitor dichotomy 109, 121
revalorising 154
Right of Public Access 78, 80
River City 56, 57
Russia 4, 139–49

sagas 5
Sámi
    culture 139, 140, 43–50, 153, 221, 225
    entrepreneurship 225
    tourism 139–49, 224

Sámpi 4, 139–50, 154, 223, 225
Samsø 113, 115, 117, 158
Samsø Energy Academy 115
Scandinavia 11, 71, 72, 74
Scandinavian 40–47, 175–87, 201–25, 229, 245
    Airlines (SAS) 47–9
    institutionalism 13, 68
Scandinavism 71, 175, 177, 179, 181, 185–9
Schondia 68, 73–4
screen tourism 92, 99–104
second-home 112
sense of place 19, 244
Showcase Sweden 46
size 54–5
    of the municipality 63
skunk work 133–4
Slow food movement 81, 85, 148
small and medium-sized enterprises (SMEs) 77
social cohesion 4
social place 20
Sorsele 58–9
South by South West (SXSW) 40, 45–6
spatial
    augmentation 105
    planning 57
sportification 78
Spotify 39
State Institute for Race Biology 222
stereotypes 4, 79, 142
Stockholm 69
    Business Alliance (SBA) 69, 72
    Capital of Scandinavia (SCA) 70–72
    Mälarregionen 72
storytelling 83, 148
summerhouse 114
supranational place branding 25–8
Sustainable Development Goals (SDGs) 168
Svendborg 15
Sweden 43–4, 207–10, 228
Swedish
    Institute 44
    music export 43
    state 73, 224

tactical
  manoeuvre 93
  urbanism 96–7
Team Sweden 43
technocracies 2
television drama 104
terroir 13–14, 179–82
  fetish 14
  reversely engineered 154
  values of 22
Texas 40
The Nordic Lighthouse 46
The Nordic Perspective 26, 28, 31
The Swedish Affair 46
Top of Mind Awareness Analyses
  (TOMA) 125
tourist gaze 98, 146
touristification 82
Tove Lo 39
tradition of consensus-seeking 54
translation 12–13
translocal
  engagement 110
  lifestyle 115
translocality 110
transnational 82

ultra-local 114
underdog 154
unique value propositions 86
United Nations 168, 230
urban revitalization 133

USA 40, 208
utopia 19
  social 21
utopian 242–5

Västlänken 57
verfremdungseffekt 19
Videncentret for Kystturisme 97
Vikings 15, 209
Visby 119
Visit
  Denmark 44
  Iceland 45
  Norway 44
  Sweden 43
visual hegemony 96
Volvo 43

Wadden Sea 114
Wallander 100
Washington, DC 25, 30
welfare
  model 169, 195, 204, 228–9,
    241
  society 169, 197, 200
  state 2, 4, 100, 167–8, 200, 210,
    214–15, 229, 244
West Coast Universe 102–3
White Guide 15
wilderness 79, 142–3, 161, 222
windmill 115
wormholes 157